MW00667391

Brutal
WAR

Brutal WAR

Jungle Fighting in Papua New Guinea, 1942

James Jay Carafano

LYNNE
RIENNER
PUBLISHERS

BOULDER
LONDON

Published in the United States of America in 2021 by
Lynne Rienner Publishers, Inc.
1800 30th Street, Boulder, Colorado 80301
www.rienner.com

and in the United Kingdom by
Lynne Rienner Publishers, Inc.
Gray's Inn House, 127 Clerkenwell Road, London EC1 5DB
www.eurospanbookstore.com/rienner

© 2021 by Lynne Rienner Publishers, Inc. All rights reserved

Library of Congress Cataloging-in-Publication Data
A Cataloging-in-Publication record for this book
is available from the Library of Congress.

ISBN 978-1-62637-942-8 (hc)

British Cataloguing in Publication Data
A Cataloguing in Publication record for this book
is available from the British Library.

Printed and bound in the United States of America

The paper used in this publication meets the requirements
of the American National Standard for Permanence of
Paper for Printed Library Materials Z39.48-1992.

5 4 3 2 1

For Darleen

Contents

1

A War to Remember

Buna, 1943—end of the earth. *"I had walked up the wrong trail and passed near a sniper's tree,"* wrote Robert Eichelberger, in a letter to his wife. *"When I finally realized that the bullets were coming close to me. We all dropped quickly . . . I took a Springfield rifle. . . . I then took a typical knee firing position, held my breath, aimed low for the rise of the trajectory,"* the general recalled. *"Naturally, I could not miss and the man plunged downward."*

In Papua New Guinea, even generals experienced the brutality of war firsthand. In modern war, men like General Robert Lawrence Eichelberger were supposed to be corporate warriors, not killers.[1] In Papua New Guinea, modern war was ancient history.

The Themes of Battle

A snowflake, a work of art, a car crash: no two are exactly alike. Such is battle.

Every terrible struggle deserves remembrance. Among the worst of war, those dark night terrors that never fade, the fighting in Papua New Guinea ought to hold a more singular place in our sleepless, troubled memories. Numerous studies describe this desperate melee in the Southwest Pacific between the United States and Australia against Japan during World War II. But, like an enigmatic statue unearthed by archaeologists, this clash of arms remains, in some ways, inscrutable.

Some of the toughest combat in the global conflict occurred during this campaign, killing as far removed from the popular image of "the

1

good war" as machine guns from machetes. Jungle fighting plunged men into a primitive, primordial struggle where the modes of battle seemed out of place and time. Warriors hated, suffered, and massacred like ancient Biblical tribes. Prisoners were executed, butchered, and eaten. Why would men be put to such a horrible fate in such a horrible, distant place? To answer that question, four themes offer the foundation for a renewed appreciation of this faraway and long-ago fight.

One theme situates the Papua New Guinea fighting in the context of a worldwide war. This was not a peripheral campaign. In the months after the December 7, 1941, attack on Pearl Harbor, implacable enemies battled for supremacy over the island via land, sea, and air—and for good reason.

When the Japanese were on the offense, their campaign threatened the security of Australia and the defense of the United States. Japanese prime minister and army general Hideki Tojo, for example, envisioned an imperium that stretched the width of the Pacific to Alaska and the coasts of Canada and the Northwest United States, a conception laid out in the "Land Disposal Plan in the Greater East Asia Co-Prosperity Sphere," a document prepared by the War Ministry. In turn, when the Allies went on the attack, securing the island opened the way for invading Imperial Japan and ending the global cataclysm once and for all.

In tandem with another fight in the Southwest Pacific—Guadalcanal—victory in Papua New Guinea proved a crucial turning point in World War II. For that reason, there is a lot of the "big picture" and strategy in this book, explaining why the stakes of a fight in one of the most remote regions on earth was so important.

A second theme stresses the prominence of terrain. Wars are fought on dirt and salty seas, not maps. Different ground makes war different. Over the course of World War II, US forces fought in variations of five combat environments. The battles from Normandy to Germany, the European theater of operations (ETO), represented one kind of war. Fighting in the mountainous terrain of southern Europe (part of the Mediterranean theater of operations [MTO]) was another kind of battle. The US desert campaigns in North Africa (originally called the North African theater of operations) had distinctive features all their own. On the other side of the world, land combat was distinguished by either island-hopping amphibious operations, like Guadalcanal, or protracted land campaigns, such as Papua New Guinea in the Pacific theater of operations (PTO). Each kind of war has its own story to tell.

Large-scale land campaigns across vast, rugged jungle terrain like in Papua New Guinea were a particular form of combat. The terrain on the world's second largest island dictated how battles could be fought. The goal here is to never let readers (as they reimagine for themselves the incredible trials faced by the fighters on the ground) feel far from the humid stench, oppressive heat, and constant miseries of this unforgiving land.

An authentic retelling of war also hears all the voices on the battlefield. A conflict told from one perspective is just narrative. History listens to all parties. Seeing the many sides of the fighting comprises the third theme of this history. This story gives equal weight to the US, Australian, Japanese, and Indigenous people's viewpoints.

More than 340,000 Americans that served in the theater didn't fight alone on an empty battlefield against a faceless enemy. By the end of the war about a million Australians had served in uniform; at least half fought overseas. Fighting in Papua New Guinea was their biggest and most significant contribution to the war effort. In many ways, the great jungle fight was the defining moment of the Australian experience, just as D-Day and the battles of Normandy were for Americans. Only the tragic campaign at Gallipoli during World War I stands larger in Aussies' military memory.

Meanwhile, the campaign is anything but a forgotten war in Japan—half a million fought in this campaign. Contemporary officers in the Japan Self-Defense Forces still hold Lieutenant General Hatazō Adachi, who commanded the Imperial troops in the later part of the Papua New Guinea campaign, in awe and reverence despite the fact he lost. He lost not just battles but most of his troops, starting the campaign with about 140,000 and surrendering in the end with barely 13,000 ragged, bony ghosts of an army. In Japan, the remembrance of that service and sacrifice still matters.

The story of the Papua New Guinea people also counts for much in recounting the campaign. On average, a workforce of 20,000 New Guineans supported the Allied troops during the course of operations over three years. Most carried supplies. Some fought in active service, including 800 men from the Papuan Infantry Battalion and the Royal Papuan Constabulary, who were among the first to oppose the Japanese landings in 1942. Others served the Japanese either as volunteers or forced labor. More were just caught in the middle. Civilians died (estimated at 15,000) from forced labor and abuse, as well as bombing and shelling by all sides.

These voices assembled from archival materials, personal records, and oral histories make it possible to weave many sides of the story together to form an integrated history. By choice, sharing all these perspectives makes the tale more complicated, but after all, real war can be a complicated mess—and Papua New Guinea proved messier than most.

A fourth and final theme challenges other interpretations of the campaign, which are mostly just . . . wrong. Explanations of victory and defeat in this conflict are usually ascribed to either the decisions of generals on the one hand or the mettle of the armies fighting in Papua New Guinea on the other. In the end, neither conclusion really gets to the main point. The fact is, once high-ranking generals launched their armies into the jungle, they were as remote from the fighting as sports commentators in the broadcast booth are from the game on the field. As to the quality of the fighting men, that didn't tip the balance either. Arguably, all sides fought well given their training, equipping, resources, and numbers.

That said, due consideration is given to both the captains of war and to men in the ranks. The operational choices made by generals get a balanced assessment. There is also a lot of exploration into the character, competence, and capabilities of the fighting armies—the Australian militia, Aussie regulars, the US Army, and the Japanese forces. In particular, four specific battles are covered in great detail, with investigations into the performances of each of the combatants in action.

Still, what really favored victory in this kind of fighting was the capacity to sustain force over distance. Modern armies couldn't live off the land. When an offensive outran the means to replace, rearm, feed, and care for the troops in an immense, impenetrable jungle, they were as exposed and exhausted as a long-distance runner, far from the finish line with the pack closing in. At some point the advantage of the attacker waned as their resources stretched to the limit. Then they were more vulnerable to counterattack than they were a threat to the enemy. The peril of overreach determined who won and who died.

The chapters that follow are both thematic and chronological. They delve into the aforementioned themes but also advance the story each step of the way, from the planning for the Pacific War that started months before Pearl Harbor through the end of the campaign. Taken together, this history explains why this fight could never have been anything but a most brutal war.

Notes

1. Eichelberger, Robert L., Papers, III-5, US Army Heritage and Education Center.

2

The
Allies' War

LONDON, MAY 5, 1942. *"The next two months are no doubt very dangerous in the Indian and Pacific Oceans as no one can predict with certainty what the next Japanese move will be,"* wrote Winston S. Churchill, the British wartime prime minister. *"The Australians naturally think they are going to be invaded in great force."*[1]

FEW WORLD LEADERS influenced the outcome of World War II more than Churchill. Without question, his decisions significantly shaped the course of the Asia-Pacific conflict. In May 1942, the prime minister, his Australian allies, and the Americans were all scratching their heads over what the Japanese Imperial armed forces might try next. Whither Japan?— was the key question of the day and had been for months.

Although this history properly starts in May 1942 as Churchill mused over the future of the Pacific War, the backstory is equally important. How the Allies came to this point of uncertainty, and the decisions they made as a consequence, opened the path to the distant jungle war in Papua New Guinea. It all started with an agreement called the ABC-1 report.

Meeting of Minds

In 1941, over a year before Churchill penned his letter on the Pacific situation, the US and British military staffs met in Washington, D.C., from the end of January through March. The secret consultations took place many months before the sudden Japanese attack that crippled the fleet in Hawaii and catapulted the United States into the conflict.

To this point the Americans had teetered between preserving neutrality and preparing for war. In 1939, Roosevelt ordered "neutrality patrols" to protect US shipping, cooperating with British and Canadian efforts to keep the transatlantic sea lanes to the United Kingdom open. In 1940, Congress authorized mobilizing the National Guard and establishing selective service (the draft). Whether those measures would serve as a prophylactic against war or accelerate the march to arms remained an open question.

Unquestionably, the United States was unprepared for global conflict. In 1941, the total strength of the military stood at under 2 million, a fraction of the force that would fight World War II. Meanwhile, Americans remained deeply ambivalent over the role they should play. "The pall of the war seems to hang over us today. . . . The attitude of the country seems to waver back and forth," Charles Lindbergh wrote in his diary on January 6, 1941. "Our greatest hope lies in the fact eighty-five percent of the people in the United States (according to the latest polls) are against intervention."[2] The more the war crept toward the United States, the more Lindbergh and the America First movement he helped lead stiffened their resistance against the carnage.

On January 22, 1941, Hanford MacNider, a World War I combat veteran and former assistant secretary of war, summed-up the America First argument. In a national radio address, he declared he was "unwilling to commit my sons or any of America's sons to the policing of the rest of the world. . . . The first responsibility of every American is his fellows Americans. The first responsibility of our government is the American people; not to the rest of the world, no matter how sorely beleaguered it may be."[3]

MacNider, Lindbergh, and indeed many of their fellow Americans believed US interests would best be served by staying out of this war. What they did not know was that the future weighed against them. Soon Americans would find that saving the world was indisputably their only option.

As the America First leaders made speeches, the US government was already preparing for the consequences if war became unavoidable. Only days after MacNider's fiery address, the US and the British governments started the ABC-1 talks.[4] The purpose of the staff "conversations," summarized in their report, was to "determine the best methods by which the armed forces of the United States and the British Commonwealth, with its present Allies could defeat Germany and the Powers allied with her, *should the United States be compelled to resort to war*."[5] The powers siding with Germany included, notably, Italy and Japan, which together had signed the Tripartite Pact in September 1940. By the time the ABC-1 talks convened, Hungary, Romania, and Slovakia had also joined the "Axis Powers."

To defeat this enemy confederation, ABC-1 concluded that "since Germany is the predominant member of the Axis Powers, the Atlantic and European area is considered to be the decisive theatre. The principal United States military effort will be exerted in that theatre, and operations of United States forces in other theatres will be conducted in such a manner as to facilitate that effort."[6] In short, the plan was to defeat Germany decisively—and first. Everything else was a lesser priority.

The Germany first decision made sense to the Americans. For years leading up to the attack on Pearl Harbor, army and navy general staffs along with their military service war colleges had looked at various contingencies in which the United States might be drawn into war.[7] Their plans included fighting against one or more enemies, either alone or with allies. The closer war came, however, the more they pared down the menu of practical options to match the reality on the ground.

For starters, any plans that envisioned the United States fighting only one foe were dropped. By the time of the ABC-1 meetings, it sure looked like the United States might face military threats from the east (Germany-Italy) and the west (Japan) at the same time.

In addition, if the United States had to fight against multiple adversaries just defending the Western Hemisphere (proposals favored by anti-interventionists like Lindbergh and MacNider) looked increasingly impractical. Those options were also discarded. All that was left were choices where the United States would struggle in a two-front war, one front across the Atlantic and the other in the Pacific.

On reflection, considering the global visions of America's potential opponents at the time, the military planners made the right call. The Japanese high command land-disposal plan called for Tokyo to control East Asia, the Pacific Ocean, and parts of the Western Hemisphere including lands in the United States, Latin America, and the Caribbean. Germany's Adolf Hitler had even more ambitious objectives. He planned to colonize all of Eastern Europe after exterminating or expelling the local population. Germany would rule the Reich from "Germania," the world's largest city, bridged by the greatest arch ever built by man, making San Francisco's Golden Gate look like a freeway overpass. Hitler would cleanse his lands of the handicapped, the mentally challenged, gypsies, and homosexuals, as well as Jews. They would all be killed. Germany would then bring German immigrants back from America to repopulate the homeland. These nightmare visions would have left a grim future for the United States. It is difficult to imagine how Americans could have endured as a free and independent people surrounded in a hostile world by powers that controlled most of the earth's population, productive resources, and major trade routes.[8]

Clearly while the decision to take Germany first made sense for the Americans and the British, it created no small amount of angst for Australia. The faraway land was far from the primary theater. Months before the ABC-1 conference, the Australians started peppering the British with their concerns.[9] London, dutifully, forwarded copies of the Australian military chiefs' appreciation to the British planning team at the ABC-1 talks in Washington.[10]

After the conference, the Australians honestly couldn't claim they were ignorant of the Anglo-American masterplan or their place in the big scheme. Although the Australian representatives were not allowed to attend the joint talks with the Americans, they were in Washington and worked closely with the British delegation. At the end of the conference, the Australians were given copies of the ABC-1 report to send to their chiefs of staff. The report is referenced in correspondence with the home government. Reportedly, the Australian prime minister got a copy during a visit to London. There is a copy of the ABC-1 report in the government archives.[11] Further, the chiefs sent the advisory war council a memo on the talks acknowledging "the basic principle of the strategy of the Associated Powers is that the Atlantic and Europe are the decisive theatres of war."[12] The correspondence from John Curtin, who served as a member of the council and later became prime minister, includes references to ABC-1.[13]

Australian angst aside, there did not seem a realistic alternative at the time. When the British and American staffs drafted the ABC-1 report in the spring of 1941, the situation in the West appeared bleak. Germany looked unstoppable.

Although the British prevailed in the Battle of Britain (beating back the German Luftwaffe campaign to gain air superiority in preparation for an amphibious invasion), the homefront was far from safe. On December 29, 1940 (only a month before the ABC-1 talks), the Germans launched a massive bombing raid on London, setting the skyline alight as fires raged across the capital. The United Kingdom's survival remained a concern. As the US chief of naval operations summed up, if Britain "loses, the problems confronting us could be very great, and while we might not lose everywhere, we might possibly not win anywhere."[14]

American aid helped keep Britain in the war. However, if the enemy cut the link across the sea, it would be nearly impossible for the British to fight on. At the time, the Battle of the Atlantic was far from won. German and Italian submarines and surface raiders preyed on transatlantic shipping. The British and Americans had just begun adopting changes to better protect the convoys carrying support to the United Kingdom. No one knew for sure if they would work.

Meanwhile, in February 1941, the first units of German general Erwin Rommel's Afrika Korps arrived in North Africa for a campaign that would take Hitler's legions to the outskirts of Tobruk, the port city on Libya's eastern Mediterranean coast, near the border with Egypt and the crucial Suez Canal that linked Britain to its Middle East oil supplies and the rest of the British Empire and Commonwealth. Churchill dispatched a new field commander to take over the Middle East command (whose troops included both British and Australian forces) with a warning: "You take up your command at a period of crisis."[15] The prime minister feared that German and Italian dominance of the Greater Middle East would sever the tether between Great Britain and the rest of the empire. Germany, Italy, and Japan could snatch up all the jewels in the British crown piecemeal, as well as dominions of the Commonwealth, including Australia.

Meanwhile, the German-Soviet Nonaggression Pact (signed on August 23, 1939) was still in place. The agreement—a treaty affirming that the two countries would take no military action against each other for at least ten years—diminished the danger of a two-front war for Germany. Popularly referred to by the names of Soviet foreign minister Vyacheslav Molotov and German foreign minister Joachim von Ribbentrop, the Molotov-Ribbentrop Pact allowed Hitler to focus all his military efforts on Western Europe.

While prospects in the West looked precarious at the time of drafting ABC-1, conditions in the Asia-Pacific region had not yet reached a crisis state. Here was the state of play.

War in China started in 1937. The Japanese expected to win in three months. They did not. Even after pouring in four million Imperial troops and fighting for years the war was still far from won. Chinese forces stubbornly resisted. Japanese casualties mounted. Battles stalemated.

Most of the Japanese Imperial Army remained tied down on the mainland. Japan remained only a potential threat, albeit a dangerous one. Japan had fifty-one ground divisions (not all of them committed to the China theater); more aircraft carriers than any other nation on the planet; and the third largest navy in the world. "Even if Japan were not initially to enter the war on the side of the Axis Powers," concluded the ABC-1 report, "it would still be necessary for the Associated Powers [the Allies] to deploy their forces in a manner to guard against eventual Japanese intervention."[16] Still, while the empire remained a force to be reckoned with, the general strategic concept would stay—Germany first. If the Allies had to fight the Japanese, the British and Americans expected to start on the defensive in Asia. Win in Europe, then turn toward Tokyo.

Considering the global balance at the time, the Germany first plan was reasonably prudent. Eight months later, however, when the United States finally entered the war, the question was—did the ABC-1 formula still make sense?

On December 22, 1941, two weeks after the United States declared war on Japan, Churchill arrived in Washington, D.C., for the first of almost two dozen major conferences that British and US warlords would attend over the course of the war. Code-named Arcadia, the meetings included sessions between Churchill and the US president Franklin Delano Roosevelt, as well as what would become the Combined Chiefs of Staff, the most senior military leaders of the British and US armed forces.

Arcadia reaffirmed that taking down Hitler was the top priority. At the same time, Roosevelt and Churchill began the task of assembling a global coalition to win the war for freedom, drafting the United Nations Pact—a pledge to commit resources and cooperation in the war. The first country listed among the twenty-six signatories (the benefit of alphabetical order)—Australia.[17]

The Aussies' War

Though the continent and country had a population of little more than seven million tucked into a far corner of the planet surrounded by the Indian and Pacific oceans, Australia had an outsized role to play in US and British military strategy. While the ranks of the Australian ground forces peaked at under half a million to the British, strapped for troops, the Aussies were an important pool of military manpower. Australia was also a mini-arsenal of democracy, producing food, munitions, planes, and ships as well as training pilots for the war effort. Equally crucial, Australia was part of a vital line of support, connecting the global operations aimed at defeating the Axis powers. Australia mattered, but at the time, the British and American planners assumed Australia's main military task would be to help win the war in other theaters.

Fighting the war in the Pacific without Australian aid was unthinkable. The odds that Australia could go it alone—impossible. That was the basis for a sound strategic partnership. Alliances based on a common threat are the most enduring and resilient. That said, the presence of even the most threatening enemy does not smooth over all the friction of antagonism, disagreement, misunderstanding, and mistrust that grinds on coalition allies. This truth was nowhere more certain than in the Southwest Pacific.

The Australians had been in it since the start. On September 3, 1939, shortly after Hitler's forces entered Poland, Australia declared war on Germany. On June 11, 1940, Australia declared war on Italy. Australian ground and naval forces fought in the Middle East, North Africa, and the Mediterranean.

In October 1940, hoping to consolidate political support for the war effort, the Australian prime minister and opposition leader John Curtin created an advisory war council comprising four government cabinet ministers, the secretary of the war cabinet, and three members of the opposition. With the inclusion of five cabinet ministers, as well as the country's most powerful political leaders, the council became "Australia's principal body for strategic direction."[18]

The deliberations of the council reflected the insecurities of being a junior partner in a very big war. Minutes of the first council meeting on October 29, 1940, sketched out a menacing view of Tokyo's ambitions. "Japan is anxious to be on the winning side in this war, and she views Germany as the winner," the council agreed. "She sees the possible break-up of three empires, British, French and Dutch, and is anxious to gain her share of the spoils."[19] Japan might scoop up so much territory that Australia would be cut-off, alone, isolated at the farthest end of the fighting.

Australia had a plan to deal with the worst-case contingency. It was called hope. The Australian government hoped to avoid war with Japan. A concerted and continuous Australian diplomatic offensive tried to dissuade Tokyo from a path of conquest.

The question the Australian military chiefs had to grapple with was—what if war came anyway? The chiefs were not worried about an imminent invasion of their continent. At the time, they worried more about the lynchpin of the British defenses in the theater, in Singapore. The Australians agreed with the British that the bastion off the southern Malay Peninsula remained key to blocking an advance on the imperium.[20] To support the Singapore strategy, most of the Australian forces deployed in Asia Pacific concentrated on the Malay Peninsula.

The Australians would have been shocked to learn how little faith even Churchill had in the British strategy for the Pacific. With air and naval assets strained to support operations in the Middle East and the homeland, the defense of Asia hinged on the army alone hanging on.

Churchill acknowledged his own misgivings after the war in a note. "I consoled myself by feeling that [if war with Japan did break out] that the Americans would be in it," he wrote, "and that would make amends for all."[21] Churchill's private doubts would have been cold comfort to the Australian troops, which found themselves (along with the Americans in the Philippines) to be a tripwire against a Japanese invasion.

The chiefs also fretted about defending the maritime line of transit connecting the United States to the Southwest Pacific and from Australia on to the Indian Ocean, the Suez Canal, and the Middle East. "[T]he sea routes [to the] Indian and Pacific Oceans [are of] vital importance for maintenance [of] trade and continuance [of the] war effort in Middle East and United Kingdom," the Australian military assessed. "Security South-Western Pacific [also] essential [for] safe passage to and operation of American fleet in East Indies area in event [of] American intervention."[22] As a result, the Australians wanted to keep more forces for Australia and the Far East to safeguard the vital sea lanes.

Churchill had other ideas, incessantly calling for more Australian troops for other theaters. With little hope of outside support, the chiefs determined to do their best to safeguard against the Japanese gaining a foothold in Papua New Guinea. This area was of vital importance, key to protecting the transpacific routes and Australia. With that in mind, Australia would "arrange provisions for garrisons necessary within Australian area, utilization of A.I.F [Australian Imperial Forces] outside the mainland and local personnel where practicable, e.g., Papua and New Guinea."[23] That would include shoring up the defenses of Rabaul, an important port location in the Southwest Pacific and Port Moresby, a strategic location that if seized could be used to threaten the Australian mainland. If the Japanese controlled both, even if they never invaded Australia, the country could be cut out of the war by enemy air and naval power.

Australia's defense plan for the islands to their north was also little more than a hope. The chiefs knew that the meager forces that they had scraped together would not be enough to hold out against a major Japanese offensive.

While Churchill was sailing across the Atlantic to meet for the Arcadia conference, Curtin, now Australian prime minister, wired his deep concerns. "The [Australian] Commonwealth Government has for long pressed the United Kingdom Government on the provision of the strength considered necessary for land, sea and air defence," he cabled the British prime minister on December 20. "Now that the actual threat has come and the enemy is making substantial progress on several fronts, we must press for it to be boldly met and hope it will not be attempted by dispositions of a 'penny packet' nature."[24] Curtin asked for reassurance. He got none.

When it came to war priorities, Arcadia replayed ABC-1. What changed was that unlike the ABC-1 talks, the Australians were not even invited to observe or advise. The Australian ambassador to the United States did attend some of the sessions. He pressed on the British prime minister that his country wanted to be consulted more on war policy. "Churchill replied," summarized historian John Robertson, "that the conduct of the war would not be improved by increasing the number of people concerned in any decision-making."[25] That must have been hardly comforting to the Aussies.

Now a little over four months on, when Churchill wrote his assessment of the circumstances in the Asia-Pacific theater (May 5, 1942), the world at war looked very dissimilar from when the ABC-1 report (March 27, 1941) had been typed out and when Roosevelt and Churchill reaffirmed the Germany first strategy at the conclusion of Arcadia (January 14, 1942). Here is what happened in the intervening period.

In the spring of 1942, there were some bright spots. All of them, unexpectedly, were in the war in the West against Germany and Italy.

The British firmly established air superiority over the United Kingdom and surrounding waters, ending the fear of an imminent German cross-channel attack. Efforts were also ramping-up to win back the Atlantic. The ships from the United States kept coming. In addition, the British were holding on in North Africa.

Meanwhile, after the Germans violated the Molotov-Ribbentrop Pact and invaded Russia (June 22, 1941), Soviet forces launched a counteroffensive in the winter of 1941 and by the spring of 1942 were consolidating their gains. Hitler's reversal on the Eastern Front and the increasing demands for Axis forces to hold off the Russian armies was obviously good news for Britain.

And, of course, the United States was now formally at war with Germany and Italy, removing the last barriers to full-throated cooperation in the Anglo-American alliance. In short, the situation for London was far less bleak than it had been only a Christmas before.

Conversely, conditions in the Indo-Pacific were a catastrophe, far worse than the worst assumptions in the ABC-1 report. ABC-1 had not anticipated the crushing defeat at Pearl Harbor nor how quickly Allied forces in the Far East would be rolled up. To make matters worse, after Arcadia concluded, Japan's breathtaking advance across Asia Pacific only accelerated the deterioration of the Allied situation. Here is what happened.

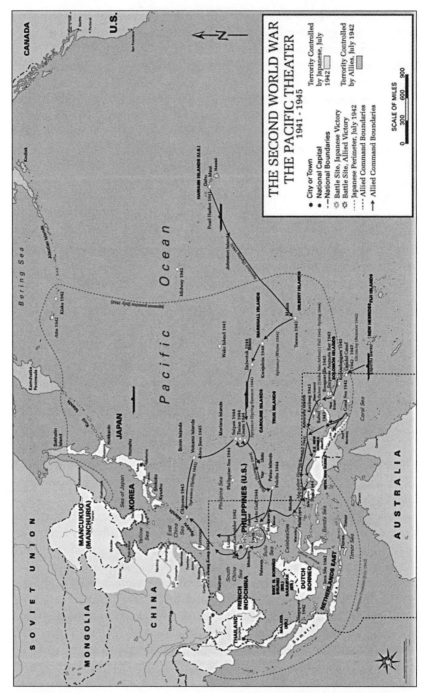

14

Source: US Army.

On January 23, 1942, Japan's Imperial Forces seized Rabaul on New Britain in the Solomon Islands, establishing what would become their main base for operations in the Southwest Pacific.

On February 15, the British surrendered Singapore in a stunning blow. The British warlords expected the garrison had the capacity to hold out for months. The fight for Singapore lasted less than a week. The British lost their firebreak against the Japanese threat to England's Empire. This disaster shook the Commonwealth as deeply as the American losses at Pearl Harbor. In the fighting on the Malay Peninsula and Singapore, the Australians had about 8,000 killed or missing in action and 15,000 taken prisoner, wiping out the preponderance of their ground forces deployed in the theater.

On March 7, Japanese forces landed at Salamaua, a settlement on the northeastern coastline of Papua New Guinea, and Lae, a large town and port located near the delta of Papua New Guinea's Markham River. The seizure put the enemy only one island away from the Australian mainland.

Trying to stabilize the rapidly deteriorating situation in the Asia-Pacific theater proved an irritant that could not be put off. While strategic squabbling rambled on, decisions had to be made. In March 1942, the Anglo-American alliance reached an agreement on how to divide responsibility for worldwide operations. The United States and Britain had equal stakes in winning the Battle of the Atlantic and victory in Europe. Developing, executing, and overseeing the combined campaign to accomplish that would all be shared between them. Churchill wanted, and got, responsibility for oversight of campaigns in the Greater Middle East and South Asia. The British and the Americans split the Asia-Pacific war. In part, the Japanese had made that decision for them. At Arcadia, Roosevelt and Churchill agreed on establishing an American-British-Dutch-Australian Command (ABDACOM) to oversee operations from Burma to New Guinea. That didn't last long. A month after the fall of Singapore, ABDACOM was history, virtually wiped out by the rampaging Japanese and leaving a wide gap between the US and British areas of operations. There was little choice over the division of Anglo-Americans responsibilities. "We see great merits in the simplification resulting from the American control of the Pacific sphere [including China] and the British control of the Indian Sphere," Churchill wrote Roosevelt on March 17, 1942, "and indeed there is no other way."[26] He was right.

That, however, did not solve all the challenges of commanding forces in the Pacific for the Americans. The US theater of operations stretched from the coast of California to the Arctic Circle to the east coast of Malaya and south to Australia, New Zealand, and on to the coast of Latin America. The army and navy agreed to divide command of the Pacific. In March, Chief of Naval Operations Ernest King and Army Chief of Staff George C. Marshall fleshed out the particulars, squabbling over the islands that pockmarked the route to Tokyo from Australia. General Douglas MacArthur got the Australia–New Guinea area and the Philippines. The navy got a wide swath of ocean, the New Hebrides, and most of the smaller islands.

The Australians viewed the new US responsibilities in the Southwest Pacific as an opportunity for renewed dissent over Allied strategy. Still dismayed over the agreement at Arcadia and the progress of the war in the Pacific, Curtin dispatched his minister of external affairs on a mission to Washington and London, arguing for a rethink that shifted more resources and priority to the defense of Australia.

In Washington, the minister launched a diplomatic carpet-bombing campaign, pigeon-holing the president; Army Chief of Staff Marshall, who the minister met with on several occasions; FDR's adviser Harry Hopkins; Supreme Court justice and Roosevelt confidant Felix Frankfurter; and Undersecretary of State Sumner Wells (another Roosevelt-man and key foreign policy adviser) as well as Admiral King.[27]

What must be done, the minister wrote Curtin, is suggesting "strongly that Churchill's method of dealing with Australia sometimes indicates party political bias and what is most essential is a broad settlement by which United Kingdom as well as United States would give immediate positive proof of their desire to assist Australia."[28] After plastering Washington, the minister took his case to London in an effort to shift the strategic emphasis from Germany first to Asia Pacific.

In this debate, Marshall was the man caught in the middle. He was losing the fight for an invasion of Europe proper sooner rather later. He could not get a concrete date for the cross-channel attack. At the same time, the army chief of staff had to referee a debate on strategy for the Pacific between Chief of Naval Operations Ernest King and the senior army theater commander, General Douglas MacArthur.

The relationship between Marshall and MacArthur required special attention. Although the army chief of staff would never relinquish his unshakeable commitment to the cross-channel attack, he deferred to King on managing the Pacific campaign while also making a sincere effort to support MacArthur. Unfortunately for Marshall, the thinking of King and MacArthur was far apart.

Over the previous two months, King had been drafting a plan for the Pacific that called for using the marines and naval air assets to seize key bases that would then be turned over to the army for occupation while the offensive hopped forward to the next target. King shared the general scheme with Marshall. Then, he sent it to the president. Marshall did not object to the overall concept, and Roosevelt approved.

In the division of responsibilities, on April 18, 1942, MacArthur was appointed supreme commander of Allied forces in the Southwest Pacific Area (SWPA). Meanwhile, King's half of the Pacific War became split between the Pacific Oceans Area (POA) and the Southeast Pacific Area. Admiral Chester Nimitz commanded the POA. The area was further divided into three subcommands (central, south, and north). Nimitz maintained personal command over the Central Pacific Area (CENPAC). These commands were intended to be joint and combined. In other words, the theater commander would oversee all the forces—land, sea, and air—operating in their region for all the Allied fighting forces assigned there. Dividing the map not only divided responsibility and provided for unity of command within geographical areas, but it also affected strategic decisions and how the war would be fought.

For starters, the division effectively ended Churchill's influence over Australia's war. His shadow would still be cast over events in the Pacific as his views continued to influence the debate over the balance of effort between East and West—but that was it. In the future, Australia's military forces would be used for the fight in the Southwest Pacific. Australia was now part of America's war.

Command arrangements aside, the controversies over strategy did not abate. On May 6, one day after Churchill wrote his assessment of the Pacific situation, the last US and Filipino forces in the Philippines sent up the white flag. The Imperial achievement was stunning. "Japan's high command by May 1942," military historian Mark Stoler summarized, "had accomplished all of its objectives and possessed an enormous empire, its diameter equivalent to half the circumference of the entire globe, with all the resources necessary for the economic self-sufficiency it desired."[29] In Tokyo, it seemed the realization of the land disposal plan was well under way.

The implications for Australia loomed large. Before this point in the war, a Japanese threat to the Australian homeland was not part of anybody's war plan. When the warring powers started to think about fighting for Australia, they were starting from scratch. Certainly, nobody envisioned fighting a protracted jungle war on the country's doorstep in Papua New Guinea.

Churchill, for one, was unmoved by the shifting strategic balance in the Pacific. Although the prime minister puzzled at what the Japanese might try next, his judgment of what the priorities ought to be remained firmly fixed. However, with an evil empire on their doorstep, Australia's warlords now had grave concerns about the "Beat Hitler first" mantra. When threats were only a possibility sketched out on a map, Australia's risks seemed tolerable. When the maps marked the location of actual enemy troops standing on the ground, risks appeared very different. Australia faced this situation in May 1942. The Australians' concerns put them at odds with London and Washington. Who was right? To answer that question, we require an assessment of the overall strategy as matters stood at the time.

Lifeline of a Guiding Idea

The dispute over Allied strategy carried on as vigorously in the paper trenches of the Combined Chiefs of Staff and the blood-red velvet covered conference tables of foreign capitals as the real battling against Axis troops raged in the field. The Allied warlords rumbled over how to win a war while they were in the middle of fighting a war—which at the time they were not winning.

The task of settling on a strategy for World War II was daunting. Making strategy is by definition hard. "Strategy concerns big things and the big people who do them," wrote Hillsdale scholar Larry Arnn.[30] If decisions were easy or the need for boldly setting a course was not required, then there would be no need for a strategy. By their nature, strategic challenges present multiple, competing, sometimes contradictory goals—and there are never enough resources to do everything (certainly conditions that confronted the British and American forces in 1942). A strategy confronts this challenge by delivering a guiding idea that dramatically shifts the priorities of what, who, and how things get done. Strategy is about making hard choices.

Strategy-making at its most basic accounts for making three interrelated decisions: ends, ways, and means. Ends are the goals, the objectives the strategy is tasked to achieve. In World War II, for example, the Allies described their war aims as the unconditional surrender of the Axis powers (Germany, Italy, and Japan).

Ways are how ends will be met. For World War II, that included everything from offensive and defensive military campaigns to strategic air bombardment, convoys across the Pacific, aid to foreign countries, propaganda, sabotage, and other covert activities as well as mobilizing the homeland with victory gardens and war movies.

Means are the capabilities and resources that will be dedicated to accomplishing the strategy. Of course, the armed forces were a big part of that, but means also included all the national assets mobilized in support of the war effort, from Rosie the Riveter on the factory floor of a Boeing assembly plant to artists in Disney studios making military training films.

A strategy is inadequate unless it interconnects and answers all three questions—what, how, and with what? But just because a strategy has all three components doesn't mean it's a good strategy. A good strategy is suitable, feasible, and acceptable.

- The first measure is whether the strategy is suitable—in other words, would the strategy satisfy the policy aims?
- Feasibility is a judgment of whether the strategy could actually be accomplished with the means available.
- Acceptability assesses the commitment to follow through and accomplish the strategy.

Satisfying all three judgments is no guarantor of victory. There is no secret sauce. After all, the enemy gets a vote. The people supporting the war get a vote. Even the troops under the general's command get a say. Still, strategy guided by a logic that satisfies competing demands is the best assurance leaders can hope for in the messy world of war.

Though the United States had started to address their woefully inadequate armed forces in 1940, America remained shockingly short of what it needed to fight a global struggle. In addition, both of America's most vital allies—Britain and the Soviet Union—required massive aid.

Further complicating priorities was the necessity of fighting German-Italian forces on one side of the planet and the rampaging Japanese on the other.

The decisions of ABC-1 and Arcadia aside, four strategic options had their advocates in the Anglo-American alliance in the spring of 1942. The choices offered and considered went something like this.

1. Hell Bent for Berlin

This course spelled out how to make "Hitler first" happen. It started with securing the sea lanes across the Atlantic as speedily as practicable, then undertaking an invasion of Europe sooner rather than later with British, US, and Canadian armed forces that would conduct amphibious landings on the continent proper and drive toward Berlin, crushing the German armies on their way while the Russians (well supported by American aid) closed in from the other side. In addition, a British-American strategic bombing campaign would pummel everything that contributed to the German war machine.

There was an argument that this approach was important for political as well as strategic reasons. Americans overwhelmingly supported the war effort. The national debate ended after the first bombs fell on Pearl Harbor. The day after, Charles Lindbergh, who led the national antiwar movement, wrote in his diary, "I can see nothing to do under these circumstances except to fight. If I had been in Congress, I certainly would have voted for a declaration of war."[31] Still it is worth recalling that despite the newfound resolve, Lindbergh and many of his fellow Americans had been against "Europe's war" only days before the sneak attack on Hawaii. If the conflict became protracted and encumbered with setback after setback, the homefront might sour again. Racing to Berlin best addressed the problem of a democracy at war. Americans would have to make real sacrifices to meet the ambitious objectives laid out by Washington and London: economizing at home, breaking their backs to build a global war machine, and anguishing as their husbands and sons were thrown into the pit of battle all over the planet. Committing to a drive to Berlin early would be a soothing reassurance, a pledge to get the boys home as soon as possible.

A hell-bent drive for Berlin, the preferred strategy of Army Chief of Staff George C. Marshall, would put the defeat of Germany first—on steroids. Crushing Germany quickly would also make dealing with Japan far easier—ensuring that the Allies could achieve their goal of complete and decisive victory against the Axis powers. To make this possible, however, the minimum amount of resources possible could be spared for the Pacific theater.

Opening an early second front in France was key. The longer the Allies waited, the tougher that fight might be. Even as the war with Russia dragged on, Hitler anticipated a counterattack from England. On March 23, 1942, the Führer issued a formal directive for what would become known as the Atlantic Wall, defenses meant to forestall an Allied force from gaining a foothold on the Continent. The longer the invasion was put off, the stronger these defenses might become.

The option to drive across the Atlantic was feasible only if the Americans could deliver the preponderance of power needed to pull off a cross-channel attack. In the spring of 1941, the ABC-1 talks just brushed out the broad strokes of strategy. At the time there seemed little sense in delving into the details of military campaigns when the United States did not know when it would fight or the conditions under which the US forces would operate. The vague, general agreements on taking Germany first proved good enough. That was then. In pressing the case at Arcadia a year later, details mattered. The business of war—mobilizing and moving millions of men and tons of material—was at hand. Suddenly, a cross-channel attack was more than a map exercise.

With little more to support the case for a quick invasion than a passion for the course of action, it was difficult to argue the feasibility of a sprint to Berlin. "We were more or less babes in the woods on this planning and joint business with the British," recalled a member of the army planning staff.[32] Scrambling in the wake of Pearl Harbor to deal with the challenges of digging into the details of fighting a global war for real, the US chiefs had no definitive answers on how the means could be marshaled for an invasion strong enough to ensure victory. That was a problem for pressing the race to Berlin.

2. Tightening the Ring

The second option, the one Churchill advocated for, also called for the preponderance of Allied power to be applied to the Western Front. But, rather than a frontal assault through France, this course looked at a more indirect approach advancing through North Africa and southern Europe. This advance offered no direct route to invade Germany, but it would tie down German and Italian forces and prevent Hitler from massing all his armies on the Russians. In addition, the Allied attacks would safeguard links to British interests in the Middle East and the Indian subcontinent—an outcome that, of course, Churchill greatly favored.

Tightening the ring depended heavily on the success of the Red Army. "Hitler's failure and losses in Russia are the prime factor in the war at this time," Churchill wrote in preparation for Arcadia in December 1941, "We cannot tell how great the disaster to the German Army and regime will be. This regime has hitherto lived upon easily and cheaply won success. Instead . . . it has now to face the shock of a winter of slaughter and expenditure of fuel and equipment on the largest scale."[33] The pressure of the Russian offensive might result in unrest among the conquered nations or even political collapse in the Nazi regime and an effort to sue for peace.

This option looked to pressure Hitler from within and without. In addition to supplementing land campaigns with propaganda, subversion, and sabotage and creating a continental blockade, strategic bombing would accelerate the collapse of Germany. Meanwhile, in Asia Pacific, Australia would largely have to fend for itself, but enough had to be done to guard against a threat to India. Maintaining the supply route through Burma to China and keeping the Chinese in the war with aid would also help hold down the bulk of Japan's land forces in an intractable struggle on the Asian mainland.

An indirect approach, Churchill hoped, would also spare the high losses the British might expect from a frontal assault in Europe, an important advantage for a nation already weary from carrying the burden of global war. Further, the British doubted the US forces were prepared for anything else but this approach. America had not sufficiently mobilized, trained, and equipped combat-experienced forces to handle a cross-channel assault anytime soon.

Tightening the ring had its detractors. Stalin wanted a frontal assault on Berlin from the West as soon as possible to force Hitler to pull the maximum number of Germans away from the Eastern Front. Roosevelt wanted Americans fighting in the West as soon as possible to show Americans he was determined to win and bring the boys home. In the Pacific, there were concerns as well. Curtin fretted that as war dragged on in Europe, Japan would consolidate its hold on a newly minted empire that lapped at Australia's doorstep.

3. Step by Step

Another option, one supported by US Chief of Naval Operations Ernest King, argued for winning the war that could be won. In the spring of 1942, there was an argument that war was in the Pacific. Of course, the Allies would have to continue to secure the transatlantic ship routes and protect America's unsinkable aircraft carrier, Great Britain, as well as to keep up aid to the Russians (who were expected to do most of the work in grinding down the German army). These actions were a prerequisite for bringing about the eventual downfall of the Third Reich. But, while those efforts were ongoing, there could be an opportunity to finish off Japan.

There was a case to be made that the Japanese had already stretched their military advance to the limits—pressing dangerously close to their strategic culminating point. In particular, if the powerful Japanese carrier fleet could be defeated, the enemy would be vulnerable to a counterstrike.

Step-by-step strategy called for shifting more resources to the Pacific—for starters, to make sure Hawaii was secure and the sea lanes to Australia kept open. Then would come a systematic advance using naval and amphibious forces from the New Hebrides (an island group east of Australia in the South Pacific Ocean) to the Solomon Islands (east of Papua New Guinea and northwest of the New Hebrides) and the Bismarck Archipelago (northeastern coast of New Guinea in the western Pacific Ocean). After key points were seized, the army would move in to build bases and airfields in order to station pursuit planes and long-range bombers that would extend the reach of the Allied forces.

The main effort for the assault on Japan would be through the Central Pacific from the Marshall Islands to the Marianas in the western North Pacific Ocean and then Formosa (Taiwan). A second advance northward from New Guinea (bypassing the Philippines) would be a supporting effort to keep the Japanese from focusing all their efforts on the Central Pacific offensive.

For the United States, the step-by-step campaign offered the advantage of delivering revenge for the Japanese attack on Pearl Harbor and demonstrating early wins in the war. But, while that might make Americans cheer, shifting emphasis from the second front in Europe would not please the Russians. Stalin also fretted the Anglo-American powers might cut a separate peace, allowing Hitler to turn his full attention back to Moscow. Delays in a commitment from the Americans and the British on a cross-channel attack would put additional strains on the alliance.

Further, there was a big risk in making an aggressive push in the Pacific—the Japanese carrier fleet. By the end of the war, the United States would field an incredible armada of 160 aircraft carriers of various types. But when the United States entered the war, it had only seven. If the US carrier fleet was crippled in a head-to-head engagement, preventing the Japanese from consolidating their hold on the Southwest Pacific, let alone going on the offensive, would be near impossible.

4. "I Shall Return."

Another option that would shift the balance in the priority between the Pacific and Atlantic was to push north from Australia, eliminating the massive base that the Japanese were building on Rabaul and then moving in a line from Papua New Guinea to the Philippines. This was the option pressed famously by General Douglas MacArthur. "I came through and I shall return," MacArthur declared (after abandoning the Philippines) in a statement when he disembarked at the Terowie Railway Station in South Australia on March 20, 1942. "The President of the United States ordered me to break through the Japanese lines and proceed from Corregidor to Australia," he told the first assembled group of reporters he spoke to since arriving in the country, "for the purpose, as I understand it, of organizing an American offensive against Japan, the primary purpose of which is the relief of the Philippines. I came through and I shall return."[34] This proved more than just a public relations statement. "I shall return" was the core strategy MacArthur insisted would win World War II. With the Philippines secured and Japan cut off from its Southwest Asia and Pacific conquests, the Imperial homeland would be reduced through strategic and maritime blockade while the bulk of the Japanese forces stranded in China were harassed by Indigenous forces.

Implementing this course would also require far more resources than what had been initially allocated to Asia Pacific at Arcadia. To make this strategy feasible, not only would the invasion of Europe have to be put on the backburner but support for a counteroffensive in Burma to protect India and keep open resupply routes to the Chinese would be cut back; scrapped as well would be the proposal for a second line of maritime advance (the route the navy preferred) through the Central Pacific.

While MacArthur's option was feasible (and popular with the Australians), many quarters found it unacceptable. Stalin rejected this option, seeing it as a lack of commitment to a second front. Churchill hated it, arguing it put India and the Middle East at risk. Roosevelt's top commanders questioned the wisdom of a single thrust that allowed the Japanese to focus their efforts, and their carriers, against a single Allied initiative.

Difficult Choices

By May 1942, Japanese battle flags had advanced as far as Papua New Guinea. The risks were menacingly real. No longer content to be the backwater of the war, the Australians expressed shock that the "beat Hitler first" plan was a done deal. They argued to be higher on the list of Allied priorities. The truth was—present protestations aside, before the Japanese went on the march—the war cabinet and the chiefs of staff knew where the priority stood. Once the war with Japan was under way, it was the Australians who had second thoughts. They were not satisfied to see the defense of Australia carry so little weight in Allied plans. Curtin's demands for more consideration of Australia's defense and the imperative of fighting and winning in the Southwest Pacific would only grow.

The Australians were not alone in being unhappy with the present plans. Americans had not resolved among themselves, let alone with their British and Soviet allies, conflicting service interests, the allocation of resources, and the timing of operations. In the spring of 1942, the Americans pursued bits and pieces of all four options for prosecuting the war.

This was all perhaps to be expected. In practice, the options from hell-bent for Berlin to "I shall return" did not represent four distinctly and completely different strategies. They were all variations on a basic concept—some parts compatible, some not. That is not surprising given the multiplicity of goals the global strategy was meant to achieve. Rather than distinct Manichean choices, the various plans represented a strategic supermarket from which the Allies could pick and choose as they adapted to the conditions of global war.

In a strategic appreciation written for Arcadia, Churchill reminded his colleagues that "war is a constant struggle and must be waged day to day. It is only with some difficulty and within limits that provisions for the future can be made."[35] No advice could be more appropriate to dealing with the conditions the Allies faced in the spring of 1942.

By not locking-in myopically and inflexibly on a determinant course at the outset—rather than reflecting a failure of decisionmaking—the lack of obtaining a fixed strategic consensus kept the Allies' options open without inflicting either complete chaos or paralysis in the war effort. In the end this allowed the Allies a measure of flexibility. That was to prove an immeasurable benefit. The Allies proved imperfect at predicting their capacity to prosecute the war. Delivering men and material, managing their war machine, and adapting weapons and warriors to the realities of combat in different parts of the world proved supremely difficult. Being able to adapt the course of action to those realities was a boon not a burden.

Flexibility also allowed the Allies to recalibrate their actions to best match what the enemy was actually doing—as opposed to what the Allies thought they might do. Good strategy is not a rigid line of linear activities implemented inflexibly on an inanimate adversary. In the course of conflict, enemies act and react. Good strategy has the capacity to accommodate actions by an adversary. The menu the Allies had to operate from broadened their ability to adjust.

In May 1942, the Allies keeping their options open meant that additional resources would continue to flow into the Pacific and into Australia. That was all to the good, because Japan was getting ready to make a big move.

Notes

1. Winston S. Churchill to General Claude Auchinleck, May 5, 1942, in Gilbert, *The Churchill Documents*, vol. 17, p. 630.
2. Quotes from Lindbergh, *The Wartime Journals of Charles A. Lindbergh*, p. 437.
3. Sarles, *A Story of America First*, p. 159.
4. "United States–British Staff Conversations, ABC-1, March 27, 1941," in Ross, *U.S. War Plans, 1938–1945*, pp. 67–102; Robertson, "Australia and the 'Beat Hitler First' Strategy, 1941–42," pp. 302–303.
5. "United States–British Staff Conversations, ABC-1, March 27, 1941," in Ross, *U.S. War Plans, 1938–1945*, p. 68. Emphasis in the original.
6. Ibid., p. 71.
7. See, for example, ibid., pp. 33–54; Gole, *The Road to Rainbow*.
8. The objectives of the regimes spearheading the world's militaries is summarized in Weinberg, *Visions of Victory*. See also Iriye, *The Origins of the Second World War in Asia and the Pacific*, p. 67.
9. Mr. R. G. Menzies, Prime Minister, to Mr. S. M. Bruce, High Commissioner in London, January 3, 1941, document 243, Papers of the Department of Foreign Affairs and Trade, http://dfat.gov.au/about-us/publications/historical-documents /Pages/volume-04/243-mr-r-g-menzies-prime-minister-to-mr-s-m-bruce-high -commissioner-in-london.aspx; Record of Meeting at UK Foreign Office, 26 February 1941, document 324, Papers of the Department of Foreign Affairs and Trade, http://dfat.gov.au/about-us/publications/historical-documents/Pages/volume-04/324 -record-of-meeting-at-uk-foreign-office.aspx; Mr. R. G. Menzies, Prime Minister, to Mr. A.W. Fadden, Acting Prime Minister, March 4, 1941, document 330, Papers of the Department of Foreign Affairs and Trade, http://dfat.gov.au/about-us/publications /historical-documents/Pages/volume-04/330-mr-r-g-menzies-prime-minister-to-mr -a-w-fadden-acting-prime-minister.aspx.
10. Robertson, "Australia and the 'Beat Hitler First' Strategy," p. 303.
11. Ibid., pp. 303, 305; Legation in Washington to Department of External Affairs, March 25, 1941, document 365, Papers of the Department of Foreign Affairs and Trade, http://dfat.gov.au/about-us/publications/historical-documents /Pages/volume-04/365-legation-in-washington-to-department-of-external-affairs .aspx.
12. Robertson, "Australia and the 'Beat Hitler First' Strategy," p. 305.
13. Ibid., p. 309.
14. Quoted in Morton, *Strategy and Command*, p. 81.
15. Winston Churchill to General Auchinleck, July 1, 1941, Gilbert, *The Churchill Documents*, vol. 16, p. 878.
16. "United States–British Staff Conversations," http://www.ibiblio.org/pha/pha /pt_14/x15-049.html, p. 71.
17. Twenty-one nations later signed, making for forty-seven nations in the United Nations. See Subcommittee on the United Nations Charter, *Review of the United Nations Charter*, Document No. 87, pp. 38–39. This pact is not to be confused with the 1945 Charter of the United Nations, which was the foundational treaty establishing the United Nations as a multinational intergovernmental body.
18. David Horner, "MacArthur: An Australian Perspective," in Leary, *MacArthur and the American Century*, p. 111.
19. Advisory War Council Minute, subject: Relations with Japan, Melbourne, October 29, 1940, document 182, Papers of the Department of Foreign Affairs and

Trade, http://dfat.gov.au/about-us/publications/historical-documents/Pages/volume
-04/182-advisory-war-council-minute.aspx.

20. Commonwealth Government to Lord Cranborne, UK Secretary of State for Dominion Affairs, Cablegram 97, February 15, 1941, document 300, Papers of the Department of Foreign Affairs and Trade, http://dfat.gov.au/about-us/publications/historical-documents/Pages/volume-04/300-commonwealth-government-to-lord-cranborne-uk-secretary-of-state-for-dominion-affairs.aspx.

21. Quoted in Reynolds, *In Command of History*, p. 296.

22. Commonwealth Government to Lord Cranborne, UK Secretary of State for Dominion Affairs, Cablegram 97, February 15, 1941, document 300.

23. Ibid.

24. Mr. John Curtin, Prime Minister, to Mr. Winston Churchill, UK Prime Minister (en route to the United States), December 20, 1941, document 208, Papers of the Department of Foreign Affairs and Trade, http://dfat.gov.au/about-us/publications/historical-documents/Pages/volume-05/208-mr-john-curtin-prime-minister-to-mr-winston-churchill-uk-prime-minister-en-route-to-the-united-states.aspx.

25. Robertson, "Australia and the 'Beat Hitler First' Strategy," p. 311.

26. Winston S. Churchill to President Franklin D. Roosevelt, March 17, 1942, in Gilbert, *The Churchill Documents*, vol. 17, p. 398.

27. Dr. H. V. Evatt, Minister for External Affairs, to Mr. John Curtin, Prime Minister, March 21, 1944, document 433, Papers of the Department of Foreign Affairs and Trade, http://dfat.gov.au/about-us/publications/historical-documents/Pages/volume-05/433-dr-h-v-evatt-minister-for-external-affairs-to-mr-john-curtin-prime-minister.aspx.

28. Ibid.

29. Stoler, *Allies in War*, pp. 59–60.

30. Arnn, *Churchill's Trial*, p. 70.

31. Lindbergh, *The Wartime Journals*, p. 561.

32. Oral history interviews with Thomas T. Handy.

33. Memorandum by the Prime Minister, December 16–20, 1941, United States Department of State, *Foreign Relations of the United States*, p. 22.

34. "I Came Through, I Shall Return," *The Advertiser*, Adelaide, Saturday, March 21, 1942, Australian National Library, p. 1, http://trove.nla.gov.au/newspaper/article/48749454.

35. Memorandum by the Prime Minister, December 16–20, 1941, United States Department of State, *Foreign Relations of the United States*, p. 30.

3

Japan's War

TOKYO, JULY 1928. *"We cannot achieve real peace until we change the present irrational international state of affairs,"* declared Prince Konoe Fumimaro. *"We cannot wait for a rationalizing adjustment to the world system."*[1]

KONOE GAVE HIROHITO that advice before confirmation of the twenty-five-year-old's ascension to the Chrysanthemum Throne, over a decade before the start of the war. The quote is oft cited as foreshadowing Japan's global conquests. That was not Konoe's intent. What the prince meant was this: the international order unfairly constrained Japan with its growing population and expanding economy. Japanese policies should remove those obstacles. Konoe's appetite had limits. He saw danger, for example, in expanding by force into China, fearing a potentially larger conflict with Western powers and Russia. Conversely, the advocacy of leaders like Konoe, their rhetoric for replacing European domination with a Japanese-led "Pan-Asianism," was far from benign. Their encouragement legitimized Japan's hunger for power. Konoe normalized belligerence, helping provide justification for wars of aggression. The background of how his kernel of an idea swelled into insatiable conquest is also an important part of the context for this story.

In 1937, the prince, a rising influential politician, became prime minister. Like his words, his politics only strengthened the military's hand in the end. "The appointment of Konoe satisfied army personnel," wrote Japanese scholar Yoshitake Oja. "They had been hoping for just this development, but it was not because they expected a great deal from him . . . nor because he had approved the foreign policy the army had been promoting since 1931."[2] They intended to use the popularity of the new government to their own end. Prime Minister Konoe never mustered an effective check on the military's expansionist policies. Unable to restrain the army's determination to invade China after the infamous Marco Polo Bridge Incident (July 7, 1937), Konoe futilely worked to end the expanding conflict. He failed. Konoe resigned in 1939.

The emperor recalled Konoe to head the government in 1940. But, once again the prince could not shape policies to his liking. His political authority did not extend to disciplining the war effort. The military general staff had been granted independence from oversight from parliament with the "right to supreme command"; they were responsible only to the emperor.[3]

Konoe, reluctantly supporting the military's demand that Japan join the Axis Powers, hoped Berlin would help Tokyo negotiate a nonaggression deal with Moscow. Although Germany, Italy, and Japan signed the tripartite pact, Konoe never got his treaty with Russia. Japan and the Soviet Union eventually signed a nonaggression pact on April 13, 1941. That turned out to matter little anyway. The treaty would have had little value because at the time Tokyo did not need it. Russia, consumed with fighting the Germans, was looking to avoid war with Japan, not start one. At the time, however, the effect of the tripartite alliance rippled across Asia. Stalin was worried Japan might turn on him.

The United States imposed an oil embargo in July 1941 (after Japan seized France's Indo-China colonies). That brought US-Japanese relations to the crisis point. In addition to avoiding war with Russia, adding a conflict with the Americans seemed too grave a risk for Konoe. To mitigate against this danger, he knew the Japanese military would have to cripple the US fleet, seize the possessions needed to fuel and feed the empire (in particular the Dutch East Indies), and consolidate their defenses before the United States could respond. Perhaps even more vital, success would depend on Germany defeating its enemies or at least tying down so many forces that Japan could manage its own war. Germany was holding its own for now, but the British and the Russians were far from defeated.

Konoe was running out of options. He had hoped statecraft would find a way to avoid war. But, he could not negotiate a deal with the Americans without compromising Japan's war effort in China. China was the one issue where neither the Japanese military command nor the United States seemed to have any interest in compromise. Diplomacy hit a dead end.

The prince had dreamed big for Japan's place in the modern world. Others dreamed much larger. In a cabinet meeting on October 15,

Prime Minister Hideki Tojo (also a general in the Imperial Japanese Army) declared the effort for a negotiated deal with Washington a failure. Konoe could not muster support in the cabinet for more negotiations. He resigned. Tojo became prime minister. This fateful moment started Japan on its path to war in the wildest of places: Papua New Guinea.

Carriers at War

Months before the Imperial fleet sailed into "the day of infamy" (Roosevelt's famous description of the attack in his declaration of war address to the US Congress), Prince Konoe fretted about Japan's capacity to wage a wider war. Now out of office, on January 1, 1942, Konoe went to the palace for the New Year's greetings to the emperor. The victory at Pearl Harbor still resonated across the royal grounds. Konoe later recalled, "Everybody at the palace was celebrating . . . giving toast after toast. . . . How vulgar they are! At this rate, they will push us all the way to defeat."[4] He remained pessimistic.

Konoe's gloom was understandable. The balance of power, even after Pearl Harbor, was not in Japan's favor. "As [the historian] H.P. Willmott calculated long ago," noted Jon Sumida and Daniel Moran, "if on December 7, 1941, the Japanese had contrived to sink not just the entirety of the Pacific Fleet, carriers and all, but in addition every other vessel in the United States Navy on that day, the American navy would still have been larger than Japan's at the start of 1944, which is in fact when the 'Biblical retribution' phase of the Pacific War began."[5] Japan could never realistically match the US capacity to build and field armed forces.

The Japanese were not blind to this challenge. Winning the race against the mobilization of American manpower and the economy would be a herculean task. Yet, in contrast to Konoe's pessimism, others, most notably General Tojo, were more sanguine about the odds of victory. Tojo believed Americans were soft and weak at their core, unwilling to make enough sacrifices to mount a monumental war effort. He recalled his time in the United States, finding "the Americans of the roaring twenties as undisciplined, unmilitary, and unconcerned with anything but the pursuit of the jazzy life."[6] He watched the United States brought to its knees by the Great Depression. He believed them an indecisive, squabbling, divided people, as reflected in the unending bickering between Lindbergh and Roosevelt. They lacked the solidarity of the Japanese nation. They had nothing like the people's unshakable faith and allegiance to their emperor. If the Americans did fight, they could not match the Japanese warrior ethos, the unfailing willingness for self-sacrifice.

Still, even Tojo knew that spirit was not enough. Japan needed decisive military victory. Once the Japanese decided to expand the empire to the Dutch East Indies (providing Japan secure and abundant energy by securing oil production, refining, and shipping facilities) they made the fateful choice for war with the West. An assault directly on the East Indies would leave the Japanese seagoing supply lines flanked on one side by the British in Singapore and the Malay Peninsula and on the other by US forces in the Philippines. Both had to be dealt with. The Japanese decided their offensive to seize the Dutch possessions would have to follow advances that eliminated potential threats from Singapore and the Philippines—that decision could not but result in war with Britain and America. Capturing Singapore would neuter the British. Conquering the Philippines would immobilize the Americans. Japan would also have to crush the fleet in Hawaii to halt the American threat.

The hope of delivering a crippling blow to the United States was anything but farfetched. The Pacific fleet was not nearly the formidable force that it looked like on paper. In 1940, even after concentrating the fleet in Hawaii (meant to deter more Japanese aggression in Asia Pacific), the United States continued to strip ships and planes from the Pacific fleet for the Battle of the Atlantic. Many of the warships at Pearl Harbor were not combat ready and lacked full crews. An effective attack would further diminish the US Navy's capacity to conduct combat operations in the near term.

The United States had three carriers in the Pacific—the *Lexington, Saratoga*, and *Enterprise* berthed at Pearl Harbor—in addition to eight battleships—*Arizona, California, Maryland, Nevada, Oklahoma, Pennsylvania, Tennessee*, and *West Virginia*. As the Japanese fleet closed in on Hawaii, however, all three American carriers were at sea. All eight capital ships were moored on Battleship Row. The consequences of that coincidence proved crucial to what happened next. It also settled the debate over the importance of the offensive power of aircraft carriers and battleships that had built steadily over the course of the interwar years.

Naval capabilities evolved significantly between the two world wars. Carriers moved from experimental craft to formidable military machines. Radar and sonar expanded the ability of ships to detect and counter threats. Naval aircraft gained in range, speed, survivability, and capability. Air-delivered bombs and torpedoes packed a bigger punch and got more reliable and accurate.[7] Battleships got better too. Naval gunnery, for example, greatly advanced.[8] Further, neither battlewagons nor carriers were invincible. In fact, flattops packed with gasoline, munitions, and thin decks piled with people and planes were more vulnerable. But, the carriers had a decisive edge in the amount of ocean that could be commanded by firepower. A US battleship could throw a shell as far as twenty miles. A carrier's air arm could search, find, attack, and destroy an enemy out to 150 to 200 miles. After Pearl Harbor, it was clear battleships still had a role to play in naval warfare. The navy repaired six of the big ships attacked at Pearl Harbor and sent them back to war. The United States used them extensively throughout the conflict. But, the carrier became king.

In practice, the dominance of the aircraft carrier provided a commanding means to sail ships into adversarial waters. That was a crucial capability in the Pacific War. In land warfare, the critical advantage was often the ability to take and hold key terrain (territory that gave one side a clear advantage—like holding the high ground at the Battle of Gettysburg). Seizing a key objective could determine the outcome of a battle, a campaign, or a war. Ocean warfare was different. Although armies occupy key terrain, fleets do not occupy water. They sail through it. After they are gone, the sea they crossed is no longer under their influence. Fleets matter not because they can hold a patch of ocean but because they can move military force from one place to another.

The most powerful asset in sailing a navy wherever the admirals wanted them to sail during World War II was an aircraft carrier—a moving airfield. The day after the disaster at Pearl Harbor, the US Navy still had three carriers in the Pacific. And that meant the navy could go on the offensive. That was a big problem for the Japanese—and the reason that, even after the overwhelming success of the attack on Hawaii as well as the seizure of Singapore, the Philippines, and the oil-rich Dutch East Indies, the empire could not rest easy.

However, though the United States could take the offensive whenever it chose, the competition for a decisive advantage was still up for grabs. There was no maritime choke point that prevented a US fleet from sailing from Hawaii to Tokyo. For that matter there was nothing to stop a Japanese carrier battle group from maneuvering from the Hashirajima anchorage in Yamaguchi to the Golden Gate Bridge in San Francisco. But while a fleet might fight its way to an objective, keeping a naval task force going and lingering by faraway shores was another matter. Ships and planes needed fuel, food, munitions, and parts. Resupply was a difficult matter at sea; the resupply ships had to sail from somewhere, and the farther they had to sail, the more fuel, support, and supplies they consumed themselves and the more security and support they needed. Ships also had to be repaired. That required ports with suitable facilities.

Weather mattered as well. Even the largest and sturdiest of battleships sought to avoid severe weather. In 1944, one US task force that sailed dead-ahead into a typhoon lost three ships. Nine more were damaged. Almost 800 lives were lost. Having a safe harbor in heavy weather was the only way to avoid the danger.

In short, to give a fleet more sustained presence at sea, the more anchorages with suitable infrastructure a nation could control and defend, the more the fleet represented an offensive threat. If an attacker also held airbases for long-range heavy bombers, then an enemy could be doubly threatened.

The challenge for the United States was that it was roughly 3,900 miles from Hawaii to Japan. Closing that distance in a militarily meaningful way was a US challenge. Indeed, the Japanese demonstrated that with the raid on Pearl Harbor. After delivering disaster, the fleet had to withdraw. There was no way to stick around and prevent the Americans from rebuilding the port and preparing to fight another day.

Another concern was that any time any carrier, from either side, went into harm's way it was only one bomb away from becoming a casualty. In the spring of 1942, sinking carriers could shift the course of conflict. If a Japanese bomber scored one hit on a US carrier deck, the Japanese would have cut a quarter of the US Pacific carrier fleet (a fourth carrier, the *Hornet*, sailed to the Pacific in the spring of 1942). That would have delivered a huge advantage to the Japanese. Loss of a carrier would hamstring many of the planned Allied efforts to take the offense. In turn, a Japanese carrier victory at sea would allow time for Japan to consolidate a defensive ring or go on the offensive in follow-on campaigns.

Unsinkable aircraft carriers—that is, land-based airbases—could make all the difference in securing a decisive advantage. On the one hand, an attacking carrier might temporarily degrade or suppress a land base. Or, the fleet could simply plot a course a few hundred miles around the range of land-based aircraft, bypassing the enemy in the way a car drives around an obstacle. On the other hand, if strategic bases (i.e., ones that could not be easily bypassed) could be seized, built-up, and held, these bases could diminish or extend the space where a carrier task force could freely operate.

Carriers and land-based airstrips and anchorages formed a strategic team. Aircraft carriers could undertake raids (such as Pearl Harbor or the famed Doolittle Tokyo Raid on April 18, 1942, a carrier-launched attack of sixteen US B-25B medium bombers) or be used to attack and sink enemy carriers and ships. They could also escort an invading amphibious force to secure a land base, helping establish a permanent defense ring or a persistent offensive threat. Carriers gave commanders operational flexibility in setting the terms of where and when to fight. Land bases extended control over a geographical area.

As the war in Europe counted on Britain as a base to launch the second front in the West, an American offensive in the Pacific without Pearl Harbor was unthinkable. If the US carriers had been attacked, the final outcome might have indeed been different. In *The Pacific War and Contingent Victory: Why the Japanese Defeat Was Not Inevitable*, professor Michael W. Myers argues in the crucial months after Pearl Harbor, Tokyo had serious options that could have made a difference.

Myers is right to be skeptical of war histories that are overly deterministic. He is critical of scholars like H. P. Willmott, who argued that from day one "the defeat of Japan was assured because she was industrially, financially and demographically inferior to the enemies she raised against herself."[9] It is a fair point to argue that owning the preponderance of power is a vital factor in war. But recognizing war is a competition tempers arguments that make strategy just a math exercise.

In 1942, America's power was, for the most part, being assembled on factory floors and trained in mustering camps across the country. For the United States, every capital ship (big carriers and battleships) that fired a shot in anger during World War II was already at sea in 1941. During those desperate months, Japan had a chance to write its own history. If, argues Myers, "Japan had continued its victories long enough, war weariness might have led to Japan's enemies admitting the right of Japan to retain its desired hegemony in Asia and the Pacific."[10] Who knows if he right? In the end, counterfactuals are unprovable and unknowable—particularly for massive, complicated events like global wars. What cannot be denied, however, is that the Japanese believed they had a fighting chance and fought that way.

Tokyo's Way of War

On the surface, the structure of how the Japanese directed their war effort did not look that dissimilar from the Allies. Strategic direction came from committees that included an admixture of military and political decisionmakers. For the Allies, Churchill, Roosevelt, and Stalin approved overall direction of the war effort. In Japan, the emperor performed an analogous role. Under the emperor, the Imperial Headquarters–Government Liaison Conference, including the heads of the military services and the prime minister, foreign minister, and navy and army ministers served as the Japanese equivalent of the Combined Joint Chiefs Staff—where the Imperial Army and Navy wrestled with the big strategic choices. At the operational level, army and navy leaders (who also controlled their respective air arms) worked out their joint plans. In the theaters where one service predominated (such as China for the army or the Pacific for the navy), direction of the service commanders with the predominance of forces held sway.

The parallels in setting strategic and operational direction for the war in the Pacific masked significantly different dynamics in how the two sides directed the war. For one, the lines of civil-military responsibility and the dominance of civilian authority over the armed forces was fairly clear and unquestioned among the Americans, British, and Australians. Not so on the Japanese side. Even before Konoe took office in 1937, "the military had almost reached the point of having autonomy, keeping the government often unaware of ongoing military actions,"[11] writes Kazou Yagami, a lecturer at the University of Northern Colorado. The Japanese not only had military leaders serving in civilian leadership roles, the Imperial Navy and Army actively competed for influence over the domestic political sphere. In addition, political leaders, even the emperor, had only limited authority over operational decisions. In short, the debate among powerful and influential senior army and navy leaders was the real crucible of Japanese strategic and operational decisionmaking.

There were also divisions within the high command of the services. Like the disputes among the Americans, divergent strategic perspectives exacerbated the intense competition among the Japanese Army and Navy leadership. These differences were nowhere more apparent than in the Pacific. Like the Americans, the Japanese found themselves fighting a war they had not anticipated. For all the intense years of war planning in the decade leading up to the war, the Americans had never considered the defense of Australia. The "rainbow plans," a series of Joint US Army and Navy Board war plans color-coded by name, never addressed the fighting for Australia. Nor did the ABC-1 talks or Arcadia conference give much regard to comprehensive defense of the Southwest Pacific. Allied strategy evolved piecemeal starting in the spring of 1942. Arguably, Japanese strategy evolved from a similar beginning.

Before World War II, the Imperial Japanese Army aimed its strategic focus east at China and Russia. The Japanese Army, concludes historian Ed Drea, "had no long-range strategic concept for a war with the United States, because for the army, the Pacific War was the wrong war at the wrong place at the wrong time and with the wrong enemy."[12]

In contrast, the Imperial Japanese Navy long regarded a great war with the US Navy as a likely task and a focus for strategic planning. For its part, however, the Southwest Pacific was not a major area of concern for the Japanese Navy until months after the war started. Despite this, when it came to the Pacific, the army largely looked to the navy to set the direction. In this respect, the division of responsibilities between the services did not differ that much from how Marshall deferred to King's judgment on Pacific operations. This also left the Japanese Army, like MacArthur, the navy's grumpy junior partner. Meanwhile, the Japanese naval leaders argued among themselves. MacArthur's back and forth with Marshall was mild compared to the outsized influence that Yamamoto (as the commander of the Combined Fleet and architect of the Pearl Harbor raid) wielded over the navy general staff.

Victory Disease?

Japanese strategy in this phase of the war has been ascribed to "victory disease," extravagant self-confidence that Japanese forces would prevail regardless of the obstacles and the odds. On the one hand, there is no question that the Japanese warlords heavily relied on the resilience and perseverance of their people to support the war effort. On the other hand, the Japanese strategy was not fueled by overwhelming hubris.

Before World War II, Japan was obsessed with reimaging Japan. Victory in the Russo-Japanese war (1904–1905) was a transformative experience. For the first time in the modern era, an Asian nation had bested a Western power in war. In subsequent decades, despite a devastating earthquake and tsunami in 1923, the Great Depression, and the privations at home to support the war in China, the Japanese public continued to see an expansive future for the empire.

In 1937, in support of the war effort, the Konoe government championed the National Spirit Mobilization Movement, which promoted sacrifice and self-discipline with mottos like "Luxury is the enemy!" and "Persevere and persist!" This effort to instill conformity and public support promoted privation as a public good and exploited the increasing influence of mass media in modern Japanese society to shape popular culture.[13]

Efforts to promote conformity were strongly reflected in the national film industry. Today, these movies are almost forgotten cinema. Unlike

US war stories that still pop up occasionally on cable television, Japanese films made during the war years are virtually unknown to most contemporary Japanese people. Yet, this cinema remains a crucial artifact for illustrating the officially sanctioned pop culture of Imperial Japan. At the time, the American anthropologist Ruth Benedict, who wrote an influential study of Japanese culture used by the US government, studied contemporary cinema to learn about US enemies.[14] These films offer an opportunity to see Japan through Japanese eyes. One example was Kenji Mizoguchi's popular 1939 movie *Zangiku monogatari* (The Story of the Last Chrysanthemums) about an aspiring Kabuki actor named Kikunosuke who throws aside the woman who helps him establish his career in order to reconcile with his family and honor his father. The film resonated with the intense sentiment of service and sacrifice. "Just as a child was to be obedient and loyal to their father, so should the Japanese be obedient and loyal to their emperor," writes Olivia Umphrey in a study of Japanese prewar cinema:

> When audiences saw the obedience of the Kikunosuke to his family, they were to mirror it in their own lives. Despite their fear, sorrow, or love, they must be ready and willing to come to the aid of Japan and the emperor. The film earned an award for its representation of the family system, which points to the government's attempt to reinforce the *kokutai* [national essence] ideology through popular culture.[15]

The sanctity of family unity and obligation to the father reflected the emphasis on national orthodoxy and the public's submission to the state.

Victory would come through the unique nobility and steely willingness of the Japanese people to bear the hardships of this noble task. This narrative spelled out a dominant cultural theme that persisted throughout the war. There is little question that the Konoe government mobilized media and popular culture to explicitly emphasize the martial responsibilities of the people. For example, "members of the literary profession," concludes professor Donald Keene, "were at the outbreak of the war almost solidly united behind the militarists. They exulted in the triumphs of the first year."[16] Photographs, illustrations, popular cartoons, artwork, and even street theater emphasized military themes. Children's games and play, guided by school and military officials, promoted values and actions suitable for Imperial military service.

Harnessing the productive capacity of the society would be essential to achieving the war surge needed to extend and defend the empire. In 1941, the Ministry of Education distributed an instructional guide, *Shinmin no Michi* (The Way of the Subject). The guide admonished,

"It is unforgivable to consider private life as the realm of individual freedom. . . . A meal . . . our clothes, none is ours alone, nor are we in a purely personal capacity when at play or asleep. All is related to the concerns of the state."[17]

The capacity to fully mobilize society was critical. With more than half the population engaged in agriculture at the start of the conflict, Japan lacked the industrial capacity of other nations in preparing for modern war. Bridging this gap, the military reasoned, would require maximum participation and cooperation from the Japanese people, who would be required to make dramatic sacrifices to sustain the war effort. Promoting the spiritual mobilization of the Japanese people through official acts and the manipulation of mass media impacted how the nation would approach the war. Together, the sentiments of a moral right to subjugate foreign places and the undefeatable spirit of the Japanese people made for a powerful cocktail, steeling them for any challenge they faced after Pearl Harbor.

But were the military strategists blind to the challenges of the battlefield that spiritual beliefs alone could not overcome? Historian Bruce Gamble among others have argued that the effects of incessant optimistic propaganda "was most apparent in the actions of military planners. Often displaying a complete disregard for the capability of the Allies, they tended to spread their own forces thinly over large areas, sometimes extending them beyond their lines of supply."[18] That was one way to explain the fateful decisions that led to Imperial expansion. But, it is an overgeneralization. Not every leader blithely assumed victory. In 1941, the army vice chief of staff warned against the problems of overreach. "If we send small numbers of troops to far away isolated islands, command and control as well as resupply will be extremely difficult. It is like sowing salt in the sea."[19] The world was not just for the Imperial Army's taking. Concluding that only hubris was at the root of the high command's decisionmaking misses the point. The "Japanese overconfidence" argument, maintains Michael Myers, "has been misused as a substitute for strategy."[20] What drove the decisions of the high command in the spring of 1942 was not the sureness that they couldn't lose, but the driving necessity to find a way to win.

Fateful Choices

Japan's real problem was the struggle to find a winning strategy. In this respect, the lack of a more unified focus between the two services on the most crucial decisions of the war hamstrung the Japanese effort. Indeed, in the Southwest Pacific, which the Japanese high command referred to as the southern area, the two services had agreed on an operational plan that covered only the first five months of the war.

The army scheduled about eleven or twelve divisions (about 20 percent of Japan's ground forces) to support operations in the Malay Peninsula, Philippines, Dutch East Indies, and Papua New Guinea. At a prewar meeting of the Imperial Headquarters–Government Liaison Conference, the army chief of staff "indicated that if the sea lines of communication could be maintained, the army could establish an invincible posture in the southern areas [Southwest Pacific]. . . . Army planners simply had no means, and could discover none, to inflict a decisive defeat or subjugate the enemy in the Pacific."[21] That, he argued, was the Imperial Navy's job. Further, after supporting initial operations for securing the southern area, the army looked to reduce its commitments by the end of 1942, believing at best the Americans could not muster a serious counteroffensive in the Pacific before the later part of 1943. In the meanwhile, the army planned to reduce its Pacific forces by about half and shift those troops to strengthen defenses against a potential Russian attack.

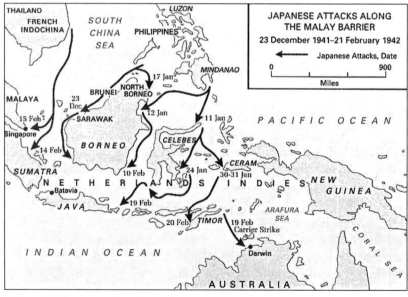

Source: US Government.

The Japanese high command cannot be faulted for not having a firm blueprint to fight the follow-on stages of the war. What was more important was the ability to adapt. Adapting to an enemy's actions is the acme of strategic skill. The facility to adapt, exploit the other side's weakness, seize an advantage, or shore-up a vulnerability is the great test of strategic judgment. Lack of a long-term plan was not an insurmountable challenge. But there was a problem. There was a strategic debate to be had over how to hold on to the empire. Japan had two choices.

1. Together the Imperial Navy and Army could secure a defense ring and wait the Americans out.
2. Alternatively, they could take the war to the United States. Japanese forces could seize and hold Hawaii, knocking America out of the Pacific fight.

There was an argument that taking the US islands made sense, but at the time the anchor of US military power in the Pacific remained beyond Japan's strategic reach. The United States would fight hard for Hawaii—and if it lost might fight even harder to take it back. In the spring of 1942, the discussion to attack or defend was academic anyway. To support either strategic option, Tokyo first needed a secure base in the Southwest Pacific. Deciding how to achieve that was the big challenge.

In March, the Japanese Imperial Navy with its commanding authority over Pacific strategy pressed for operations south into the Bismarck Archipelago (an island group off the northeastern coast of Papua New Guinea) and also to Midway in the east (an operation added to the list of priorities by Yamamoto and the Combined Fleet staff over the initial objections of the naval general staff). The only subject left to debate was over how much the army would lend to support the offensive.

After a vigorous back and forth, the army agreed to the occupation of Midway (an atoll roughly halfway between Asia and North America). Besides Pearl Harbor, Midway was perhaps the second most important base for extending US capability to conduct persistent operations in the Pacific. Taking Midway would deliver a triple benefit—take out a base the United States needed, hopefully sink the US carriers in the process, and give Japan a foothold one step closer Hawaii.

Army leaders also agreed to support further operations in the southern area, though the high command ruled out extending the offensive to include an invasion of Australia. Knocking the Aussies out of the war would eliminate any threat from the Southwest Pacific, but a conquest would be a major undertaking. Naval planners argued the operation would only require a token force. General Tomoyuki Yamashita, who knew something of fighting land campaigns (he had successfully commanded operations in Malay and the capture of Singapore), called the idea gibberish. The Imperial Army did not have enough manpower to seize and garrison the country—end of argument. At least temporarily.

What the army and navy finally agreed to was titled Operation FS. They would invade and occupy the islands groups of Fiji, Samoa, and New Caledonia, establishing a chain of "fixed carriers" (land-based aviation flying off Japanese airfields) that would isolate the Aussies and take them out of the war. At a March 4 meeting at the Imperial Headquarters, the high command agreed to a set of steps, the "Fundamental Outline of Recommendations for Future War Leadership." Invading Australia was relegated to a "future option" if everything else went well.

The boldness of the move was not surprising. At the time, recall everything was going well—on every front.

On March 20, the first Japanese marched into Burma. US forces at Bataan in the Philippines surrendered on April 20. On May 1, the Japanese occupied Mandalay. Corregidor in the Philippines surrendered on May 6.

The Japanese were close to both cutting the Allied supply line to China in the east and securing the flank of their conquest of the Dutch East Indies oil fields in the west.

Then came the Doolittle raid on Tokyo (April 18, 1942), launched from the deck of the carrier *Hornet*. This attack was one of the few setbacks to Japan's startling string of victories. For the Americans the raid had no strategic purpose other than to boost US morale, shake the Japanese sense of invincibility, and show that the US carriers could take the war to the enemy. Doolittle's raid, however, did have a strategic impact on the Japanese high command—it provoked them to become even more aggressive. The attack only reinforced the argument for pushing out the defensive perimeter, further limiting the US capacity to conduct carrier raids or long-range bomber strikes on the homeland. As a result, the Imperial Japanese Army dropped its half-hearted support for the Midway operation and moved forward with plans for the preparatory attacks for Operation FS. The army also agreed to support an amphibious invasion to secure Port Moresby and the airfields at Milne Bay in Papua New Guinea. Called Operation MO, this campaign would provide more fixed aircraft carriers to protect the flank of the main Operation FS that would follow. The invasion was set for the first week of May 1942.

Fight on the Flank

For Vice Admiral Shigeyoshi Inoue, it was long past time for Operation MO. Responsibility of the empire's flank in the Southwest Pacific fell to him. His forces in Rabaul had repulsed a raid by the US carrier *Lexington* in February. On March 10, *Lexington* was back along with the carrier *Yorktown*. They launched a strike on the Japanese bases in Lae and Salamaua. They sunk four ships and damaged several others, including a cruiser and two destroyers. At the time, it was the US Navy's most successful strike of the war. For Inoue, it was another reminder that he needed operational control of Papua New Guinea to keep out the US carriers. He also needed the protection of Japanese carriers to achieve that end and guarantee success for Operation MO.

The raids also slowed the admiral's preparations for offensive operations. "These deployments," writes Australian historian Philip Bradley, "plus the need to replace the transports lost at Lae and Salamaua delayed the Port Moresby Operation until May."[22] Ironically, the delay was mostly irrelevant. The Allies had no way of knowing the impact the raids made on Japanese forces and did nothing to take advantage of the situation. Delaying the invasion date a few weeks did not materially impact the outcome of the campaign. However, the raids did prompt a renewed sense of determination. The Imperial Headquarters assigned two carriers to the Port Moresby invasion—hoping to end the presence of US carriers in the Coral Sea once and for all.

Since the opening months of the war, Inoue had been arguing for an offensive that would take eastern Papua New Guinea and the Solomon islands, establishing a string of land-based airfields that would protect his key bases at Rabaul and Truk (in the Caroline Islands north of New Guinea), cut off Australia's links to the outside world, and secure the empire's flank. He was impatient to secure enough unsinkable aircraft carriers to offset the threat of US flattops. Finally, the delayed operation in the Coral Sea was now set.[23] For Operation MO, Inoue had two fast carriers and a light carrier, as well as cruisers, destroyers, and submarines to accompany eleven troop-carrying ships that would undertake the invasion of Port Moresby.

Meanwhile, Yamamoto reserved his big carriers for the subsequent attack on Midway. For Yamamoto, Midway was crucial. He was confident the US Navy would dispatch their flattops to defend Midway. Yamamoto anticipated he would have the opportunity to both capture the atoll and sink the US aircraft carriers. Building on the anticipated success of the seizure of Port Moresby, the emperor would rest more easily on his throne after the Imperial Navy again put the Americans on their heels.

Inoue planned to use the naval aviation from his carriers to help protect the task force and support the invasion of Port Moresby. What he did not anticipate was a carrier battle. The Japanese knew that *Enterprise* and *Hornet* were operating west of Japan, far from Inoue's operational area. After the Doolittle raid, they returned to Pearl Harbor to rearm, refuel, and refit. *Saratoga* was undergoing repairs. Inoue expected to seize his objective without the threat of bumping into a US flattop. Between his carriers and land-based air units, Inoue thought he could muster about 150 aircraft. That ought to be enough to deliver a decisive airpower advantage for his assault.

On May 3, Vice Admiral Inoue's attacking force secured undefended Tulagi in the Solomon Islands (near Guadalcanal), a precaution to cover the flank of the armada's advance. From there the Japanese could launch long-range reconnaissance flights to alert the fleet of any approaching enemy ships. He also dispatched four submarines to monitor for the approach of ships from Australia. He was ready to act with renewed confidence. Despite the complications of managing a patchwork of forces, a complex operation (including a raid on airfields on the Australian mainland—later aborted), and acting on a rushed schedule, Inoue had every prospect of success. He had the weight of force on his side—and the element of surprise.

What the admiral did not know was that thousands of miles away in a windowless room with concrete floors and lousy ventilation in a nondescript building under the command of the Fourteenth Naval District at Pearl Harbor, a team of US Naval code breakers guessed what he was up to. Throughout the month of April, Station HYPO (which the cryptologists called the dungeon) pieced together clues suggesting an impending attack on Port Moresby. On April 24, they uncovered the code word "MO" in a message. A few days later, the dungeon translated a message from Yamamoto ordering the execution of MO. HYPO concluded that an invading force was headed for Port Moresby. MacArthur's chief intelligence officer, reviewing the same information, reached the same assessment. The invasion would occur sometime between May 5 and 10.[24] It was understandable that the Americans would place such confidence in this intelligence. They had long suspected that the Japanese had set their sights on Port Moresby as a key military objective.[25]

Alerted to the impending attack, the Americans responded. Admiral Nimitz, the Pacific fleet commander, saw a chance to ambush part of the Japanese carrier fleet and to protect Port Moresby (vital to the defense of

Australia and maintenance of the lines of operation in the Southwest Pacific). He ordered *Enterprise* and *Hornet* to head for the Coral Sea. The ships, however, were still 3,500 miles away at Pearl Harbor.

General MacArthur marshaled the land-based bombers in Australia under his command to intercept the invading force. At the time, MacArthur had been in command for little more than a month. When he got to Australia, he found his air force was far from formidable. At best, for the entire theater he had 200 operational planes of varying quality with few experienced and battle-worthy aircrews.

MacArthur also dispatched available naval assets under his command, made of Australia's handful of warships and the remnants of the US Asiatic fleet that were not sunk at the Battle of the Java Sea (February 27, 1942) that precipitated the collapse of ABDACOM and the Japanese seizure of the Dutch East Indies. The little armada comprised two Australian and three American ships. For MacArthur, mustering an effective counterstrike, finding and attacking the MO occupation force in the vast expanse of the Coral Sea, would be no mean feat. In fact, it was pretty much a hopeless task.

The only effective battle team that the Allies could muster was two task forces assembled around *Yorktown* and *Lexington*. They were already at sea. Both could reach the Coral Sea in time to fight. Although the impending battle was in MacArthur's area of responsibility, when Admiral King and Marshall agreed on the division of geographical responsibilities in the Pacific, King insisted that the navy would not relinquish control of the carrier battle groups when they operated in MacArthur's area of control. Similar to the previous carrier forays into the Coral Sea by *Lexington* and *Yorktown*, the navy would run the show.

For this fight, MacArthur would have to loan his water and his ships to the navy, coordinating support from his headquarters in Australia. Combative and mistrusting personalities aside, that plan made sense. For the short time that these scarce resources operated in MacArthur's water there was little advantage to transferring their command to him. Particularly since the real operational decisions (once the task forces were committed) would be made at sea anyway.

There remained the challenge of achieving unity of effort, coordinating the forces coming from Australia with the operations of the carriers *Yorktown* and *Lexington*, but since the contribution of MacArthur's forces was so meager that was among the least of the challenges in the great battle to come.

In contrast, it made complete sense for Inoue to command the entire Japanese offensive. He commanded the preponderance of assets involved.

From his command post in Rabaul, he was reasonably close enough to influence the action. As an experienced naval officer knowledgeable in naval aviation, he was well qualified to oversee the operation.

Executing the complicated attack he envisioned would have been far easier if they caught the Allies unprepared. Still, Inoue was more than experienced enough to know that war never goes as planned. He took a number of precautions both to detect and to be prepared to defend the invasion force against a counterstrike by the Allies.

On the morning of May 7, one of those precautions paid off. Japanese spotter planes reported sighting American ships. The battle was on.

The first great carrier air-dual of the war occurred on May 7–8 in the Battle of the Coral Sea. The *Yorktown* was slightly damaged. *Lady Lex* (the *Lexington*) was less lucky. Badly damaged, after the battle the ship had to be abandoned and was scuttled, sunk by one of the accompanying destroyers. The Allies lost two other ships, sixty-nine planes, and 656 dead. In turn, the Allies sunk the light carrier and badly damaged one of the fleet carriers. The Americans also sunk four other ships and damaged four more. The Japanese also lost ninety-two planes and 966 men. Most significantly, Vice Admiral Inoue called off the invasion of Port Moresby.

The naval air war was the most high-profile part of the carrier fight, but it was not the most terrible part of the fighting. The crisscrossing of contrails, hot lines of red tracers, and swirling trails of black smoke stitched on the blue skies above the fleets were "never the face of naval battle for the great majority and it was not for the great majority during the Battle of the Coral Sea," writes retired Australian admiral James Goldrick:

> This face is very different. It is even more challenging and even more frightening. It is an experience of confined spaces, of being shut down under armoured hatches and within small compartments. Most often, it is a group experience—the stokers tending their boilers, the damage control and medical teams distributed around the ship, the turret and magazine crews ready to work their weapons and push the ammunition supplies up to the guns. But it can be a solitary experience, for the individuals who have to tend a piece of machinery in a small compartment—sometimes in spaces in which it is impossible even to stand upright.[26]

When the battles of the Southwest Pacific are told on a human scale they tend to focus on dogfights of carrier pilots or the trials of disease-ridden threadbare foot soldiers slugging it out in slimy jungles. This battle reminds us of the other faces of this war.

Seaman Otis Kight sailed with the *Yorktown* after Pearl Harbor. He was slotted as a plane pusher, part of the crew that wheeled planes on and off the carrier deck. He was with the ship as part of the hit-and-run raids on the "coconut continent" islands of the Southwest Pacific, including the successful attacks on Lae and Salamaua. Most of his war was monotonous, sweaty work in hot cramped spaces. That was his war, until the first day of war like no other: May 7, 1942.

After Coral Sea, having survived the harrowing moments of battle that waged overhead, Otis Kight also faced what came after. "I had only read in Hemingway's novels about 'the sweet smell of death,' he recalled many years later. "The area was a full disaster, and I realized what the 'sweet smell of death' really was. There were parts and particles; some ship, some shipmate." It was a grim experience. "And the thought crossed my mind then, and many more times," he remembered, "where is my number? There was sadness, and respect, for the dead, but not the wholesale celebration this present generation embraces. We gave them a military burial at sea, and went on with the business of war."[27] This unglamorous part of war hardly ever earned headlines or garnered Medals of Honor, but it was as vital to the outcome of the conflict as any.

Aftermath

What did make news was the battle itself. The Japanese press heralded the fight as a triumph for the casualities inflicted on the Allies. These reports began to appear before the Japanese ships even left the Coral Sea. MacArthur immediately jumped in as well, issuing communiqués, which at least in Australia left an outsized impression of his role in directing the battle and the contribution of MacArthur's air force in turning back the MO invasion. One Australian paper described the Battle of the Coral Sea "as one of the most important events of the war," lauding MacArthur's effort to "adequately . . . meet it, with results that have made front-page news all over the world."[28]

In the actual fight, the land-based bombers did not accomplish much. Three of MacArthur's bombers mistook MacArthur's naval task force as part of the invasion fleet and attacked one of the destroyers. Fortunately, they missed. As for combat action, the only other fighting MacArthur's navy saw was fending off a swarm of Japanese planes.

Whether from the annoyance of MacArthur grabbing credit or fears of the premature disclosure of information that might compromise the security of the ships still at sea, King and Nimitz fretted over MacArthur's press releases. In turn, MacArthur fired a dispatch to Marshall to defend himself.[29] In part, by pointing out the press releases did not include any useful information for the enemy. For their part, the US Navy withheld details of the story until after the subsequent Battle of Midway (June 4–7, 1942).

The tit-for-tat among senior commanders aside, the impact of MacArthur's press management was more than the personal aggrandizement of MacArthur. MacArthur manipulated the story to reinforce the belief that the Allies had both the capability and determination to protect Australia. The narrative played well in local papers throughout the country. One wrote:

> The fact that the Allied attacks are continuing shows that General MacArthur intends to make it as difficult as possible for the Japanese to recover their poise and bring up reinforcements for another attempt to push south. What they will try again, and perhaps very soon, need not be doubted. The fact that they were prepared to risk so much of their naval strength to isolate Australia from America shows clearly how very seriously they regard the threat of a massive Allied offensive from this country. The sample they have had of American and Australian hitting power must have convinced them more firmly than ever of the menace of Australia as an Allied offensive base and must have increased their determination to cut the Pacific route along which have come the American men and equipment so successfully used against them.[30]

This was precisely the message MacArthur wished to convey.

Crisis in Command

Following the inconclusive fight at the Coral Sea and failure of Operation MO, the Japanese were frustrated again at the Battle of Midway only a month later. Not only did Yamamoto's forces fail to take the atoll, during the sea battle the Imperial Japanese Navy lost four aircraft carriers and 240 aircraft, as well as other ship losses and casualties. On the American side, the carrier *Yorktown* was badly damaged and later sunk by torpedoes from a Japanese submarine. The Americans also had other losses including about 150 aircraft.

The Americans could make up their losses. In dockyards, airplane factories, aircrew training schools, and training bases the US arsenal of democracy was turning into high gear. That was less true for the Japanese. Japan faced the prospects of defending its widening empire with resources increasingly stretched thin and an industrial base increasingly squeezed and unable to keep up.

Japan also lost its opportunity to take Midway. The high command, however, remained committed to salvaging its strategy. Yamamoto looked to securing Guadalcanal in the Solomon Islands as the next best available target to extend his control of the Southwest Pacific to the east. Meanwhile, the Imperial Japanese Army committed to an overland campaign across Papua New Guinea to secure Port Moresby once and for all.

As for MacArthur, he would continue to press for—but not get—his own carrier force. Even after the resounding victory at Midway, King kept close control over his handful of carriers. They remained the most important asset at his disposal for influencing the course of the war. If MacArthur ever hoped to command the Coral Sea and the approaches to Australia—either for the defense of the continent or to launch the counterstrike he envisioned back to the Philippines and the defeat of the Japanese homeland—he would have to secure that base with unsinkable aircraft carriers, key interlocking land-based facilities no more than a few hundred miles apart.

By the end of spring 1942, both the Japanese and Allied high commands were at a crucial point of decision. Both sought the same goal in the Southwest Pacific—dominance over the same unsinkable ground, Papua New Guinea. Driven by that competing hunger, one of the most formidable and consequential clash of arms in the great war was about to begin in the remote jungles of a faraway land.

Notes

1. Konoe repeated the second half of this quote in an essay he published in 1933. See Rees, *Horror in the East*, p. 48; Schom, *The Eagle and the Rising Sun,* pp. 49–50. The ideas extend back to an article published in 1918 in the wake of the post–World War I settlement, which created a system that benefited the Anglo-Americans and hamstrung Japan. See Yagami, *Konoe Fumimaro and the Failure of Peace in Japan*, pp. 16–18. See also Kershaw, *Fateful Choices*, pp. 106–125.

2. Oja, *Konoe Fumimaro*, p. 47.

3. Shigeo and Saburo, "The Role of the Diet and Political Parties," pp. 321–324.

4. Oja, *Konoe Fumimaro*, pp. 161–162.

5. Sumida and Moran, "Review of *If Mahan Ran the Great Pacific War*," 1296.

6. Coox, *Tojo*, p. 19.

7. A concise description of carrier air operations is provided in Hammel, *Carrier Crash*, pp. 25–35.

8. Jurens, "The Evolution of Battleship Gunnery in the US Navy, 1920–1945," p. 246.

9. H. P. Willmott, *The Barrier and the Javelin*, p. xiv.

10. Myers, *The Pacific War and Contingent Victory*, p. 8.

11. Yagami, *Konoe Fumimaro and the Failure of Peace in Japan*, p. 9.

12. Drea, *In the Service of the Emperor*, p. 26.

13. Ishida, *Japanese Political Culture*, p. 28. See also, Oja, *Konoe Fumimaro*, p. 73.

14. Benedick, *The Chrysanthemum and the Sword*, pp. 7–8.

15. Umphrey, "From Screen to Page," p. 24.

16. Keene, "Japanese Writers and the Greater East Asia War," p. 209. See also Steele, *Certain Victory*; Orbaugh *Propaganda Performed*; Frühstück, *Playing War*.

17. Quoted in Harries and Harries, *Soldiers of the Sun*, p. 258.

18. Gamble, *Fortress Rabaul*, p. 118.

19. Quoted in Drea, *In the Service of the Emperor*, p. 35.

20. Myers, *The Pacific War and Contingent Victory*, p. 38.

21. Drea, *In the Service of the Emperor*, p. 33.

22. Bradley, *Hell's Battlefield*, p. 26.

23. Spector, *Eagle Against the Sun*, pp. 151, 155–156; Toll, *Pacific Crucible*, pp. 320–321.

24. Drea, *MacArthur's ULTRA*, pp. 15–16.

25. See, for example, "Estimate of the Situation," April 22, 1942, War Plans, CINCPAC Files, Subject: Running Estimate and Summary, US Naval War College, p. V-1.

26. Goldrick, "The Face of Naval Battle."

27. Kight, "Coral Sea and Other Reflections."

28. "Battle of the Coral Sea," *The Examiner*, May 11, 1942, p. 1.

29. Borneman, *MacArthur at War*, pp. 203–204.

30. "Battle of the Coral Sea," *The Examiner*, May 11, 1942, p. 1.

4

Of Muck
and Men

*"Most of what the American and Australian publics thought they
knew about the isles of the Southwest Pacific had been invented by
movie scriptwriters."* —William Manchester

USING THE CULTURAL clichés of the time, the journalist-turned-historian
described a place of war there never was. "Even as the Japanese were
pictured as a blinky-eyed, toothy Gilbert and Sullivan race," Manchester wrote in his expansive biography *American Caesar: Douglas Mac-
Arthur, 1880–1964*,[1] "so the South Seas were an exotic world where
lazy breezes whispered in palm fronds and Sadie Thompson seduced
missionaries, and native girls dived for pearls wearing fitted sarongs,
like Dorothy Lamour."[2] In Dorothy Lamour's dreamy eyes and soft
curves, Americans saw the Pacific they thought they knew.

Postwar culture glossed over much of the gritty reality of jungle
war. The history of the bitter land war in the Southwest Pacific lies
under a canopy of hazy memory between prewar ignorance and postwar
remembrance. Understanding the long jungle war starts with looking
past the myth, knowing the landscape of muck that men fought in and
the nature of the armies that clashed in Papua New Guinea.

The Place

Historians can debate the accuracy of Manchester's MacArthur, but not
his caricature of popular perceptions about the distant lands where GIs
would suffer and die in absolute misery. Americans, indeed all sides in

51

the bitter conflict, knew almost nothing about the hellish places where they would fight. Papua New Guinea was the farthest of faraway places.

Papua New Guinea was a poster child of colonial geopolitics. The western half of the island, West Papua (today the Indonesian territory of Papua) belonged to the Dutch. Before the war, the eastern half, a massive landmass of over 178,000 square miles, was split in half between a German colony in the north and British colony in the south. In 1905 (four years after the six colonies in Australia federated to become the Commonwealth of Australia) the British turned administration of their territory over to the Aussies.

At the outbreak of World War I, Australia captured the German colony in a minor military campaign, eventually formally receiving trusteeship from the League of Nations. When World War II broke out, the Commonwealth of Australia governed both the Territory of Papua and the Mandated Territory of New Guinea (popularly known as Papua New Guinea), the surrounding islands such as the Bismarck Archipelago (Admiralty Island, Bougainville, New Britain including Rabaul and New Ireland), as well as hundreds of small islands and archipelagos— landmasses that surrounded the Coral Sea, the gateway to Australia.

Australians knew very little about the wild place they owned. In the 1920s, the discovery of gold near Wau, a town on the southern tip of Papua New Guinea, sparked a gold rush. A modicum of mining development as well as settlements and farming followed.[3] Before the 1930s, the government had mapped little of the interior. The patrol officers who first scouted these regions, often accompanied only by a dozen or so Indigenous men recruited from the police force and bearers to carry equipment and supplies, found almost a million people who had never seen an outsider before, living lives unchanged since the Stone Age. The Indigenous people spoke hundreds of languages; there were a plethora of tribes, sometimes violent and warring. Cannibalism was commonplace. In many cases, even the tribes themselves knew little of the expanse of the highlands. For them, knowledge of the outside world might extend no farther than the borderland with the next tribe.

Although the ability to communicate among the highland tribes might not reach beyond the nearest village, for generations the lowlands and the surrounding islands developed a commonly used language—Tok Pisin (bird talk), a pidgin language derived from Indigenous Melanesian tongues with German and English words. Introduced through colonization, it was the most widely used means to communicate in the Papua New Guinea region.[4] Westerners might recognize some of the words. The average outsider, however, would find talking to the strange people in a strange land a difficult skill to master beyond the simplest of conversations.

In 1939, about 7,000 White people lived in Papua New Guinea: a smattering of Australian government officials and their families, plantation overseers, missionaries, miners, and shopkeepers. They were the only link to the wider world. And, unlike the natives they knew war was coming. The Whites also understood their remote island stood between Japan and her imperial dreams.

Even in the remotest corner, settlers could see that the war clouds were not beyond the horizon. Lloyd Purchase, a government official in Finschhafen on the northeast coast of Papua New Guinea, was one. His wife had already returned to Australia. He kept her updated:

> Well dearest what do you think of this European affair. It looks as though the fights on this time and what a struggle she will be. I hate the thought of it as I am not in accord with war. The odds at the moment do not look too good for Britain. I dont [*sic*] expect to keep on here for very long if it is on and may be will sent down south. Whichever way it goes it is depressing thought. The Japs seem to be the chief source of worry here and in Australia and all sorts of rumors as to the outcome are circulating.[5]

In addition to overseeing the Indigenous peoples, Purchase monitored the local international community including Lutheran missionaries from Germany, rumored to be enemy agents.[6] Purchase wrote to his wife:

> The Lutheran Mission Rev Zimmerman was duly informed war broken out against his country and England. Poor chap didnt [*sic*] know whther [*sic*] I was going to shoot him or put him in a concentration camp. He went so far as to offer to let me read his letters which he was sending out to Lae his headquarters. Seeing as I cannot read German I declined with thanks. His wife is about to have a baby and was disturbed that they might not let the mission doctor in when the time is due. I gave him a tip that the Australians were not inclined to indulge in brutal practices but were most humane.[7]

By the time the fighting came most Whites had left. The non-Indigenous population dropped to less than 700. The rest either voluntarily departed or were forced to evacuate. There would be few Western observers, other than journalists and soldiers, to witness the great conflict. Vicious fighting to come, however, would not take place on an empty battlefield. In addition, to the 1 million Indigenous people scattered across the interior, another 800,000 lived along the coast.

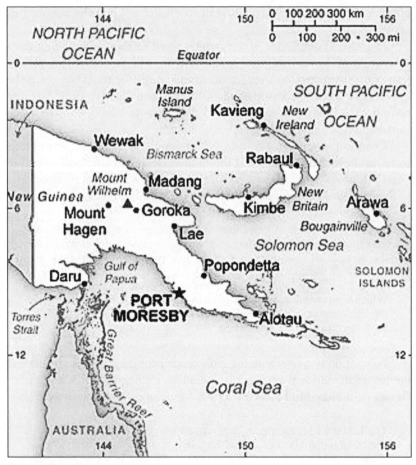

Papua New Guinea
Source: CIA, *The World Factbook.*

The Terrain

The terrain that the many peoples of Papua New Guinea inhabited was as bewildering as their numerous languages. The country is anything but a single mass of tangled jungle. A chain of mountains and steep river valleys runs the length of New Guinea Island, dividing the northern and southern halves of the landmass. The Owen Stanley Range, the dominant and from a military standpoint the most significant terrain feature in the theater of war, spans the Papua New Guinea half of the island's central mountain-chain, over 200 miles of often cloud-shrouded jagged peaks, razor-backed ridges, and steep gorges ranging from twenty-five to seventy miles wide. In many places the mountains rise abruptly from the coastal plain to 9,000 feet. The highest peak is over 13,000 feet. No army in the world trained to fight in a place like this.

The heavy rainfall and steep slopes feed raging fast-flowing rivers that plummet from the highlands to the coastal planes. Five major rivers descend from the mountains to divide the lowlands—the Mamberamo flowing northwest, the Spik and Ramu in the northeast, the Fly in the southeast, and the Digul flowing southwest. They are just the biggest ones. There are many more to vex armies trying to cross from one place to another. In places, forging the rivers could be as dangerous as braving enemy fire.

Flanking the raging rivers, a jungle so thick as to be virtually impassable drapes the mountainsides. At about 8,500 feet the jungle gives way to a tropical "alpine" environment—a tall, dark forest of moss-covered trees, giant ferns, and a floor thick and slick with vines, shrubs, and oozy mud, terrain no more forgiving than the tangle of jungle and rivers below.

Central Papua New Guinea is another world. The central highlands spread out in wide fertile valleys covered in thick kunai grass (leaves that could reach up to ten feet tall). Some of this land proved suitable for plantation farming. Before the war, there were about 500 plantations operating throughout Papua New Guinea. During the war, they were abandoned. The open spaces they left behind were inviting to the invading armies. Enemies would fight over a flat piece of ground for a resupply airstrip like knights storming a castle.

Vast stretches of mangrove swamps and coastal river deltas dot the lowlands north and south of the central mountain range. The rest of the lowlands are a spread of tropical rainforests. Wide river mouths and placid bays indent much of the low-lying coastline. Virtually all the established settlements, towns like Port Moresby, Wau, Salamaua, Lae, and Milne Bay, hugged the coastal lowlands. No roads linked the coastal towns.

Traversing this tough terrain was more difficult than a mountain hike. Michael J. Leahy recorded his account of trekking up the range in his explorations during the 1930s. His observations noted the remarkable diversity of difficult terrain. At a campsite at 8,000 feet "a heavy hailstorm hit us," he recalled, "and pounded fine damp mist right through our fly and tent." On the following march, "[w]e dropped 2,000 feet into a deep timber-covered gorge along a wet slippery native track which from years of sharp stick-dug footholds and eroding rainwater was more deep trench than track. . . .We crossed back into the headwaters of the Asaro [a river in the Eastern Highlands province] at 9,100 feet above sea level . . . through the heavy cloud cover that shrouded the top of the divide, we slipped and fell down another trench like track through the clouds to a magnificent view of the Goroka Valley [in the Papua New Guinea highlands] beneath us."[8] That was what a typical day's trek for the armies would be like.

Unlike the campaigns in Europe, where bridges and roads linked the great capitals, there was scant infrastructure in Papua New Guinea that an army could use to march to victory. Outside the copra plantations (which went untended during the war), most of the island depended on agriculture including sweet potato, taro, yams, sago, and bananas.[9] Villagers also raised pigs or fished the rivers and coastline. This was subsistence agriculture, not enough food to feed an army. Any assets that a force needed to push back the point at which an attacker would culminate, every bullet, every gallon of gas, every part, morsel of food, tin of medical supplies, all of it would have to be carried, shipped, or flown into battle.

No roads or bridges linked the sparse, dotted population centers, missions, plantations, and villages that sprouted along the lowlands surrounding the Owen Stanley Range. The portages and airstrips built to bring in supplies for plantations, support trade for a village, or deliver equipment to a mining community were not designed to host modern navies or air forces. Getting around was done mostly by boat, plane, or walking. Trails or tracks (both just muddy jungle trails) crisscrossed the highlands, often little more than crude single-file paths etched in the jungle. The most famous of these is the Kokoda trail, running some sixty miles from a point east of Port Moresby over the Owen Stanley Range to the station town of Kokoda in the highlands.[10]

At the outbreak of the war, this inhospitable and inaccessible land was also virtually unknown territory. The available maps were decades old, drafted by the Dutch, British, and Australians. If traveling by air or sea, the major islands and coastline offered some guide to navigation. But inland the maps were practically useless either for reckoning by aircrews above or a marching column on the ground. Unless troops or their guides had crossed the terrain on foot or pilots had experience flying over the cloud-shrouded peaks and jungle valleys, charting a path over the Papua New Guinea landscape was like crossing an obstacle course blindfolded.

Weather in Papua New Guinea can be as daunting as the terrain. Most of the country during most of the year is hot and humid, except in the high forests of the Owen Stanley Range where the temperatures are downright chilly year-round. The challenging and varying climate would complicate the task of properly clothing and equipping the ground troops.

It always rains in Papua New Guinea. There are two monsoon seasons, the northwest monsoon season (December to March) and the southwest monsoon season (May to October). The heaviest rainfall occurs in the highlands, up to 179 inches a year. The unpredictable and often savage weather, particularly over the Owen Stanley Range, could make for extremely hazardous flying conditions. On the ground, troops would live in two conditions—wet and hot or wet and cold. Unbearable weather is not the only concern. Typhoons can hit from December to March. The area is also prone to earthquakes, volcanic eruptions, and tsunamis.

More mundane hazards could be an even greater threat to an invading army. Tropical eye, skin, and foot infections are the most common medical concerns. Even small nicks and scratches could result in serious infections. More than an irritant, for fighting troops these infections could be serious, impairing their ability to march and fight.

In Papua New Guinea the number of vectors and the illnesses they can carry is literally an encyclopedia of tropical diseases. Mites, known as chiggers, could infect troops with scrub typhus, which could be fatal. Malaria, transmitted by mosquitos, might be less likely to kill but the chills, fever, and aches could be debilitating. Dengue fever was another painful, incapacitating mosquito-borne disease that plagued the region. Some of the swampy areas are infested with typhus-carrying parasites that can cause a severe rash, fever, and even gangrenous sores and death. Dysentery from contaminated food and water is another common concern. Ringworm, hookworm, leeches, and bacteria carrying yaws that exploded in painful skin lesions are commonplace.

All these infections and illnesses are hazards on their own. They would be doubly dangerous to troops lacking proper nutrition, hydration, rest, hygiene, and medical care. Even if the medical staff of an invading military had a full directory of every illness on the island, that alone would not prepare for all perils of the campaign. "The diseases of Aberdeen are much the same as those of London or even New York," noted a contemporary medical text; "diseases in the tropics however show marked variations from place to place and from season to season."[11] Humidity, winds, rainfall, sunshine, temperature, barometric pressure, soil, water, irrigation, drainage, deforestation, and vegetation could all affect the epidemiology of a tropical disease. In Papua New Guinea, these factors varied greatly from one part of the island to the next. In this kind of jungle warfare an enemy soldier was an enemy soldier, but tropical diseases had many faces.

Nor was disease the only danger lurking in the jungle. Papua New Guinea was home to poisonous spiders, venomous snakes, and blood-sucking bugs, in addition to any manner of hazards that could cause a broken limb, a fatal fall, or drowning. Heat stroke was another common concern for outsiders unaccustomed to the intense temperatures and humidity.

Further, the tropical conditions were not just factors that would affect the soldier in the foxhole. Humidity and temperature and harsh conditions were the enemy of the infrastructure of war. Crates of supplies would rot if not properly protected. Rats and fungi assaulted supplies. Weapons fouled. Ammunition rusted. Few environments were less hospitable to the instruments of modern warfare. During the war, no challenge was greater than long-range radio communications. Moisture and humidity damaged sensitive electronic equipment. Equipment was bulky, difficult to move and maintain in the jungle. Weather caused static and the mountains blocked radio signals.

Taken together, almost every facet of the geography and environment of Papua New Guinea had the potential to wreak havoc. The invaders would learn the jungle was neutral. Papua New Guinea equally shared its hardships and privations with all comers.

Jungle Hollywood

In military schools, such as the Command and General Staff College at Fort Leavenworth, Kansas; the Imperial Japanese Army Academy; the Royal Military Academy at Sandhurst; or the Royal Military College at Duntroon, officers were taught to gain an appreciation for the ground they might battle over and the conditions that might affect the struggle. Each military had in its doctrine a requirement to know about the ground where they would fight.

The US Army called the practice conducting an "estimate of the situation." In particular, army doctrine cautioned "that part of the commander's estimate dealing with *terrain* often exercises a decisive influence upon his decision and plan."[12] Knowing the ground was part of the knowing the business of battle.

All the information on the daunting conditions of the world where they would fight ought to have been part of each army's war arsenal. In practice, the men that would wage combat over the Owen Stanley Range knew little more about this distant theater than the average American factory worker, Australian outback rancher, or rural Japanese rice farmer—and that was not much.

An outsider's knowledge of the land was shaped more by their imagination than anything else. To Americans, writes Kelly Enright, the jungle "was decidedly a product of mass culture, born in with the rise of Hollywood and the entertainment industry."[13] The dominant aesthetic in US films was realism. The appeal of contemporary cinema was that it left theatergoers with a feeling that onscreen narratives were rooted in a real time and place. For many Depression-era Americans who had never seen a wild animal outside a circus or zoo, the jungle reality of the silver screen was all they knew. Like most of the reality peddled by American movies, tinsel town, for the most part, invented its jungle reality.

Hollywood assembled the jungle world from existing pop culture that primarily saw distant lands as places of danger and adventure for Westerners to explore and conquer, and battling evil, banishing ignorance—primitive worlds that with White fortitude would give way to Western modernity. The dark jungle place was also largely undifferentiated. Hollywood films, for example, often featured the same stock footage, carelessly mixing animals from different continents and thoughtlessly interposing shots of grasslands, rainforests, and dense jungle. For live shoots, the backdrop might be the swamplands of Louisiana substituting for Africa in the silent 1917 *Tarzan of the Apes* or Lake Sherwood, California, which provided much of the scenery for the early Johnny Weissmuller films. The same location was used for such diverse places as a medieval Sherwood Forest in the *Adventures of Robin Hood* (1938) and Tibet in *Lost Horizon* (1937).

On the eve of World War II, to most Americans all that was required to conquer a primitive world was pretty much showing up. They would learn otherwise. One GI, writing of his experiences of fighting in Papua New Guinea in 1942, concluded:

> One of the permanent effects of this war, no matter what happens at the peace tables, will be a decline in movies with the South Seas Island settings. American soldiers who have returned from the Southwest Pacific will be unable to refrain from laughing out loud at the alluring women and romantic scenery. . . . Dorothy Lamour and her luscious colleagues [might] want to get out before it's too late.[14]

The real jungle was no Hollywood. Surviving required more than making an appearance.

The Other Place

Before the war, for Japan, the jungle world of the Southwest Pacific remained an equally remote and unimportant place. The Japanese were interested in Japan. "Popular film was one means of doing this," writes Olivia Umphrey in a study of prewar cinema. "It reinforced the growing xenophobia in Japanese society."[15] Films rarely featured foreigners or foreign locals. One film historian referred to the cinema of the decade as the "golden age" of Japanese filmmaking because these movies were so obsessively about Japan. Largely overlooked now because they were profoundly antithetical to the West, in the 1930s they showed Japan how the Japanese saw Japan, creating a global identity apart from the rest of the world.[16]

Even when Japanese films moved beyond Japanese shores, they were still all about Japan. *Shina no yoru* (1940) was a very popular wartime movie. Part of a series known as the "Chinese Continental Friendship," also called the "Continental Trilogy" films, *Shina no yoru* justified Japanese expansionism and the occupation of China through the story of a youthful couple in the midst of war. In the film, a serious and courageous young naval officer meets a hotheaded Chinese war orphan. Over the course of their relationship, the civilized Japanese man tames the wild Chinese woman. She abandons her anti-Japanese attitude. At their marriage ceremony, he is abruptly called away to duty. In the Japanese version of the film, he dies in battle. In grief, she commits suicide. In the film distributed in China, he returns safely. They live happily ever after. The one ending emphasizes service and sacrifice. The other accentuates the benevolence of Japanese rule. Both sentiments were crucial to Japan's emerging global identity as an expansionist power.[17] The underlying theme of *Shina no yoru* echoed Prime Minister Konoe's clarion call that the nation was engaged in a legitimate, moral crusade to reshape the world order.

Japan's self-obsession was not just on the big screen. The National Spirit Mobilization Movement (which otherwise stressed economy and sacrifice) promoted tourism—as long as it was within Japan. The movement encouraged domestic travel as a means for the people to learn about their history and geography, gaining a greater appreciation for Japanese society and preparing them for a leadership role in a new Asia.[18] The world outside Japan was just a place to command.

The sentiments of moral right in subjugating foreign places and the undefeatable spirit of the Japanese people shaped how they would address the terrors of distant jungles. The foreigners and terrain they would encounter were all just so much blank space for the Japanese people to imprint their image upon.

Down Under

The 1920s and 1930s brought hard times to Depression-era Australia, which despite its growing significance as an Asia-Pacific nation (including its new responsibilities to administer Papua New Guinea) increasingly looked to reaffirm its identity with the West. Not surprisingly, there were far stronger parallels in Australia to the United States and British popular culture than to Japan.

Australia had its own film industry. The down-under Hollywood fell on hard times in the 1920s, largely supplanted by US and British movie companies that distributed their own works. One Aussie who bucked the trend was James Francis "Frank" Hurley. The filmmaker made two silent feature pictures in 1926 that did well at the box office in Australia and Britain. Filmed on Thursday Island off the coast of Queensland, Australia, *The Hound of the Deep* was a South Seas romance-adventure story. Hurley filmed a second feature, *Jungle Woman*, partly on Thursday Island and Dutch New Guinea. *Jungle Woman* featured explorers traipsing through exotic locales, searching for gold, escaping headhunters, and forbidden love—all the classic tropes of a South Seas drama.

Contemporary Western films also left an indelible image on their audiences. "On the eve of the Pacific War the South Seas figured prominently in popular culture across the Western world," conclude Sean Brawley and Chris Dixon in an expansive study of the influence of literature and media on conceptions of the Oceanic world. Contemporary views of the South Pacific were shaped by imaginings—portrayals of an exotic life of the South Sea Islands in places like New Britain and the Solomons. Movies such as *Jungle Princess* (1936), which starred a young Dorothy Lamour clad in a sarong (designed by famed Hollywood dress designer Edith Head), created the iconic images that both Australian and American troops carried into war, sometimes in visible form with pinup pictures of Lamour, a wild flower in her hair, long wavy tresses over naked shoulders, and the revealing sarong. These were as different from real life as Tarzan's jungle was from the actual Congo Basin.[19]

For Australians, Papua New Guinea was an exception to the popular conception of the romantic and inviting islands of the South Seas. The vast island world held a space in popular imagination far different from the breezy palm tree paradise of Hollywood's Tahiti. Since the nineteenth century, Papua New Guinea had long been a focus of imagination for Australians as both a potential source of wealth (the first gold and silver "rush" was in 1926) and a challenging new frontier as a "testing ground for the strength of the Australian character."[20] In the early 1920s, filmmaker Frank Hurley made two expeditions to Papua. His lectures, photographs, and documentary films, *Pearl and Savages* (1921) and *With the Headhunters in Papua* (1923), with their images of a strange faraway people were for many Australians the only face of the land they knew. For generations, the vast island remained a "dark and mysterious land with 'fierce and cruel' inhabitants."[21]

Papua New Guinea was a place that was at the same time inviting and foreboding.[22] In the twentieth century, the government's White Australia policy restricted Papua New Guinean immigration to the mainland. That policy remained in place until decades after the war. So even after Australia assumed trusteeship, beyond explorers, prospectors, government officials, and plantation overseers, the island people remained remote and unknown to Aussies.[23] The place where Australian soldiers would fight and die in unprecedented numbers was for most of them the place of their imagination, until they arrived at stations like Port Moresby and Milne Bay.

Unlike other foreign lands where the Australian Army might serve, writes Lachlan Grant in an overview the national military experience in World War II, "in Papua New Guinea it was the Australians rather than the British who were the colonial 'mastas' the upholder of white man's privilege. . . . Australian troops were instructed by fellow Australians to uphold an 'attitude of superiority' and where they were told they were 'superior beings.'"[24] This was their land to defend. To lose it would not only be a strategic disaster but a deep humiliation to the standing of the Australian people. The nation would be quick to fight for a place Australia barely knew.

In summary, an Australian bank clerk leafing through bills in Canberra, a Japanese soldier patrolling the streets of Nanking, or an American farmhand bringing in the harvest had no notion of what real war would be like in the wilds of Papua New Guinea. This added burden cannot be overemphasized. They might have as well been transported to fight on another planet. Not only were they unaware of the nature of jungle war of 1942, each of the armies in Papua New Guinea was unprepared for a fight in the muck.

Army at Dawn

The US Army did not enter World War II from a standing start. Long before the squabbling between Lindbergh and FDR began, the armed forces had been thinking about a big war. With limited budgets and meager forces during the interwar years, the services tried to prepare for the future. The army and navy participated in the Rainbow War plans that anticipated global conflict. The navy tested aircraft carriers. Marines toyed with amphibious operations. The army began protective mobilization planning that examined how war production and fielding new forces could be employed to rapidly increase the size of the army. In 1939, the army conducted a number of field experiments, redesigning the division, the fundamental building block of American ground warfare. In World War I, the United States had "square" divisions, each with four infantry regiments designed primarily to sustain troops at the front in attrition trench fighting. The new triangular division structure included three fighting regiments, supplemented with additional combat units such as artillery brigades and independent tank battalions. The new division structure was meant to facilitate fast-moving offensive maneuver warfare.[25]

Beginning in 1939, Roosevelt took interim steps to mobilize the military. He pressed Congress to increase funding and expand the armed forces.

In May 1940, Congress authorized selective service. Local draft boards conducted the first draft call later that year. In addition, that summer the president mobilized the National Guard for federal service.

From August to September 1941, army divisions joined in massive mock battles in Louisiana. Meanwhile, the army staff prepared the Victory Program, a document that laid out the general requirements for a global force.[26] Congress later authorized a three-month extension of the troops that had been called-up the previous year.

When Congress delivered the declaration of war there were already about thirty divisions in various states of preparation. There were almost a million and half men in army green uniforms. Only two years before there were less than 200,000 soldiers in uniform.

Still, the army was a long way from the force envisioned by the Victory Program (over 230 divisions) or the more than 8 million men in 90 divisions with modern equipment that the army generals commanded by war's end. Lindbergh, who knew a good deal about the state of rearmament mobilization, wrote in his journals only weeks after Pearl Harbor, "The newspapers are rapidly winning the war for us. I wish our military forces could keep up with them."[27] America was not prepared for a global war.

There is also the question: Could the Americans fight? Tom Brokaw's best-selling book *The Greatest Generation* (1998) and Steven Spielberg's Academy Award–winning film *Saving Private Ryan* (1998) appeared on the eve of the fiftieth anniversary of World War II's outbreak. Both book and film celebrated American grit and sacrifice. Today, the tag "greatest generation" is accepted as a matter of faith. This was not always so.

It is difficult to summarize the hopes and fears of a whole generation. There are, however, many prewar voices that give us pause. Some had serious doubts that men and women who came of age long after World War I could stand the rigors of battle. The novelist James Michener recalled that "many observers considered us a lost generation and feared we might collapse if summoned to some crucial battlefield."[28] There was also a measure of guilt. Russell Cartwright Stroup, army chaplain and a veteran of the Pacific War, wrote that he chose overseas service because he felt that, "as part of a generation that failed to prevent this war, I should suffer with those who are victims of our failure."[29] Americans were late to battle, sitting out the first two years of global conflict while the children of other nations earned their red badge of courage. Americans were yet to prove their mettle. Some did not want to be tested at all. Some fled before going to war. Others deserted on the battlefield.[30]

After Pearl Harbor, however, most Americans rallied to the challenge. Novelist and Pacific War veteran Anton Myrer wrote, "I enlisted imbued with a rather flamboyant concept of this country's destiny as the leader of a free world and the necessity of the use of armed force."[31] He started the war with supreme confidence. Others did not. But, Americans did answer the call to arms. About half of the military were drafted. The rest, millions, volunteered (including prominent leaders of the non-interventionist movement America First Hanford MacNider and Lindbergh, who both fought in Papua New Guinea).

When America declared war, US military forces were pathetically inadequate for prosecuting a global conflict. The United States would have to mobilize millions of men without any prior military experience. Despite the size of the US population, this was no easy task. About half of the 20 million Americans that had registered for the first call-up were deemed unfit for military service—mostly for health reasons or because they were illiterate. General Lesley J. McNair, responsible for training army troops for overseas combat, also fretted over the quality of the new US soldiers' "fighting spirit." In a public radio address, he lectured:

We must lust for battle; our object in life must be to kill; we must scheme and plan, night and day, to kill. There need be no pangs of conscience for our enemies have lighted the way to faster, surer, and crueler killing; they are past masters. We must hurry to catch up with them if we are to survive. Since killing is the object of our troops, the sooner we get in the killing mood, the better and more skillful we shall be when the test comes. The struggle is for survival—kill or be killed.[32]

In part, McNair's concerns stemmed from the quality of the troops he had been given to handle the frontline fighting. The best recruits went to the other services. Man for man, one historian noted, McNair's men were "far shorter, weaker, and less intellectually capable (according to the classification system's standardized tests) than the average recruit."[33] There was an argument that US ground forces were not the greatest part of the greatest generation.

McNair was not the only one who held reservations. Americans had never easily reconciled Whites and Blacks fighting together. World War II would be no different. In 1941, Hyman Samuelson was at Fort Bragg, North Carolina, training his unit, the 96th Engineer Battalion (Colored) for deployment overseas. He wrote reflectively, "very much depressed this evening. Tired of these poor negroes, tired of punishing them, trying to reason with them. Such a shame for people with education to let such ignorance exist . . . Superstitious, Emotional! . . . Men who can hardly understand English—how can they be good soldiers?"[34] It was not an unimportant question. Black soldiers were a significant part of the forces. There were over a million in uniform. Most of them, over 800,000, were in the army. Over a quarter served overseas. From top to bottom, Black and White, there was an undertow of dread over being ready to go over there. It remained to be seen if this stock was good enough for the fight.

Americans might have been the greatest generation when they ended the war, but they sure did not start that way. From the onset of mobilization, the services competed for the smartest and healthiest recruits. The services also siphoned off some of the most promising soldiers into programs like the Army Specialized Training Program where they would learn technical skills. Initially, the draft also allowed individuals to volunteer for specific services and specialties. Only about 5 percent opted for the fighting arms like infantry. Meanwhile, segregation policies limited Blacks to separate combat support units (like artillery) and service units (such as quartermaster). In the end, many of the troops sent to fill out the frontline infantry divisions met only the lowest physical and intelligence standards for recruits. Troops were mustered in with physical and educational deficiencies that could not be erased with a few months of army chow, hard marches, and stern first sergeant lectures.

None of these shortfalls meant that US troops would not be first-class jungle fighters. Technical skills mattered less in battles fought by half-naked, half-starved men with little more than a rifle and a bayonet. Further, advanced education did not equal warrior intelligence. The skills of small unit leadership were the stuff practiced by stout, blue-collar men. Physical stature was not as crucial as mental toughness and the capacity to endure hardships. Ordinary men in the end could make extraordinary jungle fighters.

Perhaps the greatest limitation facing Americans was that unlike the Japanese and Australians, the army that deployed overseas in 1942 was an army untested in battle. Papua New Guinea was a long way from Louisiana (where the troops had conducted the largest-scale military maneuvers undertaken by the US Army since the World War I armistice). The maneuvers might have been useful for offering generals and staff (men like Eisenhower and Patton) practice in handling large units, but for the average soldier there was little of practical value. Umpires managed the troops' war with rulebooks. Men fought with simulated equipment because modern weapons were not yet available. Further, though some of the troops might have tangled with a Louisiana swamp, there was virtually no specialty training in jungle fighting or for that matter any kind of specialized field training. In the end, the army would learn how to fight in the jungle *in* the jungle.

The army did have a playbook for fighting. In 1939, General Marshall dispatched McNair to take command of the staff college at Fort Leavenworth to refresh the means for training officers and to rewrite doctrine that at the time was based on the lessons of storming the trenches in World War I. That started with rewriting the basic doctrinal manual of field service regulations, which led to the publication of Field Manual (FM) 100-5, *Operations*.

FM 100-5 emphasized the destruction of the enemy by concentrating superior force at the decisive time and place.[35] Other than providing a general philosophy for conducting modern war and guidance on leadership, command, and staff practices, the manual was not much help in how to fight in a jungle. The manual ran to almost 300 pages, but FM 100-5 had only two pages on jungle war.

The army's capstone manual was most notable for what it did not cover. War on a big island in the middle of the Pacific could not be conducted without the joint cooperation of ground, air, and naval forces. The manual had little to say on that matter. Logistics, the lifeblood of warfare, which would be needed to deliver everything from bullets to bandages to a theater of war at the end of the earth, did not rate much discussion in the army's top playbook. Further, the offensive and defensive operations fit well for maneuvering the army's triangular divisions. The triangular division, however, had no place in the jungle.

The manual acknowledged that jungle fighting would be more of a close-quarters infantry fight. That was cold comfort when figuring out how battle tactics applied to the wilds of Papua New Guinea, fighting over miles of trail no wider than the shoulders of a soldier. There was also little thought of how supporting arms from machine guns to artillery and close air support would help a force reach its objectives and wipe out the enemy.

The army was smart enough to know that it might fight many kinds of war during the course of the conflict. FM 100-5 stood at the apex of a mountain of doctrinal manuals, pamphlets, and training notes. The war library included detailed guidance on jungle fighting. The only problem is the advice was terrible. FM 31-20, *Basic Field Manual, Jungle Warfare,* offered such bits of advice as "do not fear the jungle," "Do not try to bully or rush the natives," "do not drink liquor in the jungle," and "don't go barefoot."[36] That the army felt compelled to add such aphorisms to its warfighting guidance suggests how little the average American understood the austere environments they would confront. While the manual did offer basic advice on tactics and aspects of jungle warfare, including supply, communication, hygiene, and dealing with Indigenous people and tropical disease, it described a jungle as undifferentiated as a movie set, basic instruction that had only marginal utility in trudging up places like the Kokoda trail.

Nor did FM 31-20 offer many insights into how to fight the Japanese. The manual was published only a week after the attack on Pearl Harbor. Even if it had been written earlier the field manual would not have been much help. While the Japanese had been fighting since 1937, none of that fighting was under jungle conditions. The Imperial Army's most successful jungle campaigns would occur in the months ahead as Japanese forces stormed through the Philippines, the Malay Peninsula, and Burma.

War, however, would not wait for doctrine and trained troops. GIs headed to the front to learn how to fight jungle war on the job. Before the war, there were no US Army troops in Australia. When MacArthur arrived on March 17, 1942, he had virtually no army to command. That soon changed. Of the contingent of troops deployed through the first four months of the war, 90,000 went to the Pacific (almost 70 percent of all the army forces sent abroad), and most went to Australia. In contrast, only about 20,000 were dispatched across the Atlantic (15 percent of the troops deployed).

In April, another 25,000 soldiers arrived in theater. These included men to fix equipment, belt ammunition, maintain aircraft, route supplies, and all the other tasks required to get the US military into the war. In addition to the service troops, MacArthur received his first levy of US warriors, units of the 41st Infantry Division. By mid-May, just after the Japanese invasion force headed for Port Moresby withdrew (the failed Operation MO) after tangling with Nimitz's carriers at the Battle of the Coral Sea (May 4–8), these units were joined by the rest of the division, as well as the 32nd Infantry Division.

The 32nd Infantry Division was one of the National Guard units mobilized in 1940. The army's National Guard traced its lineage to the volunteer colonial militias that provided for security on the frontier. The US Constitution enshrined the authority of the states to maintain militias. These the founders assumed would be the principle instruments used to provide for public safety. Meanwhile, Congress would authorize and maintain federal troops that would serve under the president as commander-in-chief. Militia units also served or provided volunteers for national conflicts including the Mexican-American War (1846–1848) and the American Civil War (1861–1865). After the Spanish-American War (1898), in 1903 legislation converted the state militias to the National Guard. These could be, by law, mustered into federal service and serve as active-duty troops. Once mobilized, their status would be indistinguishable from the regular army.

In 1917, the National Guard, 400,000 men strong (including the 32nd Infantry Division), was mobilized for World War I. After the war, additional changes were made to provide for more training and readiness in case the National Guard was required for overseas deployments in the future.[37] The National Guard soldiers of the 32nd Red Arrow Division were from Wisconsin and Michigan, lands as remote from the jungles of Papua New Guinea as could be imagined. Constituted in 1917, the 32nd Division fought in four major campaigns during World War I. The Red Arrow shoulder patch, a line shot through by a red arrow, signified that the division had pierced every enemy line it had faced. That hardened combat division was long gone. In the interwar years, troops assembled for a few hours of delusory weekly drills, and each year for two weeks of summer training.

When war loomed, most state guards were an admixture of dedicated veterans, social clubs, and state politics. Arthur J. Kessenich knew that well enough. In September 1940, twenty-two-year-old Kessenich noticed a small article in a Madison newspaper announcing the division would soon be mustered into active service.[38] After the collapse of France in May, the possibility that Britain might concede, and growing animosity with Japan, the United States began to rearm. One way or another, citizens were going to be called up for compulsory military training, either through the mobilization of the National Guard or the draft. Kessenich had a good job at B. F. Goodrich, a chance for promotion, and recently got engaged. Volunteering for the guard seemed liked a good option: a year of service with the division and then, if there was no war, back to a normal life, job, and family. That was the plan for him and similarly many tens of thousands of young Americans who hoped the war scare was just that.

The division deployed to Camp Beauregard, Louisiana. In normal times, a summer training camp for the guard, "Camp Disregard" was little more than a motley mud-covered tent city. The division began two years of haphazard training. Stovepipes served as mortars, and stakes marked machine gun positions where the unit would have trained with machine guns if any were available.

Four months later, the division moved to Camp Livingston, Louisiana. By August 1941, the Red Arrow was fighting imaginary battles in the Louisiana Maneuvers. War stilled seemed only a possibility. Many soldiers adopted pets. One company made a stray dog, "Smoky," their company mascot. When the division went on maneuvers, many personnel were left back, including the divisional football, baseball, and rifle teams. Kessenich, who recently married, received permission to stay behind to spend time with his bride.

Then war came. On the day the Japanese attacked Pearl Harbor, Kessenich bought a small Christmas tree, and he and his wife shared their last holiday together until after the Japanese surrender four years later. For Kessenich, the real war came like a jolt from nowhere. He was not alone. Americans were shocked to their core. The annual Rose Bowl football game was immediately canceled out of fear of imminent invasion.

In February, the division moved to Fort Devens, Massachusetts, in preparation for deployment to Europe. A different sea of faces crammed the pungent, sweaty, smoke-filled troop trains. In less than a year, the character of the Red Arrow had racially changed. When the division came on active service, friends, neighbors, coworkers, and relatives filled out the ranks. All the officers including the division commander were from the National Guard. But then the division was reorganized. Soldiers left for Officer Candidate School, army specialty training programs, or as cadre for other units. Some of those who left were among the division's best and brightest (though commanders also looked on the constant levy for men as an opportunity to dump troublemakers and shirkers). In their place draftees poured in. Much of the division leadership also changed. When General Edwin Forrest Harding, a regular army officer, assumed command on February 9, 1941, some units had only a quarter of their original ranks. Men like Kessenich found themselves soldiering in the company of strangers.

Despite personnel turbulence, training intensified and war seemed a more serious business now. New orders and a change in orientation further strained preparations. In the spring of 1942, as the Japanese solidified their conquests in the Philippines and Southeast Asia, the Joint Chiefs responded to MacArthur's request for additional forces. The division was routed to Fort Ord and then sailed for Australia. Along with the marines and soldiers headed for Guadalcanal, the 32nd Infantry Division would be among the first ground troops to take the offensive against the Japanese.

But even in Australia there were distractions. The 32nd Infantry Division's hastily built camp outside Brisbane had poor training facilities. Gambling, drinking, and women seemed the primary pursuits. "Things became pretty routine," one officer recalled, "with a lot of the usual training, hiking, close order drill. Living conditions were primitive but what made it bearable was being able to see our girlfriends on the weekend." Kessenich remembered that "the female population was anxious to meet males, particularly Americans, because our spending habits were more liberal." General Eichelberger, who would later command these men in the jungles of Papua New Guinea, lamented, "The war was being fought mostly in bed," a fact resented by many Australian men. One Australian officer complained about US officers lampooning the Australian defeats at Singapore and Papua New Guinea. Their girlfriends had "repeated these jokes and they had spread over Australia." It seemed before the United States grappled with the enemy, it was making enemies of its allies.

For now, the men of the 32nd Infantry Division were living fragments of their imaginary South Pacific. Dorothy Lamour had a print dress and an Aussie accent. All that would come to an end when they crossed the Coral Sea for a battle for which they were far from prepared.

Sons of the Rising Sun

Unlike the Americans, the Imperial Japanese Army was already at war when the race across the Southwest Pacific began. Fighting in China occupied the bulk of the military forces. In addition to the twenty-seven divisions in China, the Japanese had thirteen divisions to guard the border in Manchuria against a potential Russian invasion. In 1940, divisions were also sent to Indochina. Then in 1942, troops had to be dispatched for operations in Hong Kong, the Philippines, Thailand, Burma, Singapore and the Malay Peninsula, and Dutch East Indies, and marshaled for an invasion of Port Moresby (aborted after the Battle of the Coral Sea).

As the army advanced, Prince Konoe—now out of the government and increasingly disaffected and ignored—became obsessively disillusioned, even as victories piled up. "We should note," he told an associate, "we are victorious only because we are fighting against the Malay and South Pacific islanders. It would be awful if we were losing. What is crucial is how we will do in the upcoming fights [against Western troops]."[39] He had little confidence that Japan's enemies would easily yield.

The Imperial Army staff had a different hope. In 1942, the staff started looking to rapidly draw down forces in the Southwest Pacific after consolidating the outer defense perimeter of the empire. That was a fleeting hope. Over the course of the year and setbacks in the carrier war at the Battle of the Coral Sea and Midway, the army scrambled for more troops to send into the conflict.

In addition to the polyglot forces under Vice Admiral Inoue in Rabaul (initially organized for Operation MO, the invasion of Port Moresby), the 51st and 41st Divisions, destined for battle in Papua New Guinea, were sent from China. So were the 16th and 17th Divisions, eventually stationed at Bougainville (the easternmost island of Papua New Guinea in the Solomon Sea) and Rabaul. The 20th Division was relieved from occupation duty in Korea and sent to the theater as well.

Like the Americans, the Japanese had adopted a triangular organized division as its main fighting force. The Japanese division, however, included a much higher proportion of infantry and fewer supporting arms and services. The organization of Japanese forces, concludes historian Ed Drea, was organized around the principal that "men, not machines and firepower, win wars."[40] Manpower was always the core of the Japanese fighting instrument.

The organization of combat units, in turn, reflected how Japan thought about fighting war. "One can," Drea summarizes, "search in vain to discover a jungle warfare doctrine in pre–World War II Japanese

FSRs [field service regulations]."[41] Most doctrinal thinking focused on fighting a conventional war against the Soviet Union, practices that did not easily adapt to war on jungle islands. In British Malaya, the Japanese found success in jungle warfare, employing tactics that relied on finding an open flank, usually by probing a few hundred yards into the jungle, and then advancing on the flank and striking the enemy from the rear. This became "the standard Japanese doctrine," Drea concludes, "and its successful execution gave rise to tall tales of Japanese jungle warfare."[42] In practice, later battles showed a mixed bag of skills and tactics, revealing that many Japanese units had no more affinity for jungle fighting than their Allied counterparts.

Whatever the shortfalls in tactical elegance, the Japanese compensated with grueling training, fierce discipline, and fanatical dedication. The tenacious fighting spirit of the Japanese might not have typified every soldier in uniform, but it was a consistent characteristic of most frontline infantry troops over the course of the war. Basic infantry training also included many skills and attributes that would prove useful in protracted jungle fighting, including physical fitness, endurance, and camouflage discipline.[43]

The Japanese experience in the Russo-Japanese war helped the government learn the lessons of mass mobilization, in particular how to tap the manpower of rural villages to fill out the army's ranks.[44] Even before the war, Japan had compulsory military training for males. When war came again, reservists were called up. Later, conscription provided the bulk of military troops. All recruits first went to the army and were then subsequently assigned to services. Unlike the US Army (which had the last call on the most fit and intelligent recruits), the Japanese Army could reserve the highest quality conscripts for military service. These troops served under a professional class of officers, many graduates of Japan's Military Academy.

The lion's share of Japanese conscripts came from rural communities where they were used to hard labor and hard living. Further, they were products of a society inculcated with values that called for respect and obedience to superiors, as well as a belief that their personal behavior reflected on the honor and respect of their family and country. When fused with tough, simple, realistic training, the Japanese military system produced soldiers willing to endure privation, fight hard, and never surrender.

Training for the ranks was matched with an officer corps that was taught to resolutely enforce discipline and carry out orders without question. In 1941, Tominaga Shozo was assigned as a second lieutenant in a frontline unit in China. The completion of his "special field-operations training" included executing a Chinese prisoner. "I didn't want to disgrace myself," he recalled, "I bowed to the regimental commander and stepped forward. . . . I steadied myself . . . and swung down with one breath. The head flew away and the body tumbled down, spouting blood. The air reeked with blood."[45] The incident demonstrated there were few limits to instilling brutal discipline in the fighting force.

The training of junior officers was particularly crucial, as they played a direct role in leading troops in battle. "A platoon leader always led his platoon in a direct assault," Tominaga explained. "You charged because there was no choice. It wasn't a matter of courage. My only thought was to my duty."[46] This kind of fierce dedication and discipline would prove vital in braving the hardships of leading in an unforgiving jungle.

One typical unit bound for Papua New Guinea was the Imperial Japanese Army 44th Infantry Regiment. While Konoe struggled with last minute diplomacy to avert war, at the Imperial Conference of September 6, 1941, the army decided to begin moving troops, materials, and munitions for Southern Operations. One of those units was an infantry regiment, 3,500 men strong, designated part of the South Seas Detachment and 55th Infantry Group under Major General Tomitaro Horii.

In prewar Japan, units dotted the islands, each manned by local conscripts drafted for two years of compulsory service. The men of the 44th Regiment came from the Kōchi Prefecture, the southwestern part of the island of Shikoku, a strip of mostly mountainous coastal land facing the Pacific Ocean and the far-off lands where they were destined to fight.

Sadashige Imanishi joined the regiment in 1936. His training, typical of the day, was described by Craig Collie and Hajime Marutani in a history of the Japanese campaign in Papua New Guinea.

> Recruits were subjected to any sort of physical mistreatment that their training officers' fancy. . . . Kicking and bashing were standard practice, as were a range of capricious punishments. . . . The recruits were trained to do exactly as they were told without a murmur. Although it was [a] dehumanizing process in many ways, it was highly pragmatic. It produced soldiers who would follow orders unquestioningly and who had no fear of fighting or of dying.[47]

This fierce discipline was layered on top of the socialization from popular culture and official propaganda. Even if Japanese society had not instilled blind obedience and self-service in the rural peasants that filled the ranks of the Imperial Japanese Army, harsh discipline and a strict regime of training would finish the job.

After completing his grueling tour of duty, instead of going back to tending rice paddies and vegetable plots, Imanishi returned to school. His studies were short-lived. A few months later, following the Marco Polo Bridge Incident (July 7, 1937) the regiment was called up for service. Imanishi fought in China for three years. His regiment saw an admixture of violent ugly war, filled with rape, looting, fighting, and tedious occupation duties.

When his regiment returned to Japan, Imanishi was mustered out of service. But then, he and other veterans of the China campaigns were called up again to prepare for the Southern Operations. The 44th Regiment was reorganized as the 144th Infantry Regiment. Joining a mix of experienced veterans and raw recruits, Sergeant Imanishi oversaw training intended for the troops to endure grueling circumstances they expected to face in the South Pacific, including:

> fighting at night using blindfolds; protecting a gun while swimming or wading; rope-walking over gullies in the mountains; moving silently. They did sleep-deprivation exercises; shooting at a 600-metre range set-up on the training field; and they were made to go on long runs wearing full kit, with beatings for those who did not perform up to expectations.[48]

Much of this training was sound mental and physical preparation for the campaigns, though the troops had virtually no knowledge of the conditions they would face in the heartland of Papua New Guinea. In Rabaul, the regiment continued its rigorous training regime on long marches with sacks of volcanic ash stuffed in their backpacks.[49] Despite the cancelation of Operation MO, troops continued to train for their showdown in the jungle.

Diggers at Dawn

When war came, Australians, like New Zealanders and Canadians, saw themselves as partners in Britain's Empire and were quick to march off to its defense. While Australia's warlords scrapped with Churchill over war strategy, they shared London's vision, fighting to protect the place for like-minded nations seeking to live in a liberal world order.

Over the course of the war, the Australian Army would peak at a strength of eleven infantry divisions and three armored divisions, almost half a million men. From these units, the Second Australian Imperial Force (the first was established for deployment during World War I) was organized in 1939 as an expeditionary force designed for overseas service. The force grew to include four infantry divisions. Parts of the 6th, 7th, 8th, and 9th Divisions were all deployed overseas through 1942 from Rabaul to the Dutch East Indies, Singapore, the Malay Peninsula, North Africa, the Middle East, the Mediterranean, and Greece. Meanwhile, the Citizen's Military Force, or militia, were employed on home guard for Australia (as well as its territories including Papua New Guinea and associated islands). The ranks of the militia were supplemented by conscription (authorized in 1939). Throughout the territories, local militias and volunteers aided in the defense of the islands.

The Japanese defeated the 8th Division in the fight for Singapore (a detachment from the division was also lost at Rabaul). Over the course of 1942, after much bitter debate between Churchill and Curtin, the 6th and the 7th Divisions returned to Australia. Following the Battle of the Coral Sea, if regular troops were needed for the defense of Papua New Guinea, these men would likely be the first in.

"The five months between the return of the first AIF units from the Middle East in March 1942," writes Adrian Threlfall in a comprehensive assessment of Australian military jungle fighting during the war, "and their initial despatch to Papua in August 1942 were arguably the most critical in Australian history."[50] That was all the time they had to get ready for jungle war.

Though Papua New Guinea was only an island away, the Australian Army had given scant thought to ever campaigning there or fighting the Japanese face-to-face. In the run up to the war, most of what the Australians knew about Japan came from British intelligence estimates.[51]

The primary doctrinal manuals for the Australian Army were the 1935 field service regulations and 1937 infantry training manual. Virtually nothing in these manuals was applicable for close-in jungle fighting in the tropics. Little wonder, as this was never the kind of task the Australian armed forces envisioned undertaking.

The 8th Infantry Division learned many hard lessons preparing for and fighting the Japanese in the defense of Singapore. Most of those lessons died with soldiers in the jungle or wasted away in filthy, disease-ridden prisoner-of-war camps. The training notes and the handful of survivors that returned to Australia were collected to help prepare for the next fight against Japan. But these lessons learned, concluded Threlfall, were "most applicable to combat in Malaya . . . little of value was salvaged from the Malayan campaign to help prepare forces in Papua and New Guinea."[52] All the Aussies knew for sure was that the next fight for the AIF divisions would hardly resemble their past campaigns in the Middle East and the Mediterranean.

When the 6th and 7th Infantry Division arrived home, the primary focus of training was preparing to defend northern Australia.[53] Even efforts to absorb the lessons of the Malaya campaign were tilted in that direction. Though training in Queensland, Australia, did include some basics of jungle fighting, it was in northern Australian terrain far different from the jungles of Papua New Guinea. Meanwhile, long hard marches and exercise built up the stamina and toughness of the troops, but physical conditioning alone could not compensate for the lack of experience and skill in fighting under jungle conditions.

Months of training hardened the diggers for battle, but as Bill Spencer, a young soldier of the 7th Division remembered, they "could not prepare us for the ravages of malaria, hookworm, and scrub typhus; it could not prepare us for the humid, clinging heat and torrential tropical downpours. . . . We were about to embark on an Asian war, where the conditions, weapons and tactics and the enemy were unique."[54] These were lessons soon to be learned on the job.

Blind War

Cataloging the shortfalls of the combatants bound for a tropical struggle says something about understanding why the jungle war evolved the way it did. That said, the preparations were anything but a willful march of folly.

Knowing the terrain and conditions of battle and preparing the troops appropriately seems like a simple task. The bewildering confluence of forces that bring men to battle usually makes doing that simple task pretty damn hard. While military doctrines stress knowing as much possible about the terrain, the enemy, and other conditions that affect the outcome of battles and accounting for them as much as possible in plans, preparations, and training, the reality of war is there is only so much time and so many resources. In the end, generals have to fight with the armies they have. For the Americans, Australians, and Japanese all rushing to battle, the fact that they were not more ready for this kind of war is far from surprising. In the end, the armies converging on the Papuan jungle would fight a come-as-you-are war—and pay the price.

Notes

1. Quotes in this section from Manchester, *American Caesar*, p. 278.
2. *Sadie Thompson* was a popular 1928 silent film starring Lillian Gish about a fallen woman in the South Seas. Dorothy Lamour was a popular wartime and post-war actress, best known for pictures in exotic locations costarring the singer Bing Crosby and comedian Bob Hope.
3. McGee, "The Mining Industry in the Territory of Papua in the Period Between World War 1 and World War 2."
4. Foley, *The Papuan Languages of New Guinea*, p. 36.
5. Letter "Dear Cele," dated August 24, 1939, MS 3752 Papers of Lloyd Purchase, 1939, 1944, Australian National Library.
6. See, for example, "Menace in the North: In New Guinea a Black Column Would Aid Japan for Food," undated, MS 3752 Papers of Lloyd Purchase.
7. "Letter to Cele Dear," dated Friday 8th [September 8, 1939], MS 3752 Papers of Lloyd Purchase.
8. Leahy, *Explorations in the Highland New Guinea, 1930–1935*, p. 73.
9. Bourke, "Root Crops in Papua New Guinea," pp. 121–133.
10. There is a long-standing and spirited controversy over whether the proper term is *track* or *trail*. I am not picking sides. I just use both. See, for example, "'Track' or 'Trail'? The Kokoda Debate," at http://www.flinders.edu.au/sabs/fjhp-files/2010/9_ provis.pdf.
11. Napier, *The Principles and Practice of Tropical Medicine*, pp. v–vi.
12. War Department, FM 100-5, *Field Service Regulations, Operations*, pp. 25–26.
13. Enright, *The Maximum of Wilderness*, p. 4.
14. Kahn Jr., *G.I. Jungle*, p. 103.
15. Ibid., p. 53.
16. Burch, *To the Distant Observer*, pp. 16–17.
17. Anderson and Richie, *The Japanese Film*, pp. 154–155.
18. Ginoz, "Dissonance to Affinity," p. 233.
19. Brawley and Dixon, *The South Seas*, p. xv. See also Brawley and Dixon, *Hollywood's South Seas and the Pacific War*, pp. 13–14.
20. Grant, *Australian Soldiers*, pp. 61–62.
21. Ibid., p. 67.
22. John McLaren, "Nationalism and Imperialism," p. 1.
23. Spark, "Whites Out?" pp. 213–219.
24. Grant, *Australian Soldiers*, p. 4.
25. Hawkins and Carafano, *Prelude to Army XXI*.
26. "The Victory Program, September 11, 1941," in *U.S. War Plans, 1938–1945*, pp. 103–134. On the debate on the origins and development of the Victory Program, see Stark, "Engaged in the Debate."
27. Lindbergh, *The Wartime Journals of Charles A. Lindbergh*, p. 569.
28. Bischof and Dupont, *The Pacific War Revisited*, p. 42
29. Stroup, *Letters from the Pacific*, p. 42.
30. See Glass, *The Deserters*.
31. Berry, "No Time for Glory," p, 4.
32. *Army and Navy Journal* (November 14, 1942), np. McNair's remarks generated some controversy. See Calhoun, *General Lesley J. McNair*, pp. 298–299.
33. Calhoun, *General Lesley J. McNair*, p. 297.
34. Quoted in Aldrich, *The Faraway War*, pp. 71–72.

35. Kretchik, *US Army Doctrine*, p. 144.
36. US Army, FM 31-20, *Basic Field Manual, Jungle Warfare*, p. 2.
37. Doubler, *Civilian in Peace, Soldier in War*, pp. 3–165.
38. Information of Arthur Kessenich from Kessenich, "This Is Your Life."
39. Yagami, *Konoe Fumimaro*, pp. 134–135.
40. Drea, *In the Service of the Emperor*, p. 63.
41. Ibid.
42. Ibid., p. 65.
43. Harris and Harris, *Soldiers of the Sun*, pp. 329–330.
44. Partner, "Peasants into Citizens," pp. 179–209.
45. Cook and Cook, *Japan at War*, pp. 41–42.
46. Ibid., p. 43.
47. Collie and Marutani, *The Path of Infinite Sorrow*, pp. 30–31.
48. Ibid., p. 35.
49. Ibid., p. 49.
50. Threlfall, *Jungle Warriors*, p. 74.
51. Best, "Constructing an Image," pp. 403–423; Ferris, "Worthy of Some Better Enemy?" pp. 223–256; Wark, "In Search of a Suitable Japan," pp. 189–211.
52. Threlfall, *Jungle Warriors*, p. 55.
53. See, for example guidance on the defense of Darwin in AWM52, 1/1/1 Headquarters Units, Land Headquarters, 1942, General Headquarters, GHQ Operations Instruction No. 4, April 20, 1942. Records of Headquarters, European Theater of Operations, United States Army.
54. Spencer, *In the Footsteps of Ghosts*, pp. 88–89.

5

Forward into the Jungle

LONDON, MAY 10, 1942. *"I have now served for two years exactly to a day as the King's First Minister,"* Churchill addressed the British people through the crackle of their parlor radios. *"I thought it would be a good thing if I had a talk to you on the broadcast, to look back a little on what we have come through to consider how we stand now, and to peer cautiously into the future."*[1]

IN TONE, CHURCHILL'S report seemed very different from the tense, dramatic speech on June 4, 1940, following the catastrophic defeat of the British Expeditionary Force at Dunkirk, one of the darkest days in the isle's war effort. Then, as the Germans roared across France, the prime minister roared back, "whatever the cost may be, we shall fight on the beaches, we shall fight on the landing grounds, we shall fight in the fields and in the streets, we shall fight in the hills; we shall never surrender." Two more years of trials, reversals, and setbacks followed that desperate hour. By May 1942, however, if the tide had not turned, at least the enemy was not lapping on the beaches of Brighton. Churchill's speeches added cautious wisps of optimism and visions of victory.

With the May 10 public address, coming only days after the Battle of the Coral Sea, he added another note of good fortune. "So far we have no detailed accounts," he informed the British people, "but it is obvious, if only from the lies the Japanese have felt compelled to tell . . . that a most vigorous and successful battle has been fought by the United States and Australian naval forces."

And, while the enemy many have had some early successes, "the strength of the United States, expressed in units of modern war power, actual and potential, is alone many times greater than the power of

Japan." He concluded, "I am not prone to make predictions, but I have no doubt that the British and American sea power will grip and hold the Japanese, and that overwhelming air power, covering vigorous military operations, will lay them low." Although the war was far from won, there was, Churchill remonstrated, a clearer path forward.

The prime minister's confidence masked a few of the realities of war in Asia Pacific. For Churchill, chief among them was that this was no longer Churchill's war. Survival of the Anglo-American effort in Asia now rested largely in the hands of the Yanks, the outcome largely to be determined by success in the Pacific War—and that war would be carried principally by Americans with the Australians by their side. For another, as Churchill had written just five days earlier, he had no idea what the Japanese were going to do next.

The Empire Strikes Back

A stinging setback at the Battle of the Coral Sea (May 7–8) and later at Midway (June 4–7) deprived the Japanese Imperial Navy of a key objective—seizing crucial unsinkable airfields that could have anchored the outer ring of the Pacific conquests, as well as establishing a launching pad to eventually continue further offensive operations perhaps even on to Hawaii and Australia. Yet, the Japanese Imperial Forces were far from ready to concede victory to Allied air and sea power. Nevertheless, a crushing reality had taken hold. At least for the near future, taking the war to the enemy homelands was no longer an option.

One of the most common historical themes surrounding the Pacific conflict views the defeats at Coral Sea and Midway (the sinking of four Japanese aircraft carriers and the loss of hundreds of planes and trained pilots) as *the* tipping point. "Without the fleet carrier advantage," historian Francis Pike sums up, "for the rest of the war, Japan's military and naval operations in the *Pacific* would have to march to the beat and direction of an American drum."[2] After Midway, the eventual Japanese defeat was inevitable. That view, however, is history's version of the Monday morning quarterback.

First of all, by the end of the year, the United States had lost five of the eight carriers they had put to sail at the start of the war. In addition, the *Saratoga* spent most of the year in dry dock undergoing repairs. The Japanese actually had more carriers at sea. By the end of 1943, the United States would make up the difference and surpass Japan's numbers, deploying the Essex class and Princeton class (light) carriers, but for the preponderance of 1942, the Japanese held an advantage.

Inevitable defeat was far from the minds of Japan's warlords. The emperor, who had a map room constructed in the Imperial palace so that he could follow the details of the campaign, contemplated what could be done. He was not alone. Within the palace walls, around the cramped paper-filled offices of the Imperial Japanese Army Headquarters across the street, and among the chain-smoking staff at the conference table of Combined Fleet Headquarters, there was no defeatist talk. Instead, there was a vigorous debate over how to stretch the war into a protracted conflict that might, in the end, if not produce triumph for the Axis powers, at least leave the empire standing—perhaps even prepared to fight another day.

The Japanese were realists. They knew they had the fight of their lives on their hands. The enemy's ultimate objective was their home islands. Long before the Battle of the Coral Sea, Marshall had already agreed with King that the United States could not stand pat in the Pacific. While King, Nimitz, and MacArthur quarreled over the best way forward, there was no question but that they were going forward. Meanwhile, the Imperial military staffs in Tokyo and Admiral Yamamoto and his staff at the Combined Fleet had to figure out how they could take the sting out of an expected US counteroffensive.

Among the Japanese war leaders here was a moment of rare consensus—in the near term the answer was securing more unsinkable flattops, island bases that could blunt US carrier raids and deprive the Americans from creeping forward, seizing platforms for their long-range bombers. The question for Japan was which pieces to take off the board? Where could they take control before the Allies advanced? Which islands that the Allies held could the Japanese take away?

There were several factors to assess in order to answer these pressing questions. (1) Securing an island fortress made no sense if the enemy could simply bypass the position by sailing a few hundred miles out of the way. (2) Defenses needed to be overlapping so that Japanese could marshal bombers at one outpost to defend another. (3) Having positions within a mutual supporting distance by sea was also important. The Japanese needed to be able to shift forces from one base to another. Further, installations would have to be rearmed and resupplied. That meant the Japanese had to be able to defend the lines of supply connecting the picket posts of the outer empire. In other words, Japan needed a string of bases secured like links in a fence.

Determining what to hold, picking the links in the chain, dominated the strategic discussions among the service staffs and the Combined Fleet Headquarters. As the war lengthened, however, Yamamoto increasingly had less of a free hand in setting the direction for the Southwest

Pacific war. The Imperial Army staff wanted its say—and with good reason. By the spring of 1942, the army found the soldiers of the empire had a bigger stake in the big blue ocean war than had been planned. The army had hoped to be pulling men out of the theater. Instead, more ground forces were needed to secure the airbases required to make the Southwest Pacific defensible.

The official Japanese war history summarizes the controversy.

> [The problem] developed between the army and the navy over responsibility for military administration during the FS Operation [the campaign in the Southwest Pacific]. This concerned the operation of units, guarding, placement and other key factors in the region of the operation (occupation area). The army felt it was natural for them to have the main responsibility for military administration of operational areas because army units were primarily deployed in the land operations.[3]

In short, the army wanted to control the space it was tasked to defend. Here is how they decided to address the problem.

On May 2 (on the eve of the Battle of the Coral Sea), the army contemplated establishing a higher headquarters in order to exercise more control over the forces scattered throughout the region.

On May 18, the Imperial Army staff took an unprecedented step, establishing an army headquarters to oversee operations in the Southwest Pacific. This was the first operational army organized since the start of the war. Strikingly, this new command was not for the army's chief areas of concern—China and Russia. The command was going to supervise forces where the Imperial Japanese Army had hoped by this point in the war to be pulling back. This signaled a notable shift in the conduct of the defense of the Southwest Pacific.

On May 20, 1942, the 17th Army became operational under the command of General Haruyoshi Hyakutake. The army headquarters would be at Davao on Mindanao in the Philippines. From there, Hyakutake would administer a smattering of army units including the South Seas Forces at Rabaul that had been slotted for Operation MO (the attack on Port Moresby) before the invasion fleet had turned back at the Coral Sea.

At first, Hyakutake did not have much of an army to command. Beyond himself and two senior officers, there was no staff. There were no logistical units assigned to the command. Other than what the units carried with them, Hyakutake was warned that "future supplies will be dispatched directly from Imperial Headquarters," adding that "[t]he army will plan to be completely self-reliant on the local area." Translation, there was no sustainment plans for major combat operations. Having little supply was consistent with the decision to not assign the 17th Army much fighting power. There were no fighting units larger than a battalion. With only small organizations to command, there was no expectation the army would oversee large-scale combat operations that required higher headquarters, employing reserves, or directing sustained operations over large areas. There were no army air force units. The army would have no air support unless the navy provided air cover.

"There was virtually no practical role for the 17th Army as an army," noted the official history. "The army command could only fulfil a subjugation management role after landing." In practical terms, the army was good for little more than managing occupation duties among farflung island commands. Still, while the Imperial Army staff did not expect major offensive operations, they did see the 17th Army playing an important role in the desperate race to secure the empire before the United States could press a counteroffensive. The army chief of staff informed Hyakutake "not only are your duties extremely important, you are conducting operations in areas that are essential to the enemy." As with many directives, commanders were expected to compensate for the paucity of resources with exemplary leadership and commitment. "Face counter-attacks with a fresh mind, and provide leadership to strive for completion of your duties with equal amounts of caution and a vigorous heart," the chief directed.

More than meaningless cheerleading, the Imperial staff command directive reflected the core of the Japanese approach to the conduct of the Southwest Pacific campaigns. This wasn't "victory disease." There was no overconfidence that a feckless enemy could be easily bested. Rather, there was a grim determination that there was a job that just had to be done. Their guidance reflected a core assumption in Japanese military planning that operations would rely on their greatest asset, the determination and stamina of the ground fighting forces.

There was a real question, however, if they had appointed a commander who was up to leading such a supreme effort. In the spring of 1942, between the years of fighting in China and the lightning campaign across South Asia and the Southwest Pacific, the Imperial Japanese Army had a number of seasoned senior leaders with combat experience. Hyakutake, the newly appointed commander of the 17th Army, was not one of them. Overseas diplomatic and headquarters postings marked Hyakutake's career. He led an infantry regiment for one year. When Japan invaded China, he was running army schools in Japan. Later, he commanded occupation troops in Korea. What Hyakutake had never done was direct a major military operation. The Imperial Japanese

Army staff, however, did not envision Hyakutake would be leading a fighting campaign.

Hyakutake, for his part, was dissatisfied with his new command. Although the 17th Army commander did not expect to lead a large-scale fighting campaign, he still found the order of battle for his new posting anemic. Still, though frustrated with the rag-tag composition of his command, Hyakutake determined his mission was achievable. He only thought that, however, because he was not aware of the latest progress in the war. The general had been reassured by both the army staff, as well as popular reporting in the Japanese press, that Coral Sea had been a great naval victory. The Imperial staffs had only temporarily postponed Operation MO (securing Port Moresby by amphibious invasion). With that optimistic (but disingenuous) read on events, Hyakutake concluded his "staff office did not feel future battles would be any fiercer than previous engagements." When he finally learned about the crushing defeat at Coral Sea, Hyakutake would rethink his assessment.

Even without the expectation of major ground campaigns or knowing about the setback at the Coral Sea, Hyakutake's estimate of the situation was a bit of a head-scratcher. There were still difficult tasks to be mastered. Two key, crucial links in the chain had to be secured—Guadalcanal in the Solomon Islands (northeast of Australia) and Port Moresby in Papua New Guinea. Over the course of June and July, thousands of troops garrisoned Guadalcanal and began building an airfield.[4] Port Moresby, however, remained an unattained but vital objective.

Taking Port Moresby would help reduce attacks on the key Japanese bases at Truk and Rabaul. Port Moresby would also be useful in helping isolate Australia and preventing the continent from serving as a base for a counteroffensive against the empire. Further, Port Moresby was anything but an invincible citadel. The Japanese believed they could outmatch its defenses—if they could get their forces to the fight. Unfortunately, getting troops to the front had so far proved frustratingly unsuccessful.

If the situation were to be improved, there was no question that General Hyakutake's 17th Army would play a significant role in taking, occupying, and garrisoning Port Moresby, as well as other key points. The Imperial Headquarters issued a Great Order declaring the 17th Army's primary mission was to "invade key areas in each of the islands of New Caledonia, Fiji, and Samoa and also invade Port Moresby." Meanwhile, the navy staff issued concurrent orders to the Combined Fleet to cooperate with the army and to "control the waters east of Australia and blockade the line of supply between the United States and Australia." Along with seizing Port Moresby, this joint effort would seal the flank of the southern area.

There were three options for sequencing the attacks that would help cement sealing the flank.

Option 1

In cooperation with the army, the navy could secure and occupy key islands one at a time starting with New Caledonia, then Fiji, then Samoa. This campaign had a significant advantage. Starting with the target closest to existing Japanese land bases would minimize the need for carrier-based air support. Instead, the attackers could rely on land-based air cover. The least strategic of the objectives, New Caledonia was a stepping-stone that could be used to leapfrog to the other targets. The disadvantage of a New Caledonia first campaign was that the Allies would likely react by reinforcing their defenses in Fiji and Samoa. That would mean a tougher fight to take both of the latter objectives. Still, if the offensive proceeded quickly, the Japanese might seize all the islands before too many enemy reinforcements arrived.

Option 2

A second option would simultaneously secure all three objectives (New Caledonia, Fiji, and Samoa). This bold move, which could overwhelm the Allies before they could effectively respond, was a tempting choice. However, if operations on any one objective bogged down, there would be no reinforcements to aid them. Further, simultaneous attacks would strain the capacity of theater aviation assets.

Option 3

The third option looked to secure Fiji and Samoa first. Fiji and Samoa were most crucial for the campaign to isolate Australia. Going after the most important objectives at the start would ensure that the maximum resources were focused on the most important targets. The problem was the difficulty of providing long-range air support against distant objectives from existing bases. The lack of predictable air cover due to weather and the availability of aircraft made operations even more risky.

The navy elected for the first option. This was the most conservative choice—a sequenced advance starting with securing a foothold in New Caledonia. The decision is further evidence that even if Japanese military staffs did suffer from victory disease (a doubtful proposition) before now, they had been all but cured. The Imperial Japanese Navy had started the war with bold, ambitious strokes and complicated operations, followed by daring duels such as the showdown at Midway. Now, circumstances forced the navy to husband resources with greater caution. The navy opted for modest, achievable goals. In turn, the 17th Army adjusted the allocation of its limited ground forces to support the plan for sequenced attacks on New Caledonia, Samoa, and Fiji. General Hyakutake slotted his most capable combat force, the South Seas Detachment stationed in Rabaul, for New Caledonia.

Major General Tomitarō Horii, the commander of the South Seas Force (the most capable fighting force in the 17th Army), liked the final decision. Initially, South Seas Detachment had been assigned to carry out the amphibious landings taking Port Moresby in Operation MO. "After the difficulties they encountered in the sea-route offensive against Port Moresby," the official history summarizes, they "were enthusiastic about the prospects for the New Caledonia operation, and had lost interest in the offensive against Port Moresby." New Caledonia was a much less daunting challenge. If the operations against the three islands were successful, Port Moresby could be swept up almost as an afterthought, Horii reasoned.

Hyakutake assigned the Aoba Detachment (which included a handful of infantry battalions that had been stationed at Java in the Dutch East Indies and was being redeployed to Davao on the southern Philippine island of Mindanao) to conduct the follow-on occupation of Port Moresby. He concluded that after the other victories, the Aoba Detachment ought to be sufficient to take on the isolated forces in Papua New Guinea.

The 17th Army determined that the final plan was both achievable and would finally deliver the crucial objective of Port Moresby into its hands. "Port Moresby has significance not only for being capital of British New Guinea, but for being essential base of enemy operations (especially air) for the region," the command noted. "Much of New Guinea is undeveloped, so it is thought that objectives of the operation can be achieved if Port Moresby and [nearby] Kila airfield can be occupied." Hyakutake and his small staff left for the war now confident of the way forward. There is, however, an old saying, "no plan survives contact with the enemy." That proved to be the case here. Here is what happened to the 17th Army's plans.

On June 7, Hyakutake and his chief of staff, Major General Akisaburo Futami, left Tokyo for their new headquarters at Davao in "high spirits." Their scheduled flight route would take them to Fukuoka, Japan, and then on to Taipei in Formosa (Taiwan) and then to Manila in the Philippines and finally on to Davao. When 17th Army commander arrived at Fukuoka, an ominous telegram greeted him: "Delay your departure and wait to be contacted." At 9 p.m., Hyakutake and his staff of two met with Lieutenant Colonel Imoto Kumao at Matsushima Ryokan Hotel in Fukuoka. Imoto told them everything had changed. Hyakutake learned the Imperial Japanese Navy had been defeated at Midway. The "news was a great shock," he recalled. Imoto also shared more startling information. The setback had led the army and navy staff to a cascading series of decisions that turned 17th Army's plans for the future inside out. Without adequate carrier support, the staffs jointly agreed to postpone Operation FS for two to three months. The Aoba Detachment would be held in reserve at Davao. The only significant fighting force that would be available in the area at present would be the South Seas Detachment at Rabaul.

On June 9, Hyakutake and Futami left Fukuoka. They arrived in Davao six days later with not much more baggage than their personal kit. With virtually nothing in hand, the general and his meager staff had some major tasks ahead. In their clandestine meeting, Imoto did not provide the full details of the Midway disaster and the battle's impact on the strategic direction of the war. Indeed, outside the confines of the highest level of the Imperial Military staffs, few knew of the momentous decisions that would soon ripple through Japan's fighting strategy. All Hyakutake knew for sure was that he would have to do more with less.

On July 9, the heads of the Imperial Army and Navy met for some of the most consequential talks of the war. The conversation presaged the next steps for the campaign in the Southwest Pacific. While relations between the army and navy are often portrayed as fractious partisan wrangling that undermined the effectiveness of military operations, on this occasion the chiefs saw the war in much the same way, and, for once, there was little dissention from Yamamoto and the Combined Fleet staff.

There is an old axiom in war—militaries reinforce success not failure. In the wake of the disaster at Midway, the army and navy both looked to opportunities in the east in China and India rather than the Pacific for battlefield success that would put more pressure on the Allies to sue for peace. While the navy wanted to ramp up operations in the Indian Ocean, the army wanted to pursue a major offensive on Chungking in southwest China and follow up on a successful campaign in Burma. Both suggestions had the same goal—put more pressure on Washington and London, convince them that the Pacific War could never be cheaply won. Military theorists call this a "cost-imposing" strategy: make the price of victory so high, the enemy isn't willing to pay it.

For Japan, at this point in the war, there was still a glimmer of optimism. The Germans and Italians were still advancing in Africa. The Japanese reasoned that perhaps the Axis success there and the Japanese

Navy's interest in increasing operations in the Indian Ocean could be combined into a joint conquest of India and Southwest Asia. This avenue of advance conformed, the official Japanese history notes, "to the aim at the opening of the war to break the spirit of the United States by first forcing Britain to surrender, rather than taking direct measures of this kind against the United States." This decision had big implications for the southern area. To preserve resources for other fights, the Southwest Pacific would become an economy of force operation in which the Imperial staff would seek to economize resources rather than risk more.

In his history of the Pacific War, historian Ronald H. Spector argues:

> Yamamoto had the right idea: Unless the Japanese could inflict a shattering defeat on the U.S. early in the war, she would gradually be ground down by steadily growing American power. The Japanese still had sufficient forces after Midway to again take the initiative for another try at the U.S. fleet. Instead they reverted to the defensive and allowed themselves to be drawn into a battle of attrition.[5]

Perhaps, Spector is correct; in hindsight Yamamoto should have rolled the dice on a big naval engagement one more time. But he did not. After Midway, the Combined Fleet Headquarters had made a more cautious but not unreasonable decision—instead of a climactic battle at sea, they would try to save the outer ring of the empire.

Yamamoto might have risked all on another Midway to put the US carrier fleet on its heels, but if he lost, he would have far outrun the strategic culminating point of Japanese naval power in the Pacific. Another defeat would have left the fleet vulnerable to being rolled up once and for all. By stopping short of the point of culmination, Yamamoto conserved enough force to stay in the fight.

Still, the result of the decision was that Japan's warlords had ceded the initiative of taking the battle to the enemy on the strategic level. The dream of taking Australia out of the war, let alone seeing Imperial troops march into what they called the land of British criminals, was gone.

In the coming weeks, Operation FS targeting New Caledonia, Samoa, and Fiji would be not just postponed but formally scrapped in favor of more conservative objectives. The Imperial staff, however, had far from given up on the empire's frontier. What would not change was the determination to secure and hold what were still considered two essential links for the empire's perimeter—Guadalcanal and Port Moresby.

What raised the stakes for these operations is that they would have to be accomplished with available assets in theater—limited troops, diminishing airpower, and overstretched naval forces. The first troops were already on Guadalcanal. By the end of the month, there would be an airfield in place, troops to defend it, and planes to fly off the island's airfield. But Port Moresby was still in the enemy's hands. Meanwhile, the resources available to achieve the objective were growing increasingly thin. The possibility of conducting any offensive campaign while the theater strategy shifted to the strategic defense would inherently demand that commanders assume greater risk. The decision to press on was not from the hubris of victory disease, but from the determination that there was no other course open to securing the empire's perimeter.

The Japanese had to secure the perimeter before the Allies made their next move. That was a daunting task. A campaign required planning, organizing the men and material for the task and positioning them to undertake the operation, directing the advance, making any adjustments along the way, and concluding operations—consolidating forces to hold on to the victory achieved. Those activities represented massive challenges to Hyakutake. With limited means, on a battlefield of which he knew almost nothing, the army had to put together a winning campaign.

If anything, suspending Operation FS made seizing Port Moresby more vital. "The campaign in New Guinea has developed into a war of attrition," the navy staff reasoned, and "there is no argument over the necessity in overcoming the innumerable difficulties to invade Port Moresby as soon as possible. After the invasion it will be difficult for the Allies to redeploy their air strength within the region." Securing the airbase would be a blow to the Allies' offensive punch. It would also give the Japanese a permanent platform to fend off attacks out of Australia and to help secure Truk and Rabaul.

There were only two ways to get an army to Port Moresby—land or sea. A land campaign had been something considered since the first months of the war, especially since the Japanese already had a foothold in Papua New Guinea. In February, the army had offered to attempt securing Port Moresby. Imperial forces had seized Lae and Salamaua (March 8–13, 1942), providing a land base in Papua New Guinea from which to operate from (only 170 miles from Port Moresby). Nevertheless, at the time the Imperial staffs deferred the decision. This was a wise choice. Moving major forces overland from Lae and Salamaua to Port Moresby was not practical. The march would have required crossing a near impenetrable morass of jungles, mountains, and rivers.

The Japanese could also attack Port Moresby from the sea. Rabaul put Port Moresby in range of Japanese air and naval power. With that advantage in mind, Vice Admiral Shigeyoshi Inoue had organized

Operation MO to take the objective. Even after Allied planes turned back the invasion force at the Battle of the Coral Sea, there was an argument to keep open the prospects for an amphibious landing backed by air and naval forces.

The obsession of taking Port Moresby created a serious strategic dilemma. Neither the army, navy, nor Combined Fleet staff believed a major amphibious assault without the cover of carrier aviation was feasible. Carriers were in short supply. Without carrier support, there was only one way take Port Moresby—walk over the Owen Stanley Range.

Hyakutake's operation was further complicated because though this was primarily going to be an army campaign, the operation could not be pulled off without naval cooperation. The navy would have to get troops to Papua New Guinea. The navy would have to resupply them. The navy would have to provide land-based naval support for air defense, air reconnaissance, and conducting air attacks of enemy forces and bases.

Ri Operational Study

Japan's ability to conduct joint operations during World War II has been much maligned. What often frustrated adequate cooperation, however, was not an absence of the will to cooperate but the absence of resources to make cooperation possible, particularly in the southern area where the demands for combat forces outstripped the forces available.

The army and navy conducted joint operations following a formal protocol. "Where joint command action was required in the progress of war," the protocol mandated, "Central Agreements were arrived at by the two Chiefs of the General Staffs through joint staff studies."[6] Thus, the normal practice (even under the pressure of moving quickly to regain the initiative against the Allies) would have necessitated a staff study, as well as requiring the army and navy independently to undertake extensive planning and have the operational plans approved by the Imperial staffs. The Japanese tried to follow this procedure for the campaign in Papua New Guinea.

Joint cooperation aside, however, no overland campaign against Port Moresby could be successful unless there was a route to maneuver from the coast of Papua New Guinea up to the highlands in the Owen Stanley Range and then down to Port Moresby. The Japanese had forces that were a short distance from Rabaul in New Britain and could serve as a staging base for future operations. They, however, could not serve as a starting point for crossing the Owen Stanley Range. The shortest straight-line distance across the range was farther down the peninsula. There were no roads linking where the Japanese were to where they wanted to be across the mountains. Further, since there was a paucity of coastal roads, there was no way to carry men and supplies overland to the starting point for crossing the mountains. The invading force would have to find areas with suitable anchorages for landing men and supplies to begin their trek over the mountains. There was one Japanese officer who thought he had an answer to the problem.

Prince Tsuneyoshi Takeda, a major in the Imperial Japanese Army attached to the army general staff in Tokyo, was a man of eclectic interests, singular talents, and shadowy authority. Allegedly, his duties involved traveling throughout occupied territories including China, Hong Kong, Indochina, Burma, Malaysia, Singapore, the Dutch East Indies, and the Philippines collecting valuables for the Imperial treasury. While in Manila, in the Philippines, he learned of an account of an English explorer who reported on the existence of a road to Port Moresby; he presented this report to the 17th Army staff. Armed with this information and the necessity of taking the key base on the opposite coast of Papua New Guinea, the army staff ordered a "detailed research and preparations for an overland attack." They called the effort the Ri Operational Study.

It would be too much to credit Tsuneyoshi's Indiana Jones–like discovery with launching the expedition against Port Moresby. After all, the taking of the port had been on the Japanese to-do list for some time. Both the army and navy forces had been trying to gather intelligence on Papua New Guinea. But no doubt interest from the Imperial staff and the need for an alternative to Operation FS sparked renewed interest. The tantalizing tale of an open road to a vital Imperial objective was too much to ignore. A road would have been a godsend, providing a route from the coast that the Japanese already occupied, up through the mountains to broad plateau, past the station at Kokoda, down the mountains on the other side to the Australian-held area surrounding Port Moresby.

Hyakutake had no way of judging the veracity of the information from a forgotten English explorer. The command, assembled in haste, had only been issued civil topographical maps, virtually useless for planning military operations. After the Battle of the Coral Sea, according to the official history, "the Navy's 8th Base Force and the South Seas Force at Rabaul continued investigations from documents and local testimony into the existence of roads across to Port Moresby. . . . As a result of this, an early report was submitted to Imperial Headquarters that there seemed to be a road to Port Moresby." The findings were hardly definitive. There were reports of trails along the Mambare River and Kumusi River valleys up to Kokoda and a "packhorse trail" from Buna to Kokoda. This additional intelligence was sketchy and not confirmed. Pressed to undertake an overland campaign, Hyakutake needed more information to determine if the campaign was feasible and what force would be required to succeed.

Air reconnaissance dispatched to survey the area between Buna village on the coast and the station at Kokoda delivered ambiguous results. Jungle and thick clouds obscured most of the route. The pilot sent to make the survey was on his first combat mission. The reconnaissance flight required dodging American fighters while whipping across confusing terrain. Further, the pilot could not assess the condition of the snaking lines that cut the jungle below. Despite that, the reconnaissance report stated, "There is a road passable by motor transport."[7] Nevertheless, even without knowing the conditions under which the air reconnaissance occurred, seasoned military officers knew enough to be skeptical. Aerial reconnaissance, while valuable, had limitations. Ground that might look dry and flat from a couple of thousand feet in the air could be a sea of mud or overgrown vegetation. Roads that looked fine might be potholed and rutted. The only way to judge the suitability of terrain for the conduct of land operations was to inspect the ground close up.

The findings of the aerial inspection were enough for the Imperial Army staff to press for a ground reconnaissance force to determine if a suitable route existed. The staff designated the mouth of the Mambare River as the best site for a reconnaissance bridgehead. The results of the effort, designated the Ri Operational Study, would inform the staff on the best way forward. Meanwhile, Hyakutake summoned Major General Tomitarō Horii to Davao. Horii, commander of the South Seas Detachment, could not have made more of a contrast with the 17th Army commander. Both commissioned in the infantry. There the similarities in their military careers pretty much ended. Horii had far more operational experience. In 1941, he was appointed as the commander of the 55th Division. With these forces under him organized as part of the South Seas Detachment, he directed the invasion of Guam. Afterward, the South Seas Detachment participated in the capture of Rabaul. Unlike Hyakutake, Horii was a fighting commander. He was the kind of seasoned leader needed to lead a difficult mission.

Horii's troops had been loaded on ships for the invasion of Port Moresby as part of Operation MO. When that operation was canceled, they were off-loaded. He was told to prepare to load his men back on the ships for action in New Caledonia. That mission was canceled. On June

30, 1942, Horii accompanied by a staff officer reported to 17th Army Headquarters in Davao to discuss a new mission—marching over the Owen Stanley Range to attack Port Moresby.

Horii saw serious challenges in attempting an overland campaign, particularly if there was not a road to support motor transport from Buna up to Kokoda. "From Buna to Kokoda is approximately 100 kilometers [60 miles] as the crow flies, but in fact around 160 kilometers [96 miles]," the general reported. "Likewise, Kokoda to Port Moresby is 120 kilometers [72 miles] direct but is judged to be around 200 kilometers [120 miles] actual distance. In short this route requires over 360 kilometers [216 miles] of trudging." He estimated to feed 5,000 men on the campaign would require 32,000 additional troops to serve as carriers (that was about as many carriers as the entire Allied forces employed at the height of the Papua New Guinea campaign). Horii needed an army of porters that he did not have. The only way to reduce that number of bearers to a feasible level would be to supplement them with motor transport. Motor transport, however, would only help if there were roads. Horii soon learned that it would be his task to find out.

On July 1, Hyakutake and Horii drafted a plan to insert a reconnaissance force near Buna village instead of the Mambare River (which the Imperial Army staff had recommended). They made that choice with good reason. There were anchorages near Buna for the ships. Aerial support from Rabaul and existing bases on the coast could provide over watch. Buna was also the starting point for crossing the Owen Stanley Range at its narrowest point from Port Moresby.

On his return to Rabaul, Horii organized the Yokoyama advanced force under Colonel Yokoyama Yosuke, commander of the 15th Independent Engineer Regiment. Yokoyama would lead the spearhead at Buna. This mission was appropriate for an engineer. One of the most important tasks upon landing would be to build up facilities to support the follow-on forces.

In addition to the regiment, Horii attached the 1st Battalion of the 144th Infantry Regiment (55th Division) commanded by Lieutenant Colonel Tsukamoto Hatsuo and 1st Company of the 1st Battalion, 55th Mountain Artillery Regiment. Tsukamoto's men would be the point of the spear. These troops would establish an advance line, find and make usable roads to support the campaign, and make a determination of the feasibility of main overland assault. Here is how the operation progressed.

On July 11, Yokoyama's units and supporting troops were dispatched from Davao to Rabaul to join Horii's combat forces. Meanwhile, Hyakutake gave the go-ahead to launch an advance reconnaissance.

They began planning a cautious, methodical probe for how to best traverse the Owen Stanley Range. It was a judicious start. Then, a few days later, everything changed.

On July 15, six days before the first troops of the Yokoyama advance force landed in Papua New Guinea, Lieutenant Colonel Tsuji Masanobu arrived at 17th Army Headquarters in Davao, informing the command that the Imperial Headquarters has decided to proceed with the overland attack—even before the reconnaissance had gotten under way. With this new guidance, Hyakutake immediately began planning for a full offensive with the troops available.

On July 18, Hyakutake issued a new order: "The army, in cooperation with the navy, will promptly carry out offensive operations in the key areas of Port Moresby and New Guinea." The order directed the South Seas Detachment to land near Buna and advance over the "Kokoda road" and secure Port Moresby. In addition, the plan called for securing Samarai, a small island off the southeast tip of Papua New Guinea by sea and the Louisiade archipelago to the east. (They would serve as a flanking position to help launch seaplane air attacks on Port Moresby.)

Only July 20, the first wave of the Yokoyama advanced party, two transport ships accompanied by two destroyers and two cruisers under the command of Rear Admiral Mitsuharu Matsuyama of the 4th Fleet, sailed from Rabaul for Papua New Guinea, arriving at dusk, planning the following day to complete debarkation.

On July 21, the Japanese landed. Japanese destroyers appeared on the horizon and shelled the beaches at Buna and Gona, coastal villages in Oro Province on the northern coast of the Papuan peninsula. Behind the warships two freighters steamed toward the shallow waters. A small Australian detachment assigned to watch the coast along the two villages quickly withdrew. Before they did, a wireless operator got off a message. Before the end of the day the warning was relayed to Port Moresby. "A Japanese warship is shelling Buna apparently to cover a landing."[8] Meanwhile, the villagers yelled in pidgin, "Japon E Cum!" The enemy was coming.

The first Japanese troops came ashore unopposed a short distance from Buna.[9] According to the official Japanese military history, Buna had been the intended destination but instead the force in error landed near Gona village. Through the afternoon and into the following morning, men, equipment, and supplies were unloaded.

Elements of the 5th Yokosuka Naval Landing Party from the 4th Fleet trudged ashore with the infantry to establish a landing post and construct an airbase. Even if the overland route proved impractical, the Japanese were in Buna to stay. An advanced airfield would be useful for supporting operations in the region.[10] Indeed, lack of air support was one of the biggest concerns after they got to the beaches. The landing sites were only twenty minutes flying time from Port Moresby. They had little faith that the convoy would arrive undetected. There was the unavoidable threat of the constant reconnaissance flights over Rabaul and, of course, the coast watchers. Even if the convoy successfully made the short crossing undetected, their arrival could not escape notice once the destroyers started shelling the beaches and the troops stormed ashore.

The Japanese expected serious Allied air attacks once they landed. In fact, Horii made organizing sufficient air defense among the commander's highest priorities for the waterborne assault. For the operation, South Seas Detachment had only two anti-aircraft companies allotted. It would take time to move them ashore and set them up. Even then, with limited weapons and ammunition and limited capacity to provide early warning, ground air defense would not provide much help anyway. A serious defense of the beachhead would have to come from the navy. For the initial assault, Horii would have to rely on shipborne air defense weapons and air protection from the 25th Air Flotilla, a navy combat aviation unit stationed in Rabaul. The navy allotted a group of eighteen Zeros (fighters) to protect the landings. Due to bad weather, the planes were unable to take off. The Zeros did not show up until well after dawn.

An Allied scout plane had detected the transports loading in Rabaul. Admiral Matsuyama did not know that, but it mattered little. The Allies had no indication where the transports were headed nor could they likely marshal forces in time to interdict them. But as soon as the reports of the landing reached Port Moresby, the Allies responded. The weather in Port Moresby was better. Allied planes got there before the Zeros. At dawn, the combat ships and unloading transports were attacked by Allied planes. The planes damaged the destroyer *Uzuki* (which promptly withdrew to Rabaul for repairs) and sunk the *Ayatosan Maru,* one of the transport ships, killing and wounding dozens and destroying a number of vehicles.[11]

It was as Matsuyama had feared. Experienced at convoying troops through the troubled waters of the South Pacific, he knew air attacks not surface ships, like PT (patrol torpedo) boats nor submarines, were the greatest threat. "B-17's [bombers] were the worst," he later recalled.[12]

This air attack was a setback, but still not as bad as Matsuyama dreaded. Even though Port Moresby was only a short flight away, the Allies also had to fight dodgy weather to find enough clear skies to take off, get over the Owen Stanley Range, find the target, and get back. On top of that, for many weeks MacArthur had pressed his air forces to keep up a bombing campaign to pressure the enemy. "Frequent mechanical problems, bad weather, supply shortages, and the sheer length of missions," Bruce Gamble points out in his history of the campaign, "kept aircrews and maintenance personnel on the threshold of exhaustion."[13] Mustering an all-out effort on no notice was virtually impossible. The air attacks were more a nuisance than a decisive response.

Despite the annoyance of aerial attacks, the operation proceeded satisfactorily, even though the landings did not go as planned. The ships (because of reefs off the coast of Buna) could not offload near the village. One craft disembarked at an anchorage about three miles from Giruwa, not far from Buna village. The other transport ship was to land at Basabua also near Buna, but instead wound up seven miles away near Gona. If the landings had been opposed, the scattering of the invading forces might have caused a serious disruption. But, there were no defenders on the shoreline.

Days later, a second convoy arrived unloading additional troops, a total of 4,000 men and 1,200 native civilian carriers brought from Rabaul and 500 other civilian laborers from the Formosan Takasago Volunteers and Korean laborers. They dumped troops, vehicles, and supplies. Among the troops was Sergeant Imanishi Sadaharu. He remembered carrying "a bag of rice weighing 50 pounds, 180 bullets, two grenades, a steel helmet and a tooth brush."[14] This would have to sustain him for the grueling campaign over the mountains.

Troops from 144th Infantry Regiment, naval landing support units, and the civilian workers quickly began establishing the beachhead. The only notable setback there was that they were unable to unload a contingent of fifty-two pack horses, animals that could have helped shuttle supplies or at least been food to the troops.

Meanwhile, Colonel Yokoyama selected Giruwa as the site of what would become a sprawling military base. At the same time, Lieutenant Colonel Tsukamoto's infantry battalion with an attached signal unit and an engineer company struck out in the direction of Kokoda on the high plateau of the Owen Stanley Range.

By the end of July 22, against scant resistance from a local volunteer battalion, Tsukamoto led his men seven miles inland. The next day they encountered an Australian militia company at Awala and drove them off. The Australian company then set up a blocking position at Wairupa (pidgin for wire rope bridge) on the Kumusi River. Though they destroyed the bridge, the action did not slow down the advance. The Japanese waded the river, and Tsukamoto's infantry fought through a hastily organized ambush. Then the Japanese threw up a temporary bridge and continued to advance.

By July 25, the Japanese pressed toward the outpost at Kokoda. Meanwhile, the naval landing party was busy constructing an airfield at Buna and a wharf near Giruwa for unloading supplies. Now that they had a foothold, the challenge was getting supplies inland to keep up with the advancing advanced guard.

A truck base was established six miles inland at Soputa. From there the engineers followed the road to the jungle but then the road simply vanished. Given the dense cover of the jungle and the hurried and harried flyover by air reconnaissance, there was little wonder that the planes failed to spot the road's terminus. From the beach, through Soputa, with a concerted effort to shore up a poorly constructed road that easily fell apart under heavy use or washed away in the torrid jungle downpours, trucks could get thirty-six miles inland to Sanbo. After that the trail could only be made suitable for packhorses (of which there were none) or carried by men. Still, there was a road. Although it might not extend all the way to Kokoda, at least the path traveled halfway there.

Colonel Yokoyama had much else to be pleased with. The advanced party had survived the most vulnerable stages of the campaign. They lost no ships in the crossing and fended off a concerted air attack. Meanwhile, troops were advancing toward a key objective—the Kokoda station without heavy losses. Though the road to Kokoda did not exist, the advanced force was well on its way to establishing a base of supply and support for the operation. Progress was promising.

The advance was well under way. In two days time, the next wave of troops headed for Buna would deploy on its beaches. Then everything changed. While Colonel Yokoyama pressed on, the 17th Army Headquarters received some shocking news. The 17th Army chief of staff received a message from Colonel Hattori Takushiro, head of the operations planning section in the Imperial Headquarters, stating that the command was still waiting for the results of the Ri Operational Study. Headquarters had not authorized the full operation after all. Another member of the Imperial staff, Lieutenant Colonel Imoto Kumao, who had first briefed the army commander and his staff at Matsushima Ryokan Hotel in Fukuoka the month before, recalled (after the war) that the decision to press forward was "an independent judgment of Lieutenant Colonel Tsuji." This confusing turn of events requires some explaining and some backstory.

Whether Tsuji truly acted independently or if the source of confusion between the staffs lay elsewhere is unclear. Tsuji was a well-known, brilliant, and somewhat infamous figure in the Imperial Japanese Army. One team of historians described him as "the nail that sticks and is hammered down—but no amount of hammering could flatten him for long. He seems sometimes like a Japanese Rasputin, bobbing up in every theater of war with his taste for violence and his capacity for escalating it unimpaired."[15] He was both an instigator and sometimes a convenient scapegoat to blame when things went awry.

It is clear that Tsuji's directive to drive on with the campaign is not the stuff of some Shakespearean tragedy, an independent decision by a hot-headed staff officer that propelled the command inevitably to its doom. Tsuji's actions have to be placed in context. In different armies, general staff officers played different roles. In the US, British, and Australian militaries, general staff officers were just that—officers assigned to the general staff. The German and Japanese armies, however, followed a very different model.

The modern German general staff functions included providing independent advice, exercising their own discretion, directly influencing decisionmaking in the field, and even issuing orders on their own authority when the situation demanded it. They also had permission to go around commanders and report directly to higher headquarters.

During World War II, the functions and responsibilities of the German general staff were compiled in *Handbuch fuer den Generalstabsdienst im Kriege* (1939). Japanese officers had trained in Germany since the turn of the century, where they became versed in German general staff practices.[16] Like their German counterparts, their views in the field carried great weight with commanders.

While Hitler neutered the independent authorities of general staff officers over time, in Japan their power and influence only grew as the war years dragged on and the influence of civilian leaders waned. Competition for influence in the Imperial Japanese Army was not new. In the 1930s, *gekokujo* became a more common practice among junior officers. The term implied helping superior officers to interpret and implement orders from above. As practiced by a Japanese general staff officer this method of influence could have dramatic impact on senior level decisionmaking.

In the formal command structure of the Imperial Japanese Army, "Army field commanders, though directly responsible to the Emperor, could not report directly to the Throne but presented their recommendations through the Chief of the Army General Staff."[17] This arrangement further strengthened the influence of a general staff officer in the field. A commander who complained or disagreed with a general staff officer could not assume that the army general staff commander would side with his field commander over a general staff officer. Nor, of course, could the field commander appeal directly to the emperor. Given this command arrangement, it is not exceptional at all that Hyakutake acted on Tsuji's guidance.

To be fair, the controversy mattered little to the outcome of the campaign. If the Imperial Headquarters had wanted to wait for the full results of the advanced party, they had time to order a delay in the deployment of Horii's main force. At the same time, the 17th Army Headquarters could have requested to delay the departure of the main force pending the outcome of the advanced party operations. General Hyakutake, the 17th Army commander, however had little reason to do so.

Further, pressing forward was completely consistent with how Japanese officers were trained to make combat decisions. "Influenced greatly by the old Prussian-German traditions," writes Alvin D. Coox in an assessment of the Japanese operational thinking, the army "headed to the sound of the enemy guns. Mission, in other words must take precedence over intelligence estimates. It became the habit for Japanese field officers or reach relatively quick combat decisions rather than ponder matters."[18] With early success in the field, it was natural instinct for Japanese field commanders to follow through rather than have second thoughts.

The troops on the ground had already determined the road to Buna only extended about halfway, petering out at Sanbo into little more than a winding jungle trail. Still, Lieutenant Colonel Tsukamoto's infantry had moved quickly, sweeping any resistance before them. There was scant reason not to press on.

It is difficult to imagine that the operation would not have proceeded anyway. The Japanese were desperate to take Port Moresby. The cancelation of operations against Fiji and Samoa made taking Papua New Guinea off the table as a base for Allied operations even more vital. A land campaign was the only practical option.

No doubt, they were going to find some route of travel between Buna, Kokoda, and Port Moresby—after all the highland plantations and mines had to have some way to move people and supplies up and down the Owen Stanley Range. If there was a way to traverse the ground, then there was an expectation that determined, toughened, Japanese infantry would find a way to make the trek.

Dismissing Horii's campaign as a forlorn hope might seem reasonable with the comfort of history to rest upon. At the time, at least from the Japanese perspective, the expectation for the campaign's success was within the realm of possibility. After all, Japanese infantry had accomplished some unprecedented feats of arms in the southern campaign from taking fortress Singapore to capturing the bastions on Bataan and Corregidor. The prospects for victory in this campaign rested not on the chimera of unfounded overconfidence but the desperate determination that there was no other way to the save the empire.

As the first days of the campaign unfolded, the Japanese troops grimly marched toward the cloud-covered hills above the jungle, brushing aside the few troops sent to block their way. Who was to tell them that their goal was beyond their reach?

Notes

1. Quotes in this section from Winston S. Churchill: broadcast, 10 May 1942, in Gilbert, *The Churchill Documents*, vol. 17, p. 661.

2. Pike, *Hirohito's War*, p. 405.

3. Unless noted otherwise, quotes on Japanese military operations are from *Japanese Army Operations in the South Pacific Area: New Britain and Papua Campaigns, 1942–43*, pp. 127–132.

4. Operations at Guadalcanal are described in Frank, *Guadalcanal: The Definitive Account of the Landmark Battle*.

5. Spector, *Eagle Against the Sun*, pp. 177–178.

6. Headquarters, United States Army Japan, Assistant Chief of Staff, G3, Foreign Histories Division, Japanese Monograph No. 45, History of Imperial General Headquarters Army Section, p. 3.

7. Collie and Marutani, *The Path of Infinite Sorrow*, pp. 55–56

8. FitzSimons, *Kokoda*, pp. 171–172.

9. Milner, *Victory in Papua*, p. 55, incorrectly states that the advance force landed at the Basabua anchorage.

10. *Japanese Army Operations in the South Pacific Area*, p. 123.

11. Japanese Officials [OPNAV-P-03-100]; *Japanese Army Operations in the South Pacific Area*, p. 124.

12. Interrogation Nav 57, Rear Admiral Mitsaharu Matsuyama, 31 Oct. 1945, United States Strategic Bombing Survey (Pacific).

13. Gamble, *Fortress Rabaul*, p. 196.

14. Ham, *Kokoda*, p. 9.

15. Harries and Harries, *Soldiers of the Sun*, p. 343.

16. Bassford, *Clausewitz in English*, pp. 72, 73.

17. Headquarters, United States Army, Japan, Assistant Chief of Staff, G3, Foreign Histories Division, Foreign Histories Division, Japanese Monograph No. 45, p. 4.

18. Coox, "Flawed Perception and Its Effect Upon Operational Thinking," pp. 239–240.

6

The Jungle's
First Battle

MELBOURNE, DECEMBER 27, 1941. *"Without any inhibitions of any kind, I make it quite clear that Australia looks to America, free of any pangs as to our traditional links or kinship with the United Kingdom."* —John Curtin

CURTIN PENNED THIS line in an editorial, shortly after America entered the war.[1] Six months later, in the summer of 1942, as Japanese soldiers bayoneted Australia's boys in the jungles of Papua New Guinea, the declaration by Australian prime minister John Curtin made perfect sense. As the war closed in, what else could he do? He had to stand side-by-side with his American ally—General MacArthur.

Breaking with Churchill and the British people was, however, not foremost on Curtin's conscience when he wrote his editorial about throwing Australia's lot in with the Americans. Curtin was not an ideologue. "To Australians he conveyed," writes Australian historian Ross McMullin, "a genuine concern for the nation and its people, and a willingness to ensure that in Australia's time of trouble his government would take the drastic measures that were appropriate."[2] Above all, he had a war to win. That was why Curtin welcomed MacArthur and his Yanks with open arms, and why he and MacArthur remained brothers-in-arms (though sometimes fractious brothers) through the most difficult months of Australia's war.

Though Curtin had MacArthur on his side, the first battles of the jungle war would be carried on by the Australian militia. MacArthur might swagger, but it was the Australians who would do the fighting and dying to protect the Allied foothold in Papua New Guinea. In the summer of 1942, MacArthur was not ready for war. Every troop he employed to defend something distracted from the forces available to go after the enemy. Every fight he took on in one place was a fight he could not make somewhere else. He had vast expanses of ocean to cover, dotted with terrain that offered little in the way of resources to sustain his armies in the field. He watched the Japanese stretch their forces across the Pacific like a rubber band, pushing themselves to the edge of exhaustion. MacArthur did not want his return to repeat their mistake. Instead, he wanted to reserve the bulk of his combat power to take the fight to the enemy. This greatly influenced how he and Curtin would fight to defend Port Moresby.

Next Move

Port Moresby was crucial for both protecting the ability of the South West Pacific Area (SWPA) forces to move on Rabaul and using it as a base for supporting the offensive to follow. The question was how. The answer was Australia's militia. The militia troops, unlike the volunteers of the Second Australian Imperial Force (AIF), were conscripts. By law, militia forces could not be deployed overseas in the manner the regular troops were dispatched to defend the corners of the empire in Singapore, the Middle East, and the Mediterranean. But Papua New Guinea, since it was under the dominion of Australia, was not considered an overseas deployment. Militia troops found themselves dispersed for "tropical service" at strategic points like Port Moresby and Rabaul. Here is how they accomplished that mission.

In the spring of 1941, the government authorized dispatching one battalion of the militia (the Citizen Military Force) to safeguard Port Moresby and Thursday Island. The main body arrived in March 1941. Their principal task was to protect the coastal artillery battery overlooking the port.

In May 1941, all the troops in Papua New Guinea were placed under the newly organized 8th Military District commanded by a long-serving regular army soldier, Major General Basil Moorhouse Morris. On the day after Pearl Harbor, a little over 1,200 militia garrisoned the port, with the 49th Battalion from Queensland being the main combat unit.[3] They called them *chocos*—and that was not a term of affection. Everyone expected the militia troops to melt away if they had to face the Japanese, much like a bar of chocolate in the tropical heat. As Peter FitzSimons wrote in his history of the campaign, many considered "the militia was naught but a shelter for those weak-kneed individuals too piss-weak to expose themselves to a real fight. . . . [N]ow that the war had begun, real men had long ago left the militia to join the real army. The leftovers in the militia were considered as just one notch better than those worse-than-useless 'conscientious objectors.'"[4]

Concern about the capabilities of the militia units, however, was about more than just their moral fiber. The militia forces did not receive priority for training, equipment, or leadership. General Morris wrote in his diary, "At this time everything about the unit was wrong—efficiency, discipline, etc. . . . it must quite be the worst battalion in Australia."[5] Their state was the rule, not the exception. Preparing the militia to defend the homeland before the war received little urgency. After the conflict started, the government had to race to catch up. For the men at a distant front and already in harm's way, that was cold comfort.[6]

While Morris was less than thrilled with his command, his men were no more enamored with him. Neil Robinson, then a nineteen-year-old trooper, recalled Morris as "the idiot in charge of Moresby."[7]

Backing up these troops was an infantry battalion organized with Indigenous people, overseen by Australian officers, and noncommissioned officers. These men were even less well trained and equipped than the Australian militia. In April 1940, A Company of the Papuan Infantry Battalion was first formed. B Company was raised in April 1941. C Company was added in November. These troops spent most of their time on mundane garrison duties that could be performed with minimal skills—guarding buildings and manning roadside checkpoints, not preparing for battle.

After the disaster at Pearl Harbor and the rapid advance of the Japanese in the Southwest Pacific, the Australians bolstered the defenses of Port Moresby, quadrupling the size of the garrison—with more militia, 3,721 men. They were organized into the 30th Brigade commanded by another World War I veteran, Brigadier General Neville Hatton. In addition to the 49th Battalion, the brigade included elements of the 39th Battalion from Victoria and the 53rd Battalion from New South Wales along with the 23rd Heavy Anti-Aircraft Battery and the 13th Field Artillery Regiment.

Despite its strategic significance, the port seemed like the backwater of the war. Enduring primitive conditions and poorly supplied, when the Japanese first bombed Port Moresby on January 21, 1942, the troops raided the town, in part out of ill-discipline, but in part out of desperation to find anything to improve their meager lot.

When the Australian reporter George H. Johnston arrived at the front, he found it hardly appeared like a front at all. "Port Moresby looks entirely unsuited to war. The bomb craters and shattered houses and the coconut palms shredded by blast, the sun-bronzed men in khaki hats and khaki shorts, naked to the waist, hewing gun pits and filling sandbags. All these sights don't fit the Moresby scene. It's still a quiet, sleepy tropical port."[8]

Nor was the security of this crucial stronghold much to speak of. One officer told Johnston in confidence if the Japanese attacked, commanders estimated the garrison could hold out for thirty-six hours and no more.[9] Only gradually was the port roused from this drowsy state.

In the interminable months before the first Japanese troops landed in Buna, the troops at Port Moresby unloaded ships like stevedores. They swatted an armada of mosquitos. They were soaked to the bone. They cramped. They sweated. They suffered the runs and burned with fever from tropical diseases. Lined up for sick parade. Monotonously guarded airfields and munition dumps. Filled more sandbags than they could count. Dreaded the periodic Japanese bombing raids.

What the troops did not do was much training for war. "We infantry were still largely employed in labouring tasks," recalled Victor Austin, a young noncommissioned officer with the 39th Battalion, and "there was little time for training at platoon or company, let alone battalion or brigade level."[10] These men were not ready for a real fight.

In addition to garrisoning the port, the Australians were busy transforming the governance of Papua New Guinea from civilian to military administration and establishing under them units largely composed of native irregular forces. These troops included the battalion at Port Moresby, the Kanga Force harassing the Japanese at Lae and Salamaua, and others scattered throughout the territory. Originally they comprised the Papuan and New Guinea administrative units. By April 1942, they were amalgamated into the Australian New Guinea Administrative Unit (ANGAU), the "third force" of Allied landpower. The other two being the Australian and US ground forces.

Meanwhile, efforts to protect the base modestly improved. The Australians added a searchlight company so they could actually see and shoot back at enemy planes during night attacks. The facilities at Port Moresby also continued to expand with US engineer, anti-aircraft, and service troops helping build and expand a multi-airfield complex not just to defend Australia but to start to take the air war to the enemy. Port Moresby's prewar airport, Kila Kila Airfield, was designated 3 Mile Drome (denoting its distance from the town). In January 1942, the Australian Air Force had taken over full control of the field. That was just the start. They added Jackson Field (7 Mile Drome), which became one of the largest airstrips on the island, hosting the heavy bomber squadrons that would pound Rabaul. They also began construction on another major facility at Berry Airfield (2 Mile Drome). Durand Airfield (17 Mile Drome) was constructed to host frontline fighter aircraft defending Port Moresby. Over the course of the war, four additional airfield complexes were also built. What SWPA did not add was more troops to defend the burgeoning military platform.

On April 25, 1942, MacArthur issued his first overall directive on the disposition of forces in the theater. The order included no additional troops for Papua New Guinea—none.[11] The ground forces on hand would have to protect the additional airfields as well as the increasingly sprawling port facilities, warehouses, and garrison buildings. That was a problem. Morris and Hatton had done little to whip the Port Moresby defenders into fighting shape.

In mid-April 1942, Brigadier General Selwyn Havelock Watson Craig Porter, who served in combat with the Second Australian Imperial Forces during the Syrian campaign, replaced Hatton. Porter was dismayed at the state of the brigade. Not only had not enough been accomplished in the months since Pearl Harbor, "there were tasks of undoing what had been done and organizing almost every aspect of command, administration and preparation for battle," Porter recalled.[12]

In the wake of the Battle of the Coral Sea, SWPA dispatched more reinforcements to Port Moresby including the 3rd, 36th, and 55th Battalions from New South Wales under the 14th Brigade—more militia troops. The brigade was perhaps the least battle-worthy of the militia forces available. Between them they totaled barely four months of continuous training before being sent to the front.

On May 27, the brigade and all the other US and Australian air and naval forces in Port Moresby were placed under the command of New Guinea Force.[13] After the Japanese naval defeat at Midway, MacArthur pondered what the enemy's next move might be. One possibility was some kind of overland advance across the Owen Stanley Range against Port Moresby.[14] To counter that, MacArthur had options. He could dispatch seasoned veterans from the 6th or 7th AIF divisions. Perhaps the best troops available at the time. He could send one of his two US divisions, untested but well-equipped, fresh forces. MacArthur decided on neither. MacArthur looked at the maps. He looked at the air and sea situation. He doubted the Japanese could pull off a Singapore—march over the mountains and take Port Moresby from the landward side. Port Moresby was far beyond their culminating point. While the Allied codebreakers had delivered some warning that the Japanese might try an overland attack, MacArthur made little of it. He decided to save the regular combat forces for offensive action, the campaign of liberation that would begin the journey toward Japan's doorstep.

The defense of Papua New Guinea would have to make do with the militia. If the enemy came, it would be dealt with by the force on hand. Indeed, rather than strengthen the garrison at Port Moresby, MacArthur looked to expand the Allied footprint elsewhere. On June 25, a detachment was dispatched from Port Moresby to Milne Bay on the eastern tip of the peninsula. The force—including two companies from the 55th Battalion, some anti-aircraft units, and a company from the 46th US Engineer Battalion—protected Gili Gili, an airstrip that could be used to host fighters and heavy bombers. A few weeks later the garrison was expanded with elements of the 7th (Australian) Brigade group and additional artillery, engineers, and an anti-tank battery.

The buildup at Milne Bay reflected a larger scheme; MacArthur's top priority had long shifted to preparing to take the offensive. Expanding control over the northeast coast would block opportunities for further Japanese advances on Papua New Guinea, but it would also begin the task of isolating Rabaul. Meanwhile, the garrison at Port Moresby was ordered to begin to set up a line of supply that would run from Port Moresby up and over the Owen Stanley Range and down the other side where MacArthur wanted to establish a forward airbase at Dobodura near the village of Buna. From there the Allies could conduct air attacks more easily on all the Japanese on the northeast coast as well as raid Rabaul.

Getting to Buna started with a march along a narrow, often-rutted dirt road from Port Moresby through gradually rising foothills to the rubber plantation on Ilolo (about twenty-five miles), often called McDonald's Corner since it was once the site of a plantation run by New Guinea old-timer P. J. McDonald. From there a steep narrow track led to a point called Owers' Corner.[15] That's as far as could be driven in a jeep. From there the only way forward was to trek up and down switchbacks, plunging into forested ravines, forging fast-flowing ice-cold streams, and then trudging relentlessly upward to a towering ridge and Isurava village. The track plummeted from there through rough terrain to the village of Deniki and then followed a long level walk to Kokoda, situated on a plateau topping the northern foothills of the Owen Stanley Range. A final treacherous march through jungle, into valleys, across streams, and over razor-topped ridges led down to the northeast coast and Buna.

In early June, Morris dispatched the Papuan Infantry, about 280 barefoot soldiers and their 30 ANGAU officers to the north coast spread out from Awala to Ioma to over watch the coastal points where the Japanese might land. That might be enough troops to keep an eye on the likely landing points, but it certainly was not enough force capable of defending anything. Meanwhile, here is what the Australians did to begin securing an overland route to Buna.

On June 20, Morris was ordered to secure the route up to Kokoda.

On June 24, Morris reorganized the 39th Battalion as the "Maroubra Force." This practice of militaries was not uncommon during World War II, reorganizing fixed organizations like battalions and brigades—mixing and matching combat and support units to conduct specific missions. Different militaries had different practices on how to name these task forces. The Germans, for example, named them after the commander. "Maroubra" was a beach town in New South Wales, Australia (hometown for the troops about to march up the Owen Stanley Range), a faraway place for Australia's sons, one that got farther with every step they took.

On July 2, the US Joint Chiefs of Staff issued an overall directive for the conduct of the Pacific War. Among the tasks for SWPA were taking back the territory in Papua New Guinea on the northern coast. Chief of Naval Operations Admiral King and MacArthur disagreed about much—but not about the need to take the offensive in the Pacific. While King still favored a drive through the Central Pacific, at this point in the conflict he saw merit in supporting operations in the Southwest Pacific. MacArthur wanted to move as well, but the massive Japanese base at Rabaul was a major obstacle in his path. The Joint Chiefs signed off on a concept plan that advanced both their goals, the "Joint Directive for Offensive Operations in the Southwest Pacific Area." The chiefs called for twin offensives in the Bismarck Sea and Papua New Guinea, prerequisites for a move on Rabaul. For the Allied forces in Australia the scheme meant that, for starters, they would have to establish a foothold on the northeast coast of Papua New Guinea where the Japanese had held the ground since the spring of 1942.[16]

Of course, the natural question was why weren't the Allied forces already there? Why would they leave the enemy an open foothold a short flight from Port Moresby and in easy reach by air to the Australian mainland? The answer was simple. To this point in the war, the Allies lacked the resources to reinforce their perimeter in force, let alone take the offensive against the Japanese at Rabaul. The best the Americans and Australians could do, for example, was to harass Salamaua and Lae (which the enemy seized in March 1942) with aircraft carrier raids and pester the Japanese with attacks from an ad hoc guerrilla force. Now MacArthur was ready to move against the Japanese and take back all of Papua New Guinea. For that, he needed his best troops, the Australian regulars and the US divisions. The preparations for the way forward? Well, they would have to be handled by the *chocos* that were already in the theater.

The first steps of MacArthur's move were already in motion. In Papua New Guinea, General Morris had already task-organized the Maroubra Force for its mission over the Owen Stanley Range, detaching one infantry company and adding supply and medical detachments, assigning them the task of securing the route to and the area around Kokoda. Morris also had a seasoned veteran slotted to take over the battalion for the operations that would unfold over the weeks ahead. He was Bill Owen.

Lieutenant Colonel William T. Owen had already seen a lifetime of war in his brief military career. Before it all, he worked in a bank—he was already in his mid-fifties—and served in the militia. He commanded a company at Rabaul the day the Japanese landed. After several hours of tough fighting, Owen ordered a withdrawal. Joining the rest of the garrison trying to avoid being encircled and annihilated, Owen and his men struck out over the mountains for the coast. Some were massacred. Some died of illness. Hundreds surrendered. Owen was among the survivors to reach Port Moresby, where he was evacuated to Australia.

After a month of rest and recovery and a promotion, on July 5, he arrived back at Moresby ready to take over his new command and whip them into shape for the fight ahead. He would have less time for that crucial task than he imagined. The next day Owen got the first look at his command. He visited B Company, which had already been slated to move out the next morning, starting the long trek to Kokoda to set up the base of operations and from there conduct a reconnaissance to the forward positions that would be established at Buna.

Owen had little more than time to shake hands with Captain Samuel Victor "Uncle Sam" Templeton, one of the most respected and proficient officers in the brigade. A veteran of World War I who had sparred with the IRA while serving in the Royal Irish Constabulary, he migrated to Australia in 1923 and joined the Australian Military Forces in 1928. He volunteered to fight with the International Brigade against the communists during the Spanish Civil War. Templeton joined the Australian army in 1940. He was over forty when deployed to Papua New Guinea with his company. It was no surprise that Templeton and his men had been chosen to the lead the advance over the Owen Stanley Range. They were acknowledged as the best troops available.

Templeton knew if nothing else there was a lot of hard marching ahead. In order to support the operation, the Australians needed to build a road from Ilolo to Kokoda and then establish an airfield so that they also had an air bridge in and out of the stronghold they intended to establish high on the Owen Stanley plateau. Construction would be done under ANGAU Major Sydney Elliot-Smith and a team of surveyors, engineers, and an army of laborers managed by Lieutenant Bert Kienzle. The route would have to be defended by militia troops from Port Moresby. Work was to commence at the end of June and be completed by August 26.

Even without the intervention of the Japanese, it was a near impossible undertaking. "I have heard of superman," Kienzle later recalled, "but I have yet to see him in action. . . . Some twit at headquarters had looked at a map and said, 'We'll put a road there. . . . Had it been possible it would have ranked as one of the most colossal engineering feats in the world!"[17] And that was without contending with an enemy attacking in the other direction over the Owen Stanley Range.

On July 15, MacArthur completed the outline of a plan for establishing at base at Buna. The US 41st Infantry Division moved from Melbourne to Rockhampton in the north and the 32nd Infantry Division from Adelaide to Brisbane to prepare for the assault. Both were grouped under Lieutenant General Robert L. Eichelberger as I (US) Corps commander. The plan was an overland march from Port Moresby with a forward base at Buna in early August.

Even after the first enemy troops landed on the northeast coast in late July, MacArthur remained confident in his judgment. While he plotted an Allied overland campaign, he remained convinced that a Japanese force coming in the opposite direction was a bridge too far for the Imperial army. He was wrong. In *Kokoda*, historian Peter FitzSimons dished out disdain for MacArthur's failure to deploy regular troops to defend Papua New Guinea, particularly after receiving intelligence suggesting a Japanese overland campaign.[18] FitzSimons, no fan of MacArthur, uncritically mimics the judgments of the official Australian histories. But the argument doesn't bear up under scrutiny. The case FitzSimons argues makes perfect sense in hindsight. But commanders don't get to make decisions that way. They have to deal with what they know at the time. If MacArthur had significantly more resources, if the return of Australian troops had happened faster, or if the Americans had arrived sooner and were better prepared for battle—well, then moving sooner might have been the best move. But that was not the hand MacArthur was dealt.

MacArthur's decision was logical. It made little sense to dispatch first-class ground troops to defend the foothold in Papua New Guinea.

Holding Port Moresby was a matter of air and naval supremacy. Even the finest troops in the world could not hold the Allied position if the Allies could not command the air and water approaches. However, if the Japanese could be held at bay at sea and in the air, then any troops in Papua New Guinea would do. And, they would have to make do until MacArthur was ready to return.

Forward into Battle

In the following weeks, training to fight the enemy in the field became a higher priority for the troops garrisoning Port Moresby. On the afternoon of July 18 after a day of field exercises, Lieutenant Colonel Owen called together the commanders of the 39th Battalion to review the day's work. A dispatch rider bearing orders interrupted the meeting. The battalion, less their heavy equipment including mortars and the machine gun company, were ordered to make the long difficult trek to Kokoda. Later that day Owen ordered the first unit to be on the march by the next morning, with two additional companies joining in the following days and the rest of the battalion being airlanded at Kokoda later.

When word came, just days later, that the Japanese had beaten MacArthur to Buna, the 39th Battalion was ordered into the fight to turn them back. These troops along with the Papuan Infantry Battalion already deployed along the northeast coast were all that stood between the enemy and Port Moresby.[19]

Hyakutake had stolen a march on MacArthur with the landing of the advance force on the northeast coast of Papua New Guinea. But all was not well. Winning battles can be simple, but in the jungle the simple is difficult. That was the story of Kokoda.

Both sides had identified Kokoda as a vital piece of terrain. Not the village, of course. The villages on the Kokoda track were good for little more than orienting a map. It was the grassy flatlands outside Kokoda that the armies crossing the Owen Stanley Range eyed. Only days into the fight across Papua New Guinea and there was little question that most of the war would be carried by foot. Not only was road transport impractical, the idea that roads could be built and maintained before the fighting was done was clearly unrealistic. While the range itself presented an unending series of obstacles to transport, from raging rivers to deep gorges and mudslides after the ceaseless rains, the summit of the Owen Stanley Range was split by the central highlands that spread out in wide fertile valleys covered in thick kunai grass.

The 17th Army commander recognized the importance of Kokoda: the flat land in the highlands at the conjunction of the apex of the route from Buna to Port Moresby was an ideal spot for an airstrip that could be used to rearm, resupply, evacuate casualties, and shuttle reinforcements. The July 18, 1942, order for the offensive against Port Moresby included a requirement that a "large stockpile of munitions and supplies will be established at Kokoda."[20] The Japanese weren't the only ones who could read a map and understand how to use the dominating importance of vital terrain. Only a few days before, Bert Kienzle had been assigned a similar mission.

No one was better skilled to manage establishing the logistical lifeline to Kokoda than Kienzle. He had been a planter and miner in the Papua New Guinea highlands for over a decade. Young, fit, knowledgeable of the terrain, and skilled at working with the locals, as his biographer and daughter-in-law Robyn Kienzle wrote, "many people contend that Bert really blazed much of what was to become the war trail."[21] There is little question that her assessment is not just the impulse of family pride.

By July 15, three platoons of the 39th Battalion were established at Kokoda, led there by Kienzle. Two platoons took up position along a prewar airstrip outside the village and a third at the abandoned rubber plantation south of Kokoda. Warrant Officer Jack Wilkinson wrote in his diary, after the difficult trek up the track, "Nice place. Glad to be here." After escaping the incessant tedium and squalor of Port Moresby (interrupted by the occasional enemy bombing) and enduring the difficult trek to the Owen Stanley highlands, Wilkinson reported, "Kokoda suited us well . . . plenty of fruit and vegetables . . . climate was good. Mosquitos were few. Housing was good. Life looked sweet—for a full week."[22] It was as close as they would ever get to Dorothy Lamour and paradise.

Meanwhile, Captain Sam Templeton of B Company, 39th Battalion, had gone forward to reconnoiter preparations at Buna. What he didn't know was that the Japanese would be there in force before the defenses of Kokoda were ready for them.

More than any other, Lieutenant Colonel Tsuji Masanobu, one of the army general staff's most talented and influential tactical planners, was the driving force to shift the Japanese mission in Papua New Guinea from reconnaissance to a determined invasion across the Owen Stanley Range. While the Yokoyama advance force under Colonel Yokoyama Yosuke stormed toward Kokoda, Tsuji played a supporting role, hammering out an arrangement among the air, ground, and sea commanders. The army concluded an agreement with the 11th Air Fleet and the 8th (Naval) Fleet (signed on July 31) to land additional ground force elements by sea near Port Moresby as the column from Kokoda crossed over the Owen Stanley Range and down the other side as the South Seas Force closed on the objective. This would allow for massing additional forces for the attack without the logistical burden of supporting yet more troops crossing over the range.

Tsuji wasn't content to watch the fight from afar. On July 25, he left Rabaul for Buna to press operations forward from the front end. On the one hand, General Hyakutake was glad to see the back of him taking his high-pressure micromanagement with him. On the other hand, Hyakutake fretted the colonel might cause even more turmoil at the front. General Futami Akisaburo, the 17th Army chief of staff, recorded—with restraint—in his memoirs that "the day after Tsuji's heavy-handed departure from us, I heard from the Army commander . . . that Tsuji had been the cause of several difficulties."[23] Fate intervened. On July 27, Tsuji was injured near the coast of Buna and had to be evacuated back to Rabaul, where he continued to monitor operations and interject himself where he saw fit.

As Tsuji relentlessly prodded and browbeat Horii and other staff and commanders, the 17th Army pressed forward with its campaign to take Moresby. Meanwhile, as the Yokoyama advance party continued its rapid advance, the army and navy formally jointly committed to the overland campaign with the issuance of Great Army Instruction no. 1318 on July 28, 1942.[24]

In contrast to Horii's skepticism over the capacity to sustain an invasion force across the ridges, valleys, jungles, and rivers, Colonel Yokoyama reported optimistically that the road to Kokoda could be made passable and with sufficient transport, "if each soldier carried a total of 12 days' supply—four days to Kokoda and eight days to Port Moresby— then an attack on Port Moresby would be possible at one stretch."[25] Brushing aside, the concern that his troops were essentially going into battle without a logistical supply line behind them, Yokoyama plunged forward into battle. It was not an irrational decision. But it was bold risk. It didn't matter that the Australians had not put up a strong defense. What mattered was if the defenses could be swept aside, the jungle mastered, and Port Moresby reached before his men starved to death.

On the ground, optimism was tempered by reality. The Japanese brought bicycles. They had been handy in the Malay campaign for relaying messages and patrolling. Sergeant Imanishi carried one of them—but not for long. As the trek uphill quickly turned difficult, he was laughed at for pursuing the thankless duty of carrying useless equipment and threw it into the jungle. Remarkably, when the Japanese reached the plateau, the Australians spotted some of the enemy still carrying bicycles. They had shouldered them up the incredible trek to the top.[26]

For a week, the Japanese had been pressing forward against elements of the 39th Battalion that had advanced down from Kokoda, joining up with the remnants of the Papuan battalion from ANGAU. That the Australians hadn't been able to stop them wasn't much of a surprise to either side. That was not their job.

The Australians started the war in Papua New Guinea without much doctrine to suggest how they ought to fight. In May 1942, the military published a training memorandum, "How to Fight the Japanese," though it contained little practical advice on jungle fighting. Not until 1943 would the Australian military start to publish warfighting doctrine based on lessons learned from its fighting experience. For small unit combat training, they mostly used the imperial publication *Infantry Training: Training and War 1937*. Though updated over the years, it was already outdated and included nothing useful about jungle fighting.

Both Owen and Templeton were seasoned enough professionals to know the manual did sketch out general guidance on how to fight a "rearguard action." A force retiring "covers itself, against enemy pursuit by a rear guard." It was expected that such a body would be outnumbered. The principal task was to buy time for the main body of a friendly force and prevent them from being surprised by an advancing enemy. Time and security would allow the main body to either withdraw, prepare for defense, or counterattack against the advancing enemy.

Beyond general guidance, the manual offered that when pressed by the enemy, "the task of a rear guard is to keep the enemy at a distance from the main body, and at the same time to be able to withdraw without becoming seriously involved."[27] Owen had experienced this kind of fighting firsthand in the disastrous withdrawal from Rabaul.

At this point a rearguard action was the only option to slow the Japanese advance. The enemy was already on the march. On July 24, Owen flew into the field at Kokoda where he met Templeton and both immediately set out to join the two forward platoons and the elements of the Papuan Infantry Battalion, all that was available to slow the enemy's drive toward Kokoda. They planned to organize a series of ambushes and defensive stands to slow the Japanese down. River crossings and spots where the trails to Kokoda were hemmed in by thick underbrush were natural places to pick a fight. These were places where the Japanese would have difficulty moving quickly, maneuvering forces, or using their machine guns and mortars.

That the fighting was harrowing and chaotic was to be expected as a matter of course. Such missions were difficult for well-trained, experienced troops in open terrain. In a claustrophobic jungle, managing a novice thrown-together force against a battle-experienced enemy was no mean feat. They were fighting on ground they barely knew without any maps. That they conducted any coherent effort at all was a bit of a minor military miracle.

To make matters worse, they would have to finish this fight without Templeton. After five harrowing days of battle, on July 26, he disappeared while trying to link up with one of the platoons. It was presumed he had been killed in action. There is some evidence to suggest he was taken prisoner and later died in captivity.[28] More than the death of a brave man, more than another widowed bride and fatherless children, the tragedy of the moment was that Owen would have to carry on without one of his most dependable and talented commanders.

Unquestionably, the sacrifice was not in vain. The rearguard fight had required the Japanese to use up precious food and munitions. Further, they bought the battalion some time. On July 27, Owen withdrew his men from Kokoda to set-up defenses at Deniki, a village a few hours to the southeast, destroying the supplies they could not take with them. The last thing Owen wanted was for the enemy to press their advance thanks to Australian food and ammunition.

The remnants of the rear guard stumbled into Kokoda, exhausted and famished, finding the position deserted. The next morning, on July 28, they reported to Owen at Deniki that there was no enemy at Kokoda. The Japanese, in fact, had moved slower than Owen feared. That gave Owen time to make a choice. He could resume a fighting withdrawal from Deniki, or he could move forward to secure Kokoda and the all-important landing strip, holding on until more support arrived.

At Owen's command was an admixture of men he hardly knew. There were the exhausted remnants of Templeton's platoons and the Papuan infantry, the troops that had been garrisoning Kokoda, as well as a handful of reinforcements, thirty men that had been rushed from Port Moresby and flown in to Kokoda on July 25.

Owen wasn't just short of men. They had destroyed most of the stores at Kokoda. The rest had been moved to Deniki. They would have to fight with what they could carry.

Even if they could hold the airfield, for now it would be useless for resupply. The field was across the creek outside the defensive perimeter and well within range of enemy small arms. They would never be able to fly in supplies or reinforcements while the Japanese were pressing the position. But if they couldn't hold the field, the only help they would ever get would be by foot up the Kokoda trail.

In every fight, however, there is more to think about than how many troops, bullets, and cans of bully beef were available. The enemy gets a vote. Owen was not only lacking men and firepower and had limited supplies, but he also had scant intelligence on his adversary, other than the initial reports of the landing from the Papuan battalion and what could be gleaned from the five days of running battle with the Japanese as the Australians retreated from Buna to Kokoda station.

Owen did know that the enemy had machine guns and mortars and at least one artillery piece. (The Japanese mountain battery had only one gun and only 200 rounds that had to be hand carried.) Clearly, the Australians would be outgunned. Still, they had not yet seen the Japanese employ the kind of firepower or air support that would easily overwhelm a prepared position. Perhaps, the Japanese advance guard did not have these assets.

Owen decided. "We'll go back and re-occupy Kokoda," he ordered.[29] They would try to hold their ground. Past histories describe the colonel's initial decision to abandon Kokoda and destroy the supplies as a mistake. That was the conclusion of the official Australian account. Ham labelled it "a rash scorch-earthed policy."[30] These are judgments that could only be made with hindsight, knowing that the Japanese were not pressing the heels of the rear guard when they reached the station. In fact, risking the supplies falling into the hands of the Japanese would have been a far graver sin. Owen was never going to be able to stop the Japanese—only running out of food and ammunition would do that.

Going back was not atoning for an error. What he saw was an opportunity to regain the initiative—not just hold the airfield but defend on good ground, where a stiff defense even if it couldn't hold for long offered the prospects of slowing the enemy more than fighting a running rearguard action. Owen did what commanders are supposed to do—read the conditions on the battlefield and adjust accordingly.

It was a courageous albeit risky choice—but not an uninformed one. Owen had fought these kinds of battles before in Rabaul. He been on the scene in the Papua New Guinea highlands long enough to see the ground for himself, to measure the Japanese and the men under his command. And he knew what had to be done.

The valley was some ten miles wide. Owen appraised the terrain when he first landed at the airstrip. There was no way he could stop a Japanese force of any size from maneuvering around the plateau—but he knew the ground well enough to know how to slow them down.

Owen also knew how the Japanese attacked in the jungle. If they bumped up against a prepared defense position, they would try to sweep around it to the flanks, encircle, cut off, and annihilate the defenders. Putting up a defense at Kokoda only made sense if they could hold ground that could be defended—and if they had a secured path to retreat after.

If they were going back to defend Kokoda, they had to get there fast and set up a prepared defensive position that the enemy couldn't easily bypass, otherwise the Kokoda defense wouldn't matter anymore than a stop sign. After a brisk march at 11 a.m., Owen's force was back at Kokoda. The station was still deserted. The problem was Owen didn't know how long they had until the enemy would start pushing up from the valley below. There was little time to waste; if a coherent defensive position wasn't prepared before the enemy arrived, the Australian's forlorn hope would likely be swept from the plain.

The position Owen elected to defend had the advantage of open ground to its front. The Japanese would have to cross the Mambare River and a wide grassy area that rose forty feet from the valley floor to the edge of the embankment in front of the Australian position. The east of the embankment was bordered by the Madi Creek and on the west by more dense jungle.

The government station around which the defense organized took the shape of an inverted U, a prominence of high ground bordered by a six-foot embankment with the point facing north toward the direction of the approaching enemy advance. Behind the position was a grove of rubber trees and the trail to Deniki.

Owen couldn't take everyone forward. If they couldn't hold Kokoda, they would have to fall back to Deniki. Troops had to be left to guard the rear and the supplies at Deniki.

The colonel left two sections of 16 Platoon for the task. That left less than eighty men to defend Kokoda.[31] The remnants of the Papuan Infantry Battalion (about twenty men) and 10 Platoon under Lieutenant A. G. Garland covered the right flank. Putting the Papuans with Garland's platoon made sense. They were the least trained and equipped for a stand-up force-on-force fight against experienced infantry. Best to place them in what looked like the least vulnerable part of the defensive line.

To counter what was expected to be the main enemy effort, Lieutenant A. H. Seekamp's 11 Platoon held the center of the line. A section of 16 Platoon (the rest of the platoon had been left at Deniki) under the command of Sergeant E. J. Morrison covered the left flank.

Finally, 12 Platoon under Lieutenant A. G. Mortimore was behind in the rubber trees covering the trail to Deniki. Guarding the line of retreat was 12 Platoon, Owen's reserve, but also the only troops available to throw into the line if it was breeched, mount a counterattack, or block the Japanese if they tried to swing around and encircle the position. The whole defense was about 200 yards across and about the same in depth.

Meanwhile, the station house between the trees and the escarpment would serve as a make shift aid station for the defenders. Captain Geoffrey Vernon, an ANGAU medical officer who had been a few days down the track checking on the conditions of Kienzle's bearers, had gotten word of the Japanese landing at Buna. He knew the 39th Battalion did not have a medical officer. Without orders—alone—he decided to walk up the trail and offer to serve as the battalion surgeon for the fight ahead. Vernon was cut from the same cloth as Templeton and Owen. He was no young man, but he was physically fit and mentally tough. He also had experience in battle. He was a World War I veteran.

Together with the battalion's two medical orderlies, Warrant Officers D. S. Barnes and R. E. G. Wilkinson, Vernon set up a regimental aid station to care for the wounded that would be expected in the current fight. That would mean not just recovering the injured, but if the command was forced off the position, they would have to figure out how to evacuate the wounded down the trail to Deniki. After prepping his station for battle, Vernon fell asleep. After days of trekking he was near exhaustion—and he would need his rest for the trials ahead.

Day of Battle

During the morning, a platoon of D Company was flown up to Kokoda in two transport aircraft. The pilots circled the position several times. Decided landing was too risky. The planes headed back to Port Moresby. There was little question but that the defenders of Kokoda would be on their own for the enemy's main attack.[32]

By 1:30 p.m. the perimeter was in place.[33] About an hour later the first Japanese appeared in the valley below, followed by sporadic enemy mortar and machine gun fire. Owen's command was ready for the fight— with only an hour to spare.

The Japanese had not been slowed nearly as much as Owen might have hoped. They had to cross a major obstacle, the Kumusi River, even though the Australians had managed to drop the only bridge at Wairopi (Tok Pisin for wire rope bridge) before retreating. But, the river crossing was unopposed and Tsukamoto's troops quickly managed it with makeshift boats and few casualties. The first men reached the clearing at Kokoda not long after Owen reoccupied the position.

Probing, the Japanese advance force quickly determined they had come up against a prepared enemy defense position, not a fleeing rear guard. By the end of the day, Tsukamoto brought a considerable force for the assault on Kokoda, estimated between 180 and 400.[34] Whatever the actual number, they dwarfed Owen's force. Western officers were trained that traditionally for a successful attack the offensive force ought to outnumber the defenders by three to one. Neither side knew exactly how many the other had, but both suspected that the Japanese had sufficient forces to carry the attack. In fact, the Japanese had more than enough to carry the day.

War, however, is always more than raw numbers. On one hand, both sides had been marching and fighting for days. That made the odds more even. On the other hand, the Japanese troops were more experienced, better trained, and prepared for battle. When it came to weapons, both sides would fight principally with grenades, rifles, and machine guns. The Australians, however, had the advantage of holding a defensive position with clear fields of fire (open ground that the Japanese would have to close exposed to the fire from the Australian positions without the benefit of any cover). The Australians not only held the better ground, they knew the area better. Neither side benefited from having any usable maps, so the commander who had walked the ground before the fighting held that edge over his enemy.

Any minor "home field" advantage was cold comfort. The diggers knew they were facing a determined and relentless enemy. For his part, Tsukamoto did not know if more enemy reinforcements were on the way. He didn't know if Allied air support might show up to bomb and harass his troops.

Tsukamoto did know that time was not on his side. Colonel Yokoyama had reported that he thought the campaign could be completed in twelve days.[35] They were already at least three days in and a long way from Port Moresby. Every day the troops consumed more supplies and ammunition. The more they pressed forward, the longer the Japanese supply lines stretched and the shorter the distance for the defenders to be resupplied from Port Moresby. The longer the campaign lasted the more it disadvantaged prospects for success. But risking a frontal assault against a prepared position that could not be swiftly bypassed over open ground in daylight would likely result in heavy causalities. Tsukamoto could not afford that either.

Tsukamoto elected to make a massed night assault directly at the Australian position. That would diminish the disadvantage of closing open highground in daylight. An attack before dawn not only took advantage of the concealment offered by the darkness, but with luck the fighting would be over by dawn and the Japanese could use the first light to consolidate their hold on the objective. The Japanese also had little to fear from air attacks at night. A night charge was also a tactic that the Japanese were practiced and trained at executing.

Tsukamoto ordered a massed assault before dawn. As night closed, the Australians knew full well that an attack was coming. They could hear the Japanese in the valley below. Occasionally there would be a rip of machine guns and rifle fire. After dark, Japanese mortar fire started to range the position (that meant they were adjusting firing so mortar rounds did not land long or short of the Australian defense emplacements). Fortunately, for the Australians, most of the rounds fell behind their positions, detonating in the trees. Likely the Japanese did not have a good vantage point to accurately direct the mortar fire onto the defenses around Kokoda. If they had or had coordinated the mortars with the assault, Owen would have had a much tougher time holding his ground.

As night closed in, the mortars were less of a threat; the Japanese could not assault the position in the dark and lob mortar fire without the risk of hitting as many of their own men as the enemy. Although the Japanese harassing fire did little to threaten Owen's defenses, it certainly kept the men on edge. Everyone felt it. A big attack was coming. The exchange of fire between the two sides built up until the moment of the predawn attack.

"No one knew there was a hill," recalled Sergeant Imanishi. "We knew nothing of the terrain. But we were very good at executing night attacks. We had experience of this in China." Imanishi's 2nd Company was held in reserve when the main attack began at about 2:30 a.m. on July 29. "We could hear soldiers' voices," he remembered. "Someone shouted 'Charge!' then the sounds of hand grenades and gunshots continued after that. It stopped sometimes, but again you hear sounds of twenty or thirty shots and then someone screams, 'Move and Charge!'"[36] Even though the Japanese were crossing open ground it was difficult to follow the action. While there was a full moon cutting the darkness, there was also a light mist hovering over the valley that, combined with the smoke of explosions, left the whole battlefield blanketed in a haze.

As the battle was joined, leaders on both sides were pretty much fighting in the dark, commanding by sound, observing flashes of fire, depending on experience and intuition as much as anything. The commander's place is always where he can most influence his command. Tsukamoto was in the rear pushing his men relentlessly forward. Owen was with Seekamp's 11 Platoon. That was where he expected the main attack.

Holding off the enemy's charge was the principal task at hand. Japanese mortar fire had been relatively ineffective at ranging the Australian positions. Likewise the Japanese machine guns aiming uphill had difficulty hitting the defenders' position behind the top of the embankment. In addition, there were no signs of the Japanese mountain guns, which could have been used to pound Owen's defenses into submission. The greatest threat was the enemy pressing up the hill. If Owen's men could hold their ground until daylight, then the prospects for holding out a little longer would greatly improve.

The Japanese closed in quickly, scrambling up the escarpment, firing and throwing hand grenades as the Australians fired with rifles and machines guns into the dark mass, then lobbing grenades as the Japanese climbed up. Some of the combat was hand-to-hand, swinging rifles like clubs and jabbing with bayonets.

In the melee, Owen was shot in the head. He fell forward off the escarpment. After a brief search he was spotted lying in one of the weapons pits dug as part of the defensive position. Vernon led a group scrambling down to recover the body. While the battle raged around them, they dragged him back to the aid station. Owen was still alive.

Lighting a lantern to gauge the extent of injury attracted a withering wave of Japanese machine gun fire. Vernon recalled, "Wikinson held the lantern for me and every time he raised it a salvo of machine gun bullets was fired at the building." Firing uphill, in the dark, the Japanese fire mostly hit the thatched roof of the hut, showering the Australians below with dried grass. The steady rain of fire continued for about forty-five minutes. But like much of the Japanese machine gun fire against the high-ground positions, bullets sailed overhead.

Meanwhile, Vernon and his small team worked on Owen and the other wounded. When it came to caring for the colonel they found there was little that could be done. There was an entry wound, but no exit injury. Owen had a bullet lodged in his brain. Wilkinson recalled in his diary, "Breathing light and shallow. Twitching body at times. Hopeless case." The colonel was clearly dying.

Owen's death was more than a personal tragedy. In the heat of battle, command matters more than ever. The colonel had correctly set up his defense leaving a path for withdrawal through the rubber trees to the fallback position at Deniki. But without a leader directing an organized defense, holding the position would be nearly impossible against a determined frontal assault. If the Japanese tried to sweep the defenders' flanks, a disciplined retreat in the chaos of night-fighting would be equally problematic. The entire command could easily get wiped out.

Major W. T. Watson was next in line for command. Watson had helped drag Owen to the station building. Once there, he could see there was no question but that Owen could not issue commands, and he would likely die within minutes. Watson shifted his attention to the great task at hand: commanding his men. What to do next?

Watson ordered the reserve section forward to help Seekamp's platoon hold off the enemy's main assault. By 3:20 a.m., however, with the vicious battle still less than an hour old, the outcome was clear. Not only were the Japanese pushing Seekamp's 11 Platoon off the embankment, by the firing Watson could tell the enemy was around the flanks encircling the position. There was little option for the Australians but to withdraw by their line of retreat through the rubber trees and down the trail to Deniki.

Word was sent to the aid station that the defenders were pulling back. Vernon recalled in his diary, he took a few minutes, "before leaving. . . . We fixed up Colonel Owen, who was now dying, as comfortable as possible—moistening his mouth and cleaning him up." Then he gathered up what he could of his medical instruments, and withdrew with the walking wounded in the direction of the rubber trees.

As dawn approached, the mist on the plateau thickened. Now instead of obscuring the enemy's advance, the concealment provided an advantage to the Australians who used the blanket of white to mask their withdrawal.

Remarkably, despite the ferocity of the fight, the Australians had only six dead and five wounded, and a number of the Papuan infantry were missing.[37] A small rear guard blocked the trail while the rest withdrew carrying the wounded. The last man stood at the edge of the clearing firing full clips from a Bren gun into a charging group of enemy soldiers before falling back into the tree line and down the trail. Listening intently there was no sound of an enemy pursuit, the din of battle replaced by stillness. Vernon paused, exhausted, propped up against a tree smoking a cigarette, waiting for the last men to start down the trial, confirming that all the wounded had been accounted for. He recorded in his diary:

> the thick white mist dimming the moonlight, the mysterious veiling of trees, houses and men, the drip of moisture from the foliage, and at the last, the almost complete silence, as if the rubber groves of Kokoda were sleeping as usual in the depths of the night, and men had not brought disturbance.

The battle was over.

By 4:30 a.m. the last Australians had withdrawn. Tsukamoto ordered his forces to clear and hold the objective and the airfield. The battlefield was littered with Australian ammunition and weapons, including, according to a Japanese after-action report, 180 grenades, 1,850 rounds of ammunition, and five machine guns. The Japanese would gather this bounty up as their own supplies dwindled. Later, they would turn the captured arsenal on the enemy. The Australians had already seen that happen. The battalion war diary reported that at the Battle of Kokoda the Japanese hurled Australian hand grenades up the embankment that they had evidently recovered earlier in the campaign.

But more important than the supplies reaped from the Australians, the battle had cost another day of their food rations and gave the enemy another twenty-four hours to stiffen the defenses of Port Moresby

Meanwhile the Australians retreated to Deniki where they arrived by first light. Setting up another defensive position, Watson took stock of what was left of his command. After the losses at Kokoda, there were seventy-two men left standing between the enemy and Port Moresby.

After the Battle

In the aftermath of the small fight in the dark at the top of the world, there was scant time to ponder the greater reasons for the fight. Yet, what drove the combatants was more than just a raw impulse for survival or the bonds of comradeship, that cohesive effect that binds small units together. Both sides knew it was a fight of consequence for the future in this great war—and both sides knew the fight was far from over.

It would be a mistake to criticize the men and leaders of ANGAU and the 39th Battalion for failing to do something for which they were neither trained, equipped, or sufficiently manned to do—stop the Japanese. That said, the leaders and troops accomplished what could have been asked: they slowed the Japanese offensive, costing the enemy men, material, and food commodities that were essential to sustain their offensive.

It is hard not to argue that the glue that held the whole operation together was the steady leadership of men like Owen, Templeton, and Vernon, experienced hands who made sound tactical judgments and also brought a measure of mental toughness needed to keep generally inexperienced and overmatched troops together in the face of a determined enemy. Sprinkling the command with these officers in the weeks before the Japanese landed at Buna made a huge difference. In opposition, the Japanese advance reflected the strengths and abilities of their ground forces—relentless pursuit, the capacity to endure hardships, and the discipline to press the attack.

That the fight over the trek to Port Moresby was even a match at all has to be credited to the far-off hand of MacArthur. The general might not have sufficiently given credence to reports of an impending invasion, but he was never complacent in pressing to take the offensive to the Japanese. He did look to push the Australian defensive envelope forward to Buna even before the enemy made landfall. That happenstance resulted in enabling the Australians to throw up some defense, denying the 17th Army an open path to Port Moresby's backdoor. Grading generalship in battle is far less about whether a commander guessed exactly right or wrong than whether they positioned their forces to deal with the conditions of battle and enemy actions as they unfolded on the place of battle. It is hard not give MacArthur a passing grade at this point in the campaign.

The campaign, however, was far from over. As the last exhausted men retreated from Kokoda, in Port Moresby commanders scrambled to throw more of the same in front of the Japanese. What remained to be seen was if they would run out of troops or ground to defend before the Japanese reached the port.

Notes

1. John Curtin, "The Task Ahead" *The Herald*, December 27, 1941, National Library of Australia.

2. Ross McMullin, "Dangers and Problems Unprecedented and Unpredictable," in Dean, *Australia 1942*, p. 92.

3. Estimates of the number of troops vary. In the government official, McCarthy put the number at 1,088 "including some Papuans and some 30 A.I.F." McCarthy, *South-West Pacific Area—First Year Kokoda to Wau*, p.12.

4. FitzSimons, *Kokoda*, p. 49.

5. Quoted in Powell, *The Third Force*, p. 8.

6. Albert Palazzo, "The Overlooked Mission: Australia and Home Defence," in Dean, ed., *Australia 1942*, pp. 57–58, 62–64.

7. "No Glory, but Truth Is They Had Guts," *Sunday Morning Herald*, August 26, 2006, at http://www.smh.com.au/news/opinion/no-glory-but-truth-is-they-had -guts/2006/08/25/1156012735768.html.

8. Thompson, *The Toughest Fighting in the World*, p. 16.

9. MS 6538 George Johnston Diary, entry, January 15, 1942, Australian National Library. Johnston was an Australian writer and correspondent for the *Sydney Morning Herald*, *Melbourne Age* and *Daily Telegraph* (London). He published his wartime diaries in 1943. A censored edition was published in 1984.

10. Austin, *To Kokoda and Beyond*, p. 58.

11. McCarthy, *South-West Pacific Area*, p. 29.

12. Austin, *To Kokoda and Beyond*, p. 63.

13. AWM52, Australian Military Forces, Army Headquarters, formation and unit forces, 1/1/1 Headquarters Unit, Land Forces headquarters, war diary entry May 27, 1942, Australian War Memorial; McCarthy, *South-West Pacific Area*, pp. 111–112.

14. Ibid., p. 114.

15. In late August, Lieutenant N. Owers led a survey party scouting out alternative routes past this point. The location was popularly known after that as Owers' Corner. This is not to be confused with Lieutenant Colonel W. T. Owens who commanded the 39th Battalion.

16. "Joint Directive for Offensive Operations in the Southwest Pacific Area, July 2, 1942," in Ross, *U.S. War Plans, 1938–1945*, pp. 267–268.

17. Kienzle, *The Architect of Kokoda*, p. 123.

18. FitzSimons, *Kokoda*, pp. 172–173. See also, Spector, *Eagle Against the Sun*, p. 188.

19. AWM52, 2nd Australian Imperial Force and Commonwealth Military Forces, unit war diaries, 1939–1945 War, Item Number: 8/3/78, 39th Infantry Battalion, July–December 1942, p. 3; Austin, *To Kokoda and Beyond*, pp, 85–86. The battalion war diary states that Owen was first called to Brigade headquarters on the morning of July 18 and issued orders for the battalion movement to Kokoda.

20. *Japanese Army Operations in the South Pacific Area*, p. 121.

21. Kienzle, *The Architect of Kokoda*, p. 126.

22. Ibid., p. 128; Austin, *To Kokoda and Beyond*, p. 84.

23. *Japanese Army Operations in the South Pacific Area*, 128.

24. Ibid., pp. 126–127.

25. Ibid., p. 131.

26. Collie and Marutani, *The Path of Infinite Sorrow*, p. 70; Austin, *To Kokoda and Beyond*, p. 86.

27. Welbum, *The Development of Australian Army Doctrine, 1945–1964*, p. 6; Threlfall, *Jungle Warriors*, p. 12; *Infantry Training: Training and War 1937*, pp. 93–94.

28. Johnson, *Mud over Blood Revisited*, pp. 79–83.

29. Austin, *To Kokoda and Beyond*, p. 95.

30. McCarthy, *South-West Pacific Area*, p. 127; Ham, *Kokoda*, p. 47.

31. McCarthy, *South-West Pacific Area*, p. 127, puts the number at "some 80 men."

32. Ibid., p. 80. War Diaries, 39th Infantry Battalion, July–December 1942, p. 8, says this flight took place on July 27, not July 28.

33. Unless otherwise noted, the narrative of the battle of Kokoda comes from McCarthy, *South-West Pacific Area*, p. 80; War Diaries, 39th Infantry Battalion, July–December 1942, p. 8; Powell, *The Third Force*, p. 45; Collie and Marutani, *The Path of Infinite Sorrow*, p. 72–74; Austin, *To Kokoka and Beyond, pp. 95–98.*

34. Collie and Marutani, *The Path of Infinite Sorrow*, p. 72; Ham, *Kokoda*, p. 49.

35. *Japanese Army Operations in the South Pacific Area*, p. 131.

36. Ham, *Kokoda*, p. 49; Collie and Marutani, *The Path of Infinite Sorrow*, p. 73.

37. Reports of casualties vary. The official history (McCarthy, *South-West Pacific Area*) put the number at "about 2 killed, 7 or 8 wounded."

7

Fuzzy Wuzzy Angels

OKIUFA VILLAGE, 1930. *"I saw my first white man when I was a child. I was not old enough to cover my genitals. . . . I was very frightened," recalled Tate Sarepamo. "The men were directed to our graveyard thinking that the new arrivals had somehow risen from there. My people killed pigs and presented them as presents."*

BATTLES DO NOT occur across an empty void. People and place are anything but extraneous details in the clash of arms. Even in Papua New Guinea, as modern armies warred among the most remote places on earth, fields of innocents populated the field of battle. The Indigenous peoples of Papua New Guinea were not mere victims or bystanders. They played a significant role in the fight over the mastery of Port Moresby from the first desperate militia battles to the end of the war.

In an age of modern conflict ruled by machines such as aircraft carriers, bombers, and tanks, human muscle dominated the fight for places like Papua New Guinea and Guadalcanal. Jungle war demanded jungle fighters. In the summer of 1942, the Allies were looking for men of any skin color they could add to winning the fight in a world in many ways out of time and place from the Western way of war.

The Other World

Over the course of his lifetime, Tate Sarepamo witnessed the transformation from primitive isolation to the maelstrom of modern war. He was born into a world without White men, ruled by magic, endemic conflict, cannibalism, dance, and ritual, a universe that barely extended beyond his village. He was a young man when the great war came to the remote highlands. Seven decades after seeing his first White man, he owned his own coffee plantation that exported around the world and a local disco playing pop tunes from the United States and Asia.

His journey began in a prehistoric place, lost in time. At Tate's birth the 1920s highlands of Papua New Guinea were still virtually untouched by the presence of outsiders. He was ten years old when he saw his first White man, which most of the village assumed was some kind of being from another world, a spirit sent to them by their ancestors.

To Australians, most of Papua New Guinea recalled a world of warlike and savage places beyond the bounds of modernity. Michael J. Leahy led ten prospecting trips and explorations into the highlands between 1930 and 1935, describing a place of "Stone Age" people—thieves, murderers, and cannibals. On his first trip into the highlands, he was one of only three White men who had ever been to Tate Sarepamo's home in the Goroka Valley.

The explorers survived because of the "magic" natives attributed to them. Villagers were "overwhelmed by the European's seemingly endless and startling complex appurtenances—bits of stick that spurt fire when scratched on a box." Leahy and others brought back reports of a wild and unruly place, but also one with significant economic potential for agriculture and mining that could be tamed by a determined, realistic guiding hand. The results of such explorations ensured others would follow.

The more Whites penetrated the dense reaches of Papua New Guinea, the more the Whites' view of the Indigenous population shifted from wild, untamed brutes living from beyond the pale to eyeing the natives as a workforce, albeit one with little potential. An official report concluded the people were "lazy" with scant skills suitable for labor.

As commercial interests in Papua New Guinea expanded, however, attitudes toward the population changed as well. "It seemed to be in the natives' own interest," summed up one colonial administrator, "to introduce them to civilized ways by periods of supervised work." The coercive component of binding natives with indentured contracts was especially critical, as "casual or contract labor could not be depended on among such primitive, irresponsible people. Without European industry the natives would also revert to savagery." The colonial economy became a self-serving cause, profit in the name of rescuing the natives from their savage existence and turning them into productive workers.

It was never envisioned that the Indigenous peoples would be the equals of their overseers. A one administrator wrote, "No amount of giving up dancing and other foolishness, no amount of embracing Christianity, no amount of going to work, or learning English could make the Papuan an equal." An official assessment of labor policies concluded that "the use by European enterprise of native labour, indentured and casual, seemed to be part of the natural order, a fixed piece of social landscape taken for granted." The racial and cultural boundary between natives and Whites was set. Papuans would be molded into a useful working class that mimicked the Western world.

While not equals, the Indigenous populations were not open to unchecked ruthless exploitation either. "By 1940," writes Alan Powell in his history of ANGAU, "most of the evils that made earlier indenture practices little better than slavery had been eliminated." Still natives were seen as little more than a source of workers for mining, plantation agriculture, supply bearers, and coastal transport. Nor did they serve as "free" labor; indentured labor practices remained in place. And the treatment of Indigenous peoples was not always egalitarian. Cases of abuse by overseers or extortion and bullying by government officials and law enforcement were not uncommon.

Over the decades, Sarepamo saw this evolution. Recurring visits of Whites grew into a permanent enclave that established Goroka as the local administrative center for the Eastern Highlands. The authority of "big men" like his father, who had achieved notoriety and wealth because of their prowess as warriors and skill as orators, was supplanted by the colonial authority. In turn, the authorities were replaced by the military who eyed the villagers as valuable assets for jungle fighting.

Attitudes toward the Indigenous people changed little even after war threw them and the White men together as compatriots. "The native is nearly, if not quite, as good a man as you are," an Allied pamphlet carefully explained. While the guide counseled troops to "always maintain your position of superiority," it also provided seventeen pages of pointers on how to manage the native population in order to ensure their willing cooperation and support.

The two worlds awkwardly merged. Harnessing the Indigenous peoples as an obedient workforce would have unforeseen but crucial consequences for how the coming war in the jungles would be fought. Before Pearl Harbor, the backbone of authority and administration was the colonial police force, the Papuan Armed Constabulary (later the Royal Papuan Constabulary) and the New Guinea Police Force. Police patrols were the mediating force between the civilian administrators and the Indigenous people. While the patrol officers were White, the ranks and interpreters were from the Indigenous population. The police forces offered the thinnest veneer of oversight. The entire force amounted to about 1,300 officers to oversee a population that numbered well over a million, many of them in remote, isolated villages.

After Pearl Harbor, the Australian government evacuated most of the White population. In 1941, government oversight was transferred from the civilian authorities to the military. Police units and volunteer defense units were amalgamated into supplementary security forces. One of these units included the Papuans who fought at the battle of Kokoda.

During the course of the war the auxiliary ranks swelled, adding recruits like Tate Sarepamo. As the son of the village big man, Tate was more likely to join to advance the status and influence of his family, attracted by the prestige of wearing a uniform and carrying a gun. Rather than the police training provided to earlier legions of recruit, Sarepamo and others were sent to Port Moresby for military training administered by ANGAU and then thrown into the war against the Japanese.

Australian newspapers reported that the island's "Allied forces are being assisted by native troops, specially trained for scouting and jungle fighting, at which they are immensely skillful." That description was a bit of myth making. The modicum of instruction the Indigenous forces received was not meant to capitalize on their native abilities to move and fight in the jungle. Nor were they trained like traditional combat troops. Rather than learning the skills of fighting in formations with combined arms weapons like machine guns and mortars, the emphasis was physical training—making for good bearers, stretcher carriers, messengers, and scouts coupled with a modicum of firearms training and only the most basic English skills—like telling time, counting, and responding to military commands. The nature of this training goes far to explain why the Papuan infantry had such limited utility in set piece battles like Kokoda.

Organized forces were not the only Indigenous assets in the combat zone. In addition to the regularly constituted units, Whites with the aid of locals provided a network of coast watchers and air spotters, who helped provide human intelligence on Japanese movements and aided in the search and recovery of air- and seamen across the remote expanse of the theater. A handful of other Whites remained behind, some captured by the Japanese during the lightning spring campaign. These included principally Catholic and Lutheran ministers in New Guinea and Anglican missionaries in Papua. The handful that remained, all men (women missionaries were evacuated), continued their pastoral duties as best they could. During the Japanese advance, most withdrew to the southern half of the island, not returning to the north until 1943.

Papuan patrol in the highlands. *(Credit: Australian War Memorial, Reference 016083-1-)*

Enough of the church remained to be a witness to war. One downed Allied flyer recalled reaching a village where he met Father Luscombe Newman. The Anglican priest explained:

> We have sent our families out, but most of us elected to stay. After all, the natives need us now more than ever. We can do a great deal to keep up their morale. If the fighting becomes too intense in this area, there will be wounded to look after. Most of all, we want to be on hand for the work of reconstruction that must get under way as soon as the Japanese are driven out.

Throughout the war, the church maintained a thin thread that crisscrossed the island's Christian communities. They were both—pastors and victims. Over 300 of them (including both Whites and Indigenous people) were killed in the course of the war.

The foreign community also included a small number of enemy aliens, including Japanese and German settlers. They were interned by the Australians on the mainland during the conflict and deported after the war.

In addition, there were former government officials like Lloyd Purchase who joined ANGAU and remained in Papua New Guinea to lend their expertise on the people and the land to support the Australian forces. Purchase remained in the Finschhafen area to monitor Japanese movements. "Still here, playing cat and mouse game with our mutual friends," he wrote in a letter that reached his wife in 1942, "so far it is pretty great but have to be careful."

The ANGAU men were more crucial than what they contributed to the fighting ranks. Their greatest utility was in managing the native labor force. In January 1942, ANGAU employed thirty-eight native laborers. In August that numbered swelled to almost 5,000. At peak employment in June 1944, ANGAU's workforce included almost 38,000 workers.

Native labor dragged the supplies up the Kokoda trail blazed by Bert Kienzle. Captain Geoffrey Vernon, the ANGAU medical officer, who found himself in the middle of the fight at Kokoda, had been in the area performing his primary duty, inspecting the health and hygiene of the "fuzzy wuzzy" workforce recruited to labor for the allies.

The Indigenous labor that served the Australians, like every other resource in the South Pacific, was fair play for the Japanese. Oil and rubber were not the only prizes swept up under the shadow of the rising sun. Manpower was another commodity that the empire harvested from its expanding coprosperity sphere. For the Papua New Guinea campaign, civilian workers and carriers supplemented the Japanese forces. Approximately 500 members of the Formosan Takasago Volunteers and Korean laborers as well as about 2,000 natives commandeered from New Britain supported the Japanese invasion at Buna. That represented a fraction of the manpower needed to support and sustain the trek over the mountains. The Japanese would have to obtain workers in Papua New Guinea as well as buy or seize food supplies from local sources.

Arguably, in terms of racial attitudes, the Japanese approach to the Indigenous peoples was not much different from the Australians. Although Japanese propaganda portrayed their mission as liberating peoples from the oppressive White races, in practice as overlords the Japanese did not treat the natives as equals. They wanted the same from the natives as the Australians—a usable workforce.

In addition to the natives recruited or drafted to support the war effort, on both sides, there were many others, the people in the middle— raising children, herding pigs, growing vegetables, dancing, worshiping, and surviving while the war raged across their path. As Lachlan Grant summarizes, the Indigenous peoples "sided with those whom they felt offered the best opportunities for survival for themselves and their families."[1] That was not always their Australian overlords. War reporting lauding the cooperation of the natives also included concerns about behavior and allegiance. "In the strange lexicon of pidgin English, which is the working language of New Guinea," one news account ran, "there is no word for Fifth Columnist." But the article reported that natives sold information to the enemy for *kaikai* (food) and *kuku* (tobacco).

Had the armies come to war over Papua New Guinea a decade earlier, they might as well have been waging battle in the midst of alien creatures on another planet. But by 1940 the interactions of the native peoples and the strange "others" with their magic and spirit connections had bridged the gap between their worlds enough to make the Papuan New Guinea an integral part of the tumult thrust upon them. This happenstance made all the difference.

Natives at War

Both sides scrambled for labor as much as they did for food and bullets. After their initial successful landings, the Japanese had delayed the advance to bring up more logistical support. General Horii's decision to slow his campaign until his logistics caught up was prudent. Without food and ammunition, even if the Japanese swept all in their path, they would have arrived at the gates of Port Moresby as a helpless, starving rabble.

As part of the logistics buildup, the South Seas Detachment also moved rapidly to enlist native labor.[2] Horii recognized that he would need the support of the Indigenous peoples. "Do not wantonly kill or injure them," he warned, and don't treat them as "pigs " because the army would need their support and cooperation.[3] For the most part, official policies prohibited mingling with the natives except when overseeing labor details or conducting official civil military affairs duties.

The Japanese had a mixed record of dealing with the Indigenous population that included acts of ruthless exploitation and violence. Remembrances of the war include accounts of torture and execution. One witness recalled interrogations where "people were made to drink water and were then jumped on, they were hung upside down and bashed about the face and buttocks." In another instance, reportedly Japanese officers ordered Papuans to massacre ninety-six villagers suspected of collaborating with the Australians. In contrast to these incidents, there were also practices of bartering for supplies and labor—no different from the methods employed by the Allies.

The response of the natives ranged from ambivalent to positive. "On the whole," one New Guinean remembered, "we had very good relationships with the Japanese. We often danced for them, and they performed sword dances for us." Some actively sided with the Japanese, others remained firmly loyal to the Australians, still other were willing to switch sides or scrupulously tried to avoid the war between the peoples with the strange skins. In general, however, natives remained supportive or at least tolerant and obedient of the side that occupied the ground where they lived. A good example of that was the Japanese occupation of New Britain. An oral history project on one village concluded the people were:

> bystanders caught in the ebb and flow of war, the Japanese occupation was . . . a time of some excitement, of some amusement, and perhaps bewilderment, but it was not a particularly difficult time. All of the people [with] whom I discussed this matter agreed that the village suffered no atrocities at the hands of the Japanese. There were no reported rapes. There were no half-Japanese children left from the time. No one was killed or mutilated, and gardens and pigs [were] usually safe from confiscation.

Japanese soldiers offered similar remembrances. Ogawa Masatsugu, who fought in New Guinea, recalled, "I think the natives and the Japanese got along well. They'd dance in a circle when the moon was full. Those of us who were from farming or fishing villages would casually join in and dance, too, as if they were dancing in the Japanese countryside."[4] In contrast, the life of villagers closer to the frontline fighting were no doubt more disrupted and included more harrowing experiences, but in general the Indigenous peoples attempted to accommodate the war raging around them.

On the Australians' side of the war, the Indigenous peoples were an equally vital labor pool that played a crucial part in keeping the diggers in the fight. As the dark days of summer for Australia's military fortunes lengthened with the shadow of the rising sun ever closer to Port Moresby, no contingent was more important than the more than 2,500-man labor force supervised by Bert Kienzle.

One of the most crucial contributions, Kienzle and his "fuzzy wuzzy angels" (so-called because of the Indigenous people's wiry bushy hair) came during the crucial pause in the fighting on the trail. The Australians needed an alternative to the loss of the field at Kokoda. Losing the airfield meant there was no air bridge into the highlands for delivering supplies or evacuating casualties. Kienzle and his boys hacked a trail to Myola (which he named in honor of the first name of the wife of his friend and company commander) where the Australians established a drop zone in a dry lakebed.

By August 15, enough supplies had been parachuted into the makeshift field to provide the forward forces a stockpile of thousands of tins of beef and biscuits, crates of ammunition, and stacks of medical supplies. The supply base gave the diggers a crucial advantage. In contrast, the Japanese had to haul their supplies from the coast all the way to the fight in the mountains.

The supplies at Myola, however, were only an advantage if Kienzle could get the provisions to the troops that were still farther up the trail. For that task, Kienzle had to organize an army of bearers to carry supplies on the two-to-three day march to the front and, at the same time, set up bearers to evacuate the sick and wounded. For the next few weeks, Myola and Kienzle's operations were the lifeline to the front.

In managing his shoestring supply chain, Kienzle drew on both his prewar expertise in handling native labor and his exceptional abilities as a natural leader of men. Kienzle oversaw the work teams with extraordinary skill, a mix of relentless taskmaster and caring steward. He pushed the bearers "to the limit physically, they were cold, hungry and just plain exhausted." The human effort required to sustain operations was daunting. Evacuating one stretcher-borne soldier required eight bearers. At the height of the action, 336 stretcher-bearers (almost 15 percent of his entire workforce) carried men down the torturous switchback trail.

Every laborer on stretcher duty meant one less carrier for other duties, increasing the workload for those ferrying food and ammunition to the front. Further, desertion, sickness, and insubordination added to the difficulties of keeping enough laborers at the front. Both Kienzle and Doc Vernon "continually argued for improvement of the conditions for these 'angels' and expressed deep concern for their welfare. Bert ensured they received a daily ration." The care and leadership they showed helped sustain the labor force during the most difficult times.

Their practices became doctrine. An Allied pamphlet went on for twenty-three pages describing how to care for and manage carriers, including guidelines on loads, rest periods, rations, clothing, and medical attention. The guide admonished that the native carrier "has given his willing service to the white man for the last 50 years, and his help is absolutely vital now." If they are "slave-driven" the guide warned, the bearers might go over to the enemy. They might break down or go on strike, or they might just go home and "it will be no joke finding them."[5] They were, after all, an important military asset.

In practice, arguably the care and commitment shown by Kienzle and Vernon were more the exception than the rule. An investigation in 1943 concluded that many laborers were ill cared for and poorly supervised by troops "unfit to be in charge of natives. . . . [T]o judge from some of their conversations some of the old hands regard brutality as part of the regular routine." About of one third of the ANGAU field staff reportedly was "without experience with natives." In turn, the investigators found many laborers to be "bitter," "hostile," and "homesick."[6]

Though Kienzle may have treated his charges better than others, he could not protect them from the travails of backbreaking work, food shortages, sickness, and the harsh and dangerous conditions along the track, bringing supplies up the trail and taking injured soldiers back down. In the face of these hardships, it is hard to overestimate the value of the effort of Kienzle and the fuzzy wuzzy angels.

As the war lengthened, not only would the role of the Indigenous people prove pivotal, the war would have a transformative impact on the people of Papua New Guinea. In the wild highlands, for example, where Whites were barely seen before the battle of Kokoda, everything changed. One study concluded:

> many hundreds of Allied soldiers occupied the Valley in anticipation of a threatened Japanese invasion. Village life was disrupted as men were conscripted as carriers and labourers and whole communities were obliged to grow food to assist the Allied war effort. Those living close to military airfields . . . were subject to Japanese aerial attacks and the entire population was exposed to an epidemic of bacillary dysentery introduced by the combatants.[7]

The other's war had come to their world.

Battle for the Mind

One understudied aspect of the campaign was that the Allies waged war with more than bullets. They also fought a war of ideas.[8] One of the principal campaigns was influencing the local population.

The United States conducted psychological warfare operations during World War I. Virtually none of that capacity, experience, or doctrine carried into the postwar army. There was no psychological warfare office in the War Department before 1941. Only one officer on the army staff had psychological warfare experience from the previous war. After the disaster at Pearl Harbor, most of the operations and capability were built on the fly in theater.

MacArthur's command established the Far East Liaison Office (FELO) to oversee psychological warfare. FELO was established in June 1942 with a staff of five. Originally the office came directly under SWPA, then it was moved to the Australian chiefs of staff, and then under the commander-in-chief of Australian Land Forces. The headquarters was always far behind the front. They started in Brisbane. And they grew only modestly over time.[9]

For such a small group, FELO had a big task, charged with all combat propaganda with a mission to: lower enemy morale, mislead the enemy regarding military intentions, and influence subject populations in enemy-occupied territories to impair the enemy's war effort and assist Allied forces. In order to accomplish this daunting list of objectives, FELO had a handful of resources: (1) leaflets, (2) frontline broadcasting units, (3) mobile propaganda units, (4) agents working in enemy territory, (5) radio, and (6) distributing rumors by various methods for psychological warfare purposes.

The leaflets were the main method that FELO used to get its message out. Over the course of the war, FELO claimed to have delivered over 795,075 leaflets in pidgin aimed at the local population, in addition to targeting the Japanese troops. The leaflets intended for the Indigenous people overwhelmingly emphasized the importance of not cooperating with the enemy. For example, one pamphlet translated as:

> Message for the Coastal Natives. The Japanese have attempted to capture a place near Samarai and also Port Moresby, but we defeated them. At Buna there are no Japanese. We buried them all. . . . Only Allied troops are in Buna and Wau. At Lae, Salamaua, Madang and Wewak we have not fought yet, but later will kick out the Japs just as we did at Buna. . . . If you assist the Japs and stay near them you will be destroyed by the planes. You will have no one to blame but yourselves.

Some of the guidance was very specific. One advised, "Do not assist the Japanese. Hide your canoes. Make distant gardens and hide them from the Japanese."

Texts were prepared in English by a leaflet editor then translated into pidgin or Japanese. They were prepared and printed in Brisbane. FELO then had to get the air force to fly them to the war in big brown paper packets, then cut the string and throw them out of the plane.

In some cases, when the Allies targeted a specific location, like the last-ditch Japanese defenses at Buna, FELO needed something that could deliver their propaganda with greater accuracy. They used a

"Weigall," named after the FELO officer who invented the device. A Weigall had a circular bursting charge with a small firing mechanism (detonator) strapped over a box with the string wrapped through the detonating device. When the firing pin is pulled, it detonates the charger, burns through the string, and the box falls apart releasing the leaflets. The Weigall was used to drop leaflets from medium to high altitude.

FELO acknowledged, "It is difficult to assess the full effect of psychological warfare on enemy morale, partly because there are other factors that contribute to the lowering of morale." Other assessments were more critical. The US after-action report from Buna concluded, "Statements by prisoners of war agree that the leaflets, particularly those which were poorly written, had no effect." Over the course of the campaign, the office claimed at least one operational success at a critical time. "The most outstanding case of native reaction to FELO leaflets," the office reported, "was during the Huon Peninsula Campaign in 1943 when thousands of natives took to the hills as a result of instructions contained in leaflets." If true, the accomplishment was not immaterial since it deprived the Japanese of aid during one of their most desperate times. One of the leaflets the Allies distributed translated to "[t]he government knows that the Japs have compelled you to work for them. Never mind that now you run away. We do not blame you. Our quarrel is with the Japs." Yet, as FELO acknowledged under the often desperate conditions in the theater, it is difficult to assess how leaflets added that much more to the stress and fear of life at the front.

In addition to the leaflets, frontline broadcasting units played records of battle noises, direct messages to enemies, messages and records with songs and music to make the Japanese homesick, and messages offering food and good treatment and surrender instructions. The equipment, however, was poor; machines broke often; parts were hard to come by; and it was difficult to manhandle everything in the wet jungle terrain.

Another major asset were "field parties" dispatched to survey local conditions, influence the locals, and gain intelligence on the natives. The seven documented parties deployed over the course of the campaign yielded mix results. Two were rated successful. In the others, the teams withdrew after the White officers were attacked, killed, or taken ill. These efforts were supplemented by ANGAU officers in the field who aided in the propaganda effort to threaten or cajole natives not to cooperate with the Japanese and share intelligence on enemy activities. The contribution over the course of the campaign was marginal at best, but the fact the Allies made the effort at all reflected the importance they placed on winning hearts and minds.

The Manpower War

The heavy reliance on the Indigenous population, particularly in the early days of the ground war, was an absolute necessity. The Australian militia backed by the native population mustered by men like Kienzle had to carry the fight while MacArthur assembled his war machine. They were, however, not enough to stem the Japanese advance. The front needed more manpower and that challenge created controversy for MacArthur and his Australian allies.

MacArthur put so much reliance on the thin crust of militia, native volunteers, and bearers protecting Papua New Guinea because when MacArthur arrived in Australia most of his military was on paper. What shocked the commander of SWPA when he took over SWPA was how little of SWPA there was to command. It was well short of what he needed to win the war. In addition to pestering the Joint Chiefs of Staff and the president for more forces, he intended to husband what he had for the great counterstrike that would begin with taking Rabaul and leaping forward from there.

MacArthur organized his forces into the following commands: Allied Land Forces (ALF), Allied Naval Forces (ANF), and Allied Air Forces (AAF). Together they comprised his joint and combined force, the military power that MacArthur had to challenge the Japanese on land, at sea, and in the air.

Australian Army's commander-in-chief, General Sir Thomas Blamey, was designated the head of Allied Land Forces. In addition, to the Australian troops being organized and trained for the defense of the country as well as offensive operations, Blamey had the Australian 6th Division (except for two brigades diverted to Ceylon) and the 7th Division. Both were seasoned battle units, which despite Churchill's objections had been recalled from the Middle East. The Allied Land Forces also included the recently arrived US 41st and 32nd Divisions. In total, MacArthur had about 38,000 US troops, 104,000 Australian Imperial Force (AIF) soldiers, and 265,000 Australian militia (as well as volunteer Indigenous troops).

Only days after the Japanese landed on Buna, Lieutenant General George Churchill Kenney took command of the Allied Air Forces. AAF comprised American Army Air Forces, Australian air and support units, and operational control of the remnants of the Netherlands East Indies Army Air Forces. The US contribution was about 20,000 men supporting two heavy, two medium, and one light bomber group; three fighter and two transport squadrons; and a photographic squadron. Meanwhile, the Royal Australian Air Force (RAAF) assumed responsibility for the air defense of Australia. One exception was 9th Operational Group RAAF, controlled by 5th Air Force, which supported operations in Papua New Guinea. This included the 75th Squadron, which had provided much of the air defense of Port Moresby.[10]

Vice Admiral Herbert F. Leary oversaw the naval forces. The ANF included Australian and what was left in the region of the Netherlands navy as well as US surface ships. As for undersea warfare, the Australian Navy did not operate any submarines during World War II. Submarine Forces, Southwest Pacific Area, operated American boats out of Fremantle, Western Australia, and Brisbane, Queensland.[11]

In addition to his meager forces, MacArthur also had an intelligence network that was far from impressive considering the size of the theater and the scale of enemy activity. "When it all started in April 1942 . . . the intelligence assets at Douglas MacArthur's disposal were few," writes historian Ed Drea, "newly organized cryptanalytic centers at Melbourne, a tiny translation section, haphazard aerial reconnaissance, sporadic traffic analysis of communications, the odd prisoner of war interrogation, and surely at that time his best internal source, the stay-behind Australian planters and coast watchers."[12] MacArthur's intelligence operation was a shoestring affair.

The more sophisticated and advanced intelligence capabilities were slow to make their way into theater at the end of the world. The Australians, for example, didn't deploy a field electronic intelligence collection unit until 1943.[13] Even the most important intelligence tasks had to be improvised. For instance, crucial to the air defense of Port Moresby was the ability to get early warning so that fighters could be scrambled to intercept them. Early warning radar had limited value. The Owen Stanley Range blocked radar transmission. Japanese planes could fly north along the coast, cut through a valley and be over Port Moresby before the radar would pick them up. Until the Allies could establish early warning sites on the Huon Peninsula (controlled by the enemy), they were blind to attacks from the north. A key asset was Leigh Vial, an Australian district officer who was commissioned in the RAAF. Operating from the outskirts of Salamaua, he set up a hidden treetop observation post from where he could radio when Japanese aircraft were taking off to raid Port Moresby.[14] A lone man hanging from a tree was the best air warning the Allies could muster.

Nor did the Allies have much in the way of a capacity to forecast weather. Predicting weather was a crucial capability for conducting air operations over treacherous Owen Stanley Range, as well as for maritime operations. SWPA set up an Allied Air Force Meteorological Service. The first US contribution to the effort from Army Air Forces Weather Service did not arrive in theater until August 1942. Meanwhile, the Australian Meteorological Service and the RAAF Meteorological Service handled the chores. They had virtually no way to conduct accurate forecasting. When General Kenney first inspected the office at Port Moresby, he concluded, "We could have done better by tossing a coin."[15] For an army that was dependent on flying over the hump for air power, the lack of good forecasting was a big deal.

In addition to his tactical and operational intelligence, like other theater commanders, MacArthur also had access to ULTRA and Magic decrypts, the most sensitive Allied code breaking of high-level German and Japanese communications. For the most part, this information was extremely useful in understanding the enemy order of battle (the organization and location of major units), but normally far less useful for immediate operations. The Allies for instance could not decode the Japanese Army water transport codes, which would have provided advance warning of troop and resupply convoys. They could not read other military traffic that would have given a clearer picture of the enemy tactical situation.[16]

Early in the Pacific War, the Allies did get some intelligence coups that warned of impending enemy operations such as the Japanese attack on Midway, advance notice of troop landings on Guadalcanal, and the first enemy landings at Buna, but in the first year of the war such intelligence prizes were the exception not the rule. This shortfall was exacerbated by the controversial and suspect abilities of his chief intelligence officer, General Charles Willoughby, an officer who seemed distrusted and disliked by almost everyone but MacArthur.[17]

Meanwhile, despite the reassuring presence of American troops steaming down under in the months after Pearl Harbor, Curtin continued his incessant sparring with Churchill, pressing for the return of Australian troops from the Middle East. On July 30, the day Colonel Owen's command was being driven off key terrain at Kokoda, Curtin harangued the British prime minister with a cable warning: "Japan is now consolidating her position in New Guinea and the Solomon Islands and has made a landing in Papua which threatens our important advanced base at Port Moresby, which is vital to the defence of the north-eastern coast against enemy landings and the maintenance of the passage through Torres Strait for the supply of Darwin."[18]

The situation could allow for only temporary extension of the 3rd Division in the Middle East that the British had promised to return for the defense of Australia. Curtin also pressed for more aircraft. A few weeks later he would remind Churchill, "though Australia was placed in an American sphere of strategic responsibility you did not regard your obligations to do what you could to help Australia as being lessened in any way."[19]

In the summer of 1942, Curtin knew that the Combined Chiefs of Staff had recently met in London to rehash strategy for the war. Before the trip there had been a flurry of exchanges between Roosevelt and his chiefs, anticipating British resistance to pressing forward with a direct amphibious assault on France and a drive into the heartland of Nazi Germany. While the British were advocates for the "defeat Hitler first" agenda, they were skeptical of the direct approach desired by the Americans who wanted boots on the ground in Western Europe as soon as possible. The US Joint Chiefs informed FDR that if the British could not commit perhaps they should shift the weight of US effort to the Pacific where it might have a demonstrable effect on the outcome of the war. FDR asked the chiefs for an estimate of what redirecting America's power might look like.

The president later acknowledged to Marshall that the "proposal to transfer our major effort to the Pacific as something of a red herring."[20] Perhaps the threat to shift the preponderance of American power elsewhere than Europe might spook the British into accepting the necessity of a cross-channel invasion sooner rather later. Marshall shared news of the president's gambit with Admiral King, in a July 15, 1942, memo. King was likely disappointed. The admiral would have followed through on the threat for a Pacific push, a theater where he thought America could be decisive. MacArthur would have also liked that course of action, though he and King would no doubt disagree over the axis of the main effort to defeat the Japanese. King drew more a straight line to Tokyo. MacArthur wanted to liberate the Philippines first, perhaps take Formosa, and then isolate and starve out the Japanese home islands. Neither King nor MacArthur would get all that he wanted. The European war would always remain the top priority. The suggestion of dropping the "defeat Hitler first" strategy was FDR's hollow threat—and the British knew it. Churchill called the bluff. The British were unmoved. On July 22, the British War Cabinet voted against mounting a cross-channel invasion in 1942. The main course of the strategy remained unchanged. Rather than ship the US forces built up over the year to the Pacific, the Allies eyed a limited US operation in North Africa in concert with the British effort to defeat the Afrika Korps.

The British prime minister was thrilled with the outcome of the talks, writing that they "reached decisions which cover the whole field of the war. On these we have obtained complete unity between soldiers and statesman and our two countries."[21] None of that was good news for Curtin, who still chafed at the strategy of Germany first .

Curtin's campaign (which had begun after Pearl Harbor to get the Americans and British to elevate Australia's strategic priority and shift more resources to the continent's defense) had fallen flat. He was, he felt, fighting for scraps. While he might have rocked the world with his December 1941 editorial about turning to the United States, the reality turned out to be that "there was no more point in looking to America for support of the Australian point of view than there had been in looking to Britain," writes historian Glen St. John Barclay.[22]

On one hand, naval victories at Coral Sea and Midway had calmed fears that the nation was in imminent peril. On the other hand, the Japanese landings at Buna sparked new criticisms from political opponents over government management of the war. The opposition was never sanguine about Curtin's leadership. The former prime minister Robert Menzies told an American diplomat that they would be better off if the war wasn't run by the present government. "They are scum—positive scum," he reportedly stated. "[O]ne trouble with Curtin is that at heart he is an isolationist and wants to defend Australia only, letting the rest of the Empire go."[23] With his political opponents always looking over his shoulder, a setback in the field carried political risks giving his critics something to criticize. Federal elections were less than a year away. Curtin did not want to go to the polls looking like a failed warlord.

Anger spilled out into the press. One editorial railed, the "possession of Buna, which the enemy should never have been allowed to achieve, brings Port-Moresby, the most vital bastion in Australia's Pacific rampart, already gravely pierced by the enemy within easy flying distance for the Japanese bombers." Part of the blame was fixed on London and Washington who consigned Australia to a relatively minor place in the global strategic plan of the Allies. "We are well down on the list of priorities."[24] Curtin was the man stuck in the middle.

MacArthur thought he could turn the Australian griping to his advantage. He funneled the news to Marshall, citing one editorial claiming, "Australia can no longer count on priority." He hoped, no doubt, that the negative press would add to the pressure of his demand for more resources, not just for the defense of Papua New Guinea but for the campaign to liberate Rabaul, then the Philippines, and drive toward Japan. MacArthur provoked the opposite response.

MacArthur triggered a scolding from the army chief of staff. The Australian editorials were "damaging to morale" and untrue, Marshall schooled the SWPA commander. Marshall heaped on more admonishment. He complained about press reporting (approved by MacArthur's headquarters) left the impression MacArthur objected to Allied strategy. That, Marshall fumed, could "only serve to fan the indignation and resentment that has resulted from the editorial of which you complain." Marshall counseled, "You can do much to counteract the ill effects of this editorial through the medium of press releases."[25] The army chief staff wanted MacArthur to reassure Australians about the wisdom of the Allies' priorities—not MacArthur's. Marshall deftly lobbed the ball back into MacArthur's court.

There was no question that Marshall and MacArthur were playing a political game. Both knew it. MacArthur was being mildly insubordinate. Of course, he disagreed with the Combined Chiefs' strategy. Of course, he was happy to use the Australian press to help press his case with Washington. For his part, Marshall was not naive. He knew MacArthur's game. In particular, if there was one thing the army chief of staff well appreciated it was that MacArthur was unreserved about using the media to make his case. They had testy exchanges about press releases before, like when Marshall had to referee with the navy after an SWPA press release intimating that MacArthur's air force won the Battle of the Coral Sea. The last thing MacArthur needed to be reminded of was the power of a press release. That was a little dig from Marshall.

In handling MacArthur, Marshall had to play the role of part commander, part diplomat, and a bit of a poker player. The army chief of staff was not going to allow MacArthur's scheming to undermine the resolve to defeat Germany first. Conversely, Marshall was determined to do what he could to keep MacArthur's efforts from being overshadowed by a Pacific strategy that sidelined SWPA. Finally, Marshall would not let all the squabbling upset the solidarity of the Allied cause.

Meanwhile, MacArthur had to play a balancing act of his own. He continued pleading for more, clamoring that the Southwest Pacific was the forgotten Allied stepchild and the Japanese danger far greater than Washington and London appreciated. The enemy landings in Papua New Guinea gave the supreme commander a chance to make his case again. However, he could not appear defeatist, undermining confidence in his own leadership.

In fairness to MacArthur, while the dispatches of his command no doubt could be a powerful voice in the press, management of the Australian wartime media was a hurly-burly affair not completely under the sway of the authorities.[26] The Australian Department of Information, established in 1939, struggled to find an effective role. Its management of government advertising, particularly a print and broadcast campaign on "Know Your Enemy—The Jap as He Really Is," was a disaster. The department also skirmished with the services over censorship and producing war information (such as film and photography). Meanwhile, officials also spared with the press over censorship regulations.

Throughout the war, the department tried to enforce a policy ensuring that media reports conformed to communiques issued by MacArthur's headquarters. There were, however, incessant complaints that the general's press releases were always overly optimistic and did not deliver accurate accounts of progress against the enemy.

One particular antagonist whom MacArthur seemed unable to manage was the prominent news mogul Keith Murdoch (father of Fox media giant Rupert Murdoch). Himself a former director of the Department of Information, Murdoch chafed at censorship and "the over-confident and misleading official accounts of the war's conduct." In turn, a series of articles in his paper were regarded by MacArthur's headquarters as "masterpieces of implication, suggestion and innuendo." Murdoch also earned the ire of government officials, including political opponents in the Labor Party that came to dominate the Department of Information.

It was not just Murdoch. Western audiences were not so naive as to believe everything they read in the papers. In 1948, Leonard Doob, who served in the Overseas Branch of the US Office of War Information acknowledged, "World War II produced a fine crop of lies." In comparison to Japanese press and propaganda, he pointed out the Allies "tended on the whole to contain few fabrications, but limited themselves to minor distortions, major suppressions, and overall resumes at opportune moments."[27] This certainly sounded like the Allied press effort in SWPA.

The successful Japanese incursion at Buna created opportunity for widespread criticism. On August 5, William Morris "Billy" Hughes a prominent member of the Australian opposition declared,

> there has been a lamentable lack of vision, of initiative, of coordination, of control, by our military leaders. They have failed to anticipate the enemy's movements. The spirit of the defensive has infected their spasmodic offensive strategy. They have done too little or too late. The occupation of Buna and Gona brings this home to us with startling emphasis.[28]

Neither MacArthur nor Curtin could shut down the censure. They also could not let reproaches go unanswered. Nor could they overplay their hand, showing a despondent face to the Australian people, undermining confidence in MacArthur's genius and Curtin's steady hand.

The prime minister rebutted Hughes's criticism in the Advisory War Council. Meanwhile, MacArthur and Curtin trumpeted a recent US offensive in the papers as evidence that the Allies were taking the fight to the enemy. "All the yapping critics recently inferentially blaming General MacArthur, for not carrying an offensive to the Japanese were answered at the weekend," one paper reported, "when it was revealed that Allied forces launched an offensive against the Japanese in the Tulagi area of the Solomons Friday last and that the battle was continuing right throughout the weekend."[29] Never mind that these forces were under the command of US Vice Admiral Robert L. Ghormley in the South Pacific theater and not under MacArthur's purview at all. In fact (ironically) when MacArthur and Ghormley had met in Melbourne, they recommended postponing operations in the Solomons, concerned about the lack of troops and land-based air support. It was Admiral King who insisted that the attacks proceed in early August.[30] While MacArthur may have balked at the idea, when the troops landed, the operation presented a happy distraction for MacArthur to emphasize.

At times the war of words seemed as consuming as the real war. In the end, both the general and the prime minister knew the best way to influence Australian opinion, to shape the war news was by winning battles in the field. That was the real challenge facing MacArthur. The task was clear. The warlords of Australia would have to protect Port Moresby and regain control of the northern coast of Papua New Guinea with the forces they had at hand. And while MacArthur pondered how to do that, the Japanese were still eyeing their potential conquest—holding the crucial junction in the highlands at Kokoda and staring at the winding trail down toward their objective on the other side of the Owen Stanley Range.

View from the Other Side

In contrast to Australia, the war news in Japan was uniformly positive. No wonder, since the 1941 revision to the National Mobilization Law eliminated freedom of the press. The Information and Propaganda Department under the Home Ministry had authority over all news and advertising. The army and navy also dispatched their own war correspondents to the front. In addition, the Japan Publishers Association (*Nihon shimbunkai*) agreed to fully cooperate with the government. In mid-August, three combat journalists from the *Asahi Shimbun*, one of the country's national newspapers, arrived to cover the war. Not surprising, the dispatches were as optimistic for the prospects of victory as the generals.

In fairness, not all the news from the front at Papua New Guinea was propaganda. The Japanese were winning. What was unreported was that each victory took the Japanese force closer to its culminating point, like a runner miles ahead in a marathon who hit the wall. Horii, the commander of the South Seas Force overseeing operations to secure Port Moresby, knew that despite the glowing press reports his success teetered on failure. He spent as much time battling with the 17th Army Headquarters as with the Allies.[31] Horii fretted that he did not have enough motor transport to build up supplies for an advance past Kokoda and demanded more. Major General Akisaburo Futami, the army chief of staff considered such opinions "weak-willed." On August 1, the day after the successful assault on Kokoda, he reported that prisoner-of-war interrogations revealed there were 20,000 Allied troops at Port Moresby. Futami countered the South Seas Force commander was "grossly overestimating the actual strength of the enemy." The chief of staff was only interested in results. They had already cabled Imperial Headquarters that "the Army has confidence in the success of the overland operation. We beg you not to be concerned." Horii's headquarters was not interested in bad news.

The 17th Army had other factors to weigh besides Horii's pessimism (which had hung over the campaign from the start). For one, Colonel Yokoyama, the commander of the advance party, continued to send positive reports of progress at the front. For another, the 17th Army was also distracted managing the defense of the Solomon Islands, no small task with Allied landings at Tulagi and Gavutu that would be followed by marines hitting the beach at Guadalcanal on August 7, threatening a position every bit as valuable to the Japanese defense ring of their coprosperity sphere as Port Moresby.

Still, the army took some action. First, on August 1, it ordered the 41st Infantry Regiment to Buna (with scheduled arrival on August 15). The unit would primarily provide additional logistical support, but it could serve as another fighting force if necessary.

Second, the command recognized the risk of driving on to Port Moresby without a substantial base of supply. The initial estimate was unrealistic; the troops could not carry the campaign with just the food and ammunition they had strapped to their backs. The advance of the convoy with the main body of the South Seas Forces was postponed in favor of accelerating transport for units to complete an airfield at Buna.

They were scheduled to arrive on August 7. With the addition of the air-field and the 41st Regiment, a sufficient base of operations would be in place to support the renewal of the offensive and the overland drive to Port Moresby.

Nothing, however, went according to plan. The transports carrying the construction unit turned back en route. The troops did not arrive until August 13, and then only after braving an attack by waves of Allied fighters. The 41st Regiment, coming from the Philippines did not even get to Rabaul until August 16. The main body of the South Seas Detachment didn't arrive at Buna until the 18th of August. The 41st Regiment (less one battalion left at Rabaul) did not disembark in Papua New Guinea until August 21. It was three long weeks after the success-ful attack on Kokoda before the full weight of the Japanese force joined the campaign.

Another complication to the plan occurred in late July. A Japanese reconnaissance plane spotted Australian troops occupying Milne Bay at the tip of the Papuan Peninsula. The Japanese had themselves been eye-ing the position to extend their dominance on the peninsula. The report brought alarming news.[32] The Allies were building an airfield. Appar-ently, ground troops also moved in to help bolster the position. MacArthur had directed these preliminary actions (similar to the order to send elements of the 39th Battalion to Buna) as he prepared for his campaign against Rabaul.

On July 31, Hyakutake requested the 8th Fleet capture Milne Bay and then seize nearby Samarai Island. The success of this attack could well open the way for pressing on Port Moresby from a swing around from the seaward side in addition to the overland attack. That operation was scheduled to take place in concert with the renewed ground offen-sive over the Owen Stanley Range. The Australians would be caught in a pincer—the South Seas Force coming over the mountain and an amphibious force by sea from Samarai. If both operations succeeded and the army and navy could work together to hold Guadalcanal then there was still a chance to save the empire from defeat.

While the 17th Army anxiously awaited the opportunity to renew the offensive down the Owen Stanley Range, the Allies noted the pause in Japanese offensive action after the resounding defeat of Owen's small force at Kokoda. MacArthur had to decide what to do next. He pres-sured Marshall for more aid. Not wanting to undermine the first major effort to get the army into the war with the planned invasion in North Africa, Operation Torch, but in a concession to MacArthur, Marshall agreed to scrape together another American division for SWPA. The army chief of staff also dispatched General Arnold, the commander of the US Army Air Forces, to the Pacific for an inspection tour—a show the flag and show that the Asian war still mattered much to Washington. For the immediate future, however, MacArthur would have to make do with the resources he had at hand, knowing full well that even in the Pacific theater, his needs would play second to the fight in the Solomons for Guadalcanal. He could take some solace that the 17th Army would also have to divide its efforts between the Solomons and Papua New Guinea.

That the Japanese could not focus their full attention on Port Moresby left MacArthur confident that the enemy was far closer to their culminating point than his troops.[33] That said, the Australia militia and platoons of fuzzy wuzzies would not do. He would order the Australian regulars into the fight.

Notes

1. Grant, *Australian Soldiers in Asia-Pacific in World War II*, p. 114.
2. Unless otherwise noted, quotes and details are taken from Riseman, *Defending Whose Country? Indigenous Soldiers in the Pacific War*, pp. 105–118; David Counts, "Shadows of War: Changing Remembrance Through Twenty Years in New Britain," in White and Lindstrom, *The Pacific Theater*, pp. 195–197; White and Lindstrom, *The Pacific Theater*, p. 23.
3. Quoted in Ham, *Kokoda*, p. 63.
4. Quoted in Cook and Cook, *Japan at War*, p. 273.
5. Allied Geographical Section, Southwest Pacific, *The Native Carrier*, pp. 1, 3.
6. Quotes from Stanner, *The South Seas in Transition*, pp. 80, 81.
7. Munster, "A History of Contact and Change in the Goroka Valley," p. xii.
8. Information on psychological warfare operations is from MS 9002 Propaganda Relating to the Japanese Invasion of New Guinea in World War II; ibid., Folder 3 Box 1, Australian National Library; Kituai, *My Gun, My Brother*, pp. 182–185; MS 9002 Propaganda Relating to the Japanese Invasion of New Guinea in World War II, Folder 8 Box 3, Australian National Library; "Buna Report," pp. 62–63. See also Walker, "Psychological Warfare in the South-West Pacific," pp. 49–64.
9. Never large, the team did grow over time, including personnel from all the military services. At its largest in August 1945, FELO had a staff of only 474 including service members, 105 New Guinea natives, 21 Dutch, 8 civilians, and 5 Japanese prisoners of war.
10. Richard L. Watson and Kramer J. Rohfleisch, "New Guinea and the Solomons," in Caven and Cate, *The Pacific: Guadalcanal to Saipan, August 1942 to July 1944*, p. 7; See also Gillison, *Australia in the War of 1939–1945, Air War, Royal Australian Air Force, 1939–1942*, p. 470; Joe Gray Taylor, "Air Superiority in the Southwest Pacific," in Cooling, *Case Studies in the Achievement of Air Superiority*, p. 337.
11. US submarines start patrolling out of Freemantle, Australia, on March 31, 1942. Their operational area was also huge—covering over 3 million square miles with about two dozen subs who also had to balance their ship-hunting missions with

intelligence gathering tasks, search and rescue, and special operations (mostly sup-porting guerrilla operations in the Philippines), chores that MacArthur often gave higher priority than the interdiction of shipping.

In the first months of operation out of Freemantle, the sub forces' initial contri-butions were modest. By the end of the year, the subs sank over a total of little more 17,500 tons. Arguably, the submarine fight is one area in which operations might have benefited from centralized command and control and operations out of Pearl Harbor. However, once King made the decision to give MacArthur independent command over his submarine force, there was no going back. Conversely, there is a case to be made that having a responsive sub-surface for the theater commander was an enormously valuable asset. It is no surprise that MacArthur used his subma-rine force in a manner MacArthur best thought served himself. This frustrated the Joint Chiefs of Staff, who wanted MacArthur to make attacking enemy shipping the primary objective. See Benere, "A Critical Examination of the U.S. Navy's Use of Unrestricted Submarine Warfare in the Pacific Theater During World War II"; 17 1750, COMINCH to CINCPAC, COMZAC, War Plans, CINPAC Files, Subject: Running Estimate and Summary, December 7, 1941 to August 31, 1942, US Naval War College.

12. Ed Drea, "Military Intelligence and MacArthur, 1941–1951," in Leary, *MacArthur and the American Century*, p. 186.

13. Davies, "Field Unit 12 Takes New Technology to War in the Southwest Pacific," pp. 11–17.

14. Harry Summers, "Watched Salamaua for Six Months, Golden Voice Vial Kept Vigil," undated, MS 3752 Papers of Lloyd Purchase, 1939–1944; "Voice Warns Allies of Impending Raids," undated, MS 3752 Papers of Lloyd Purchase, 1939–1944; Peter Ewer, *Storm over Kokoda: Australia's Epic Battle for the Skies of New Guinea, 1942* (Millers Point: Pier 9, 2011), Papers of Lloyd Purchase, pp. 140–142. Accounts of how Vial got to Salamaua vary. News stories claim he was flown in. In Ewer's account, Vial walked there via the Kokoda trek and then overland. MacArthur was not alone in being dependent on coast watchers and air spotters. Ini-tial air operations at Henderson Field at Guadalcanal were dependent on coast watchers for warnings of air attacks coming out of Rabaul. See Hammel, *Carrier Clash*, p. 187.

15. Kenney, *General Kenney Reports*, p. 32. See also, *Services Around the World: The Army Air Forces in World War II*, vol. 7 (Washington, DC: Office of the Air Force, 1983), p. 329.

16. See, for example, Winton, *Ultra in the Pacific*; Drea, *MacArthur's ULTRA*; and Mack, *Code Breaking in the Pacific*.

17. See Drea, "Military Intelligence and MacArthur, 1941–1951."

18. Curtin to Churchill, Cablegram, July 30, 1942, document 12, Papers of the Department of Foreign Affairs and Trade, at http://dfat.gov.au/about-us/publications/historical-documents/Pages/volume-06/12-curtin-to-churchill.aspx.

19. Curtin to Churchill, Cablegram, August 25, 1942, document 28, Papers of the Department of Foreign Affairs and Trade, at http://dfat.gov.au/about-us/publications/historical-documents/Pages/volume-06/28-curtin-to-churchill.aspx.

20. Memorandum for Admiral King, July 15, 1942, Bland and Stevens, *The Papers of George Catlett Marshall*, p. 276.

21. Churchill to Smuts, July 25, 1942, in Gilbert, *The Churchill Documents*, vol. 17, p. 998.

22. Barclay, "Australia Looks to America", p. 267.

23. Quoted in Curran, *Curtin's Empire*, p. 87.

24. "Pacific Front Now," *The Telegraph* (Brisbane), August 6, 1942, National Library of Australia, p. 3.

25. To General Douglas MacArthur, August 10, 1942, in Gilbert, *The Churchill Documents*, vol. 17, p. 296. See also MacArthur's defense at "From Cinc Swpa To: Chief of Staff," No. C-273, August 16, 1942, National Security Archive Project, George C. Marshall Museum.

26. Unless otherwise cited, details on the Australian Department of Information from Vickery, "Telling Australia's Story to the World," pp. 54, 74–78, 194–196, 205; Roberts, *Before Rupert*, pp. 241–242.

27. Doob, *Public Opinion and Propaganda*, p. 389. See also Lloyd E. Lee, "Propaganda, Public Opinion, and Censorship During the Second World War," in Lee, *World War II in Asia and the Pacific and the War's Aftermath*, pp. 206–221.

28. "Bolder Strategy," *Lithgow Mercury*, August 6, 1942, National Library of Australia p. 3.

29. "War Talk," *The Macleay Chronicle*, August 12, 1942, National Library of Australia, p. 7; Curran, *Curtin's Empire*, p. 527.

30. Borneman, *MacArthur at War*, p. 229.

31. Quotes and details of Japanese operations from *Japanese Army Operations in the South Pacific Area*, pp. 131–132, 153–154.

32. Gamble, *Fortress Rabaul*, p. 214.

33. For MacArthur's intelligence assessment of enemy capabilities, see "From: Brisbane Qld To: Chief of Staff Wash DC," no number, August 3, 1942, National Security Archive Project, George C. Marshall Museum.

8

Regulars,
by God

MYOLA, PAPUA NEW GUINEA, AUGUST 24, 1942. *"Our lads have
done an excellent job of work," Bert Kienzle wrote to his wife,
taking a short break from the frenetic effort to get the Aussie
troops ready for the next fight.*

FROM THE LETTER, it wasn't clear if Kienzle was referring to the fuzzy
wuzzy angels under his charge manhandling supplies to the front or the
fresh troops advancing, preparing to check the Japanese advance. Either
way he wrote with self-assurance or perhaps to reassure his wife. "I feel
confident," he finished, of "driving out the yellow curse."[1] As Kienzle
wrote, faraway at SWPA headquarters in Australia, MacArthur's expectation was the same.

Turning the Tide

Although MacArthur was anxious to turn to the offensive, he was
equally intent on letting the world know he was carrying the war on his
shoulders. MacArthur famously declared, "I am always to be con-
demned to lead a forlorn hope," and often asserted, "Some people in
Washington would rather see MacArthur lose a battle than America win
a war." He had to fight "on a shoe-string," neglected and spurned by
jealous, lesser men.[2]

Historian Stanley Falk has little sympathy for MacArthur. He argues,
"During most of his campaigns he controlled resources far more extensive
than those of the enemy he faced."[3] After Bataan, most of MacArthur's

151

fights were fair ones or ones where the odds were in his favor. He has a point. Although the Japanese had over fifty divisions, half of these units were in China, leaving less than a quarter of a million ground troops for all their other Pacific campaigns. Meanwhile, in the first year of the war the United States sent more supplies and troops (nearly three-quarters of a million men) to the Pacific than to Europe.

A dean of the MacArthur critics, Falk, a widely published and long-time official historian for the air force and the army, slams the general's strategic judgment. MacArthur's mission was primarily the defense of Australia, he argues. A drive through the Central Pacific, far from MacArthur's home base, was the quickest and surest route to the Japanese mainland. An attack from Australia, beyond ensuring the defense of Port Moresby, was unnecessary. The offensive in the Southwest Pacific was peripheral, Falk argues, and undertaken only because of MacArthur's insistence. Its chief accomplishment, liberation of the Philippines, would have occurred anyway after Japan's surrender.

Falk's assessment is one view, but it is vulnerable on several points. Falk does not explain well why the Japanese warlords fought so hard and committed so many resources to the Southwest Pacific. Japan's warlords saw their southern area as an indispensable part of the empire's defense. The Joint Chiefs agreed with MacArthur. They consistently supported fighting in the Southwest Pacific, if for no other reason than to prevent the Japanese from concentrating their efforts on the defense of the Central Pacific. And while MacArthur may have had superior resources over the course of the war, in 1942 the Allies often had to fight where the odds were even or perhaps not in their favor. Further, SWPA at this point in the war lacked the infrastructure to bring all the resources being marshaled in Australia to the fight at the front.

Therefore, Falk is wrong. The battle for Papua New Guinea was more than just the defense of Port Moresby. MacArthur's plan for taking the fight to the enemy included controlling the northeast coast as a platform to isolate and eventually storm the enemy stronghold at Rabaul. Arguably, the militia had done its job in slowing the Japanese advance. But, there was way more to be done. That they could defend Port Moresby against a determined attack was debatable. Certainly, they did not have the numbers, training, or equipment to fight back over the Owen Stanley Range and reclaim the beachhead at Buna. The regular forces that MacArthur had husbanded for his intended offensive would be needed for this fight.

For pressing the counteroffensive, there was an argument to make over who should lead the way. MacArthur had a handful of American and Australian divisions. After Pearl Harbor, in his furious and incessant cable war with Churchill, Curtin had been able to wrestle three divisions back from the Middle East for the defense of Australia. Two of the divisions—the 6th and the 7th—had already arrived and undergone jungle training in North Queensland. Supplemented by the arrival of the Americans, together the Allied divisions constituted the core of MacArthur's deployable land power.

The Australian regulars, MacArthur decided, would go in first. MacArthur had already slotted the Australian Imperial Force troops for the move to Buna only to be beaten to the objective by the Japanese. He decided to stick with the plan of using the Australians to secure the first phase of the offensive. In early August, the Australians dispatched parts of one brigade of the 7th Division to Milne Bay and another to Port Moresby. The first battalions began to arrive in Port Moresby on August 13. It was the same day that a complement of Japanese reinforcements reached Buna.

Desperate Hours

The arrival of the first men of the 7th Division at Port Moresby and the occupation and reinforcement of Milne Bay could not have been timed better. Once again, the Allies moved just fast enough to stay one step ahead of the enemy. The Japanese found how proactive the Allies had become when on August 25, 1942, they launched Operation RE to secure the airfields at Milne Bay. They discovered the Australians were there in force.

Likewise, when General Horii arrived with the bulk of his forces and ordered full-scale assault toward Port Moresby commencing on August 26, he would discover the Australian ranks facing him had been greatly reinforced. Horii believed he was a five-day march from Port Moresby.

All that remained was to sweep away the rear guard blocking his path. He would learn how wrong he was when he attacked his next target—the village of Isurava.

What the general did not know was that his opposite in the field would not be just a tired, ragged militia. He would be fighting AIF regulars commanded by Brigadier Arnold William Potts.

Potts was a veteran of World War I. Despite his age (forty-five at the time of the battle) and nagging injuries that had earned him a disability rating, he joined the militia, transferred to the expeditionary force, earned the Distinguished Service Order during fighting in Syria, and now held command of the 21st Brigade, 7th Division for the counter-offensive to Kokoda.

Corps headquarters ordered Potts to concentrate his forces at Isurava, where the last of the militia had withdrawn after pulling back from Deniki. In addition to his own men, Potts would assume command of what was left of Owen's Maroubra Force and "recapture Kokoda with a view to facilitating further operations against Buna and Gona." On August 15, in their hastily established bivouac, Potts briefed the brigade's plan. With the two battalions of the brigade at hand (the 2/14th and 2/16th Infantry) they would advance, link-up with the militia, cover the "gap" between the enemy and Port Moresby, and then move on Kokoda.

Potts's first challenge was quickly apparent. He knew almost nothing about the ground in front of him. When he touched down at Port Moresby on August 13, 1942, Potts could just look across the countryside and recognize his men would be fighting in far different conditions than the jungle training they had conducted in North Queensland. The jungles of Papua New Guinea were immensely thicker. The tracks meandered over treacherous, mountainous terrain, often soaked by downpours, nothing like the ground his troops had experienced in Australia.

The next morning an ANGAU officer familiar with the local topography came to brief the brigade staff. "Otherwise," the unit war diary recorded, "our knowledge was limited to infm [information] gleaned from the study of a single air photo a track report map graph which subsequently proved extremely inadequate." Potts might well be going into a fight where the invading enemy knew more about the terrain in front of him than he did. Nevertheless, his priority was to get up the trail and into the fight. The first elements of the brigade started the march on the Owen Stanley Range on August 17. They reached Myola, a staging base, on August 20.

When the lead elements of the brigade got there, they were not happy. Myola was supposed to be a fully stocked jump-off point for their offensive. While Kienzle had achieved a minor miracle setting up a forward supply depot, the supplies proved inadequate to meet the needs of the numbers marching up from Port Moresby, a shortfall Robyn Kienzle glossed over in her effusive praise for the operation. Albeit in fairness, the fault did not lay with her grandfather.

Potts was told that by the time his troops got to Myola there would be twenty-five days of supply, including 40,000 rations for 2,000 men. That estimate proved to be wildly inaccurate. The advance party reported, "Arrangements [in] Myola are appalling lax. The sup[ply] [position] was very poor." The party estimated the base had two days of rations. To make matters worse, even though the weather was clear, there had not been a supply drop in days.

What the advance party did not know was that days before, Japanese bombers raided Port Moresby, hitting the 7 Mile Drome, obliterating two Dakota transport aircraft fully loaded for a supply run to Myola. The raid also damaged five other transports, shutting down the air bridge.

Then, it rained—vicious downpours, which were legend in the jungle highlands. Not surprising weather in a place that averaged 200 inches of rain a year. That slowed operations even more.

Even if the weather had been sunny, even if the Japanese had not scored a lucky hit, the Allies would have struggled to build a supply chain on the mountain range. The flow of material had been barely able to keep up with the needs of Maroubra Force (now comprised of two militia battalions—the 39th and the 53rd). The Australians needed thousands more carriers for the six-to-eight-mile trip to support the brigade.

Even unimpeded use of the Myola drop zone did not offer an easy alternative. The difficult flying conditions on the best of days limited pilots to one or two trips. In late August, there were only about thirty air transport planes in the whole theater, merely half of which were flyable at any one time. With so few planes, maintenance breakdowns, bad weather, and enemy air attacks, the whole effort was inevitably hopelessly off schedule.

Further, there was no good option of dropping supplies closer to the troops than Myola. The dry lakebed was the only open secure drop zone the Australians had. Trying to parachute supplies directly into the jungle or to troops at the front proved fruitless. Most of the supplies were never found. Some fell into the enemy's hands. On occasion, they landed on unsuspecting friendly troops—sometimes injuring and even reportedly killing men on the ground. These drops earned the nickname "biscuit bombers." For now, the Myola air bridge was the only option.

Even then, if the Allies had a fleet of transport planes to deluge the base with supplies, they would still need hundreds of additional porters to carry food and ammunition to the forward positions. In truth, the biggest problems were of the Allies' own making. There is a well-told military adage: "Amateurs talk strategy. Professionals talk logistics." The Australians clearly violated that maxim. It was less than two weeks from the order to send the 7th Division to Papua New Guinea until Potts's brigade was expected to take the fight to the enemy. Even if the Allies had handled all the preparations with maximum efficiency, ensuring the brigade was ready for the fight was an unachievable challenge. Preparations, however, were not efficient. They were a mish-mash from the start.

Port Moresby was not even prepared for the arrival of the brigade. Supplies were not staged. The high command was almost as much in the dark as to the true status of the supply situation on the ground as Potts. Caught in the middle was Lieutenant General Sir Sydney Fairbairn Rowell, the commander of I Corps, who had arrived in Port Moresby on August 13 (the same day as the first elements of the 7th Division) to take over command of the overall military situation. He brought with him only a small administrative staff. He expected to be fighting in the field, running a tactical headquarters. His biggest problem, however, turned out to be getting past the port. The greatest challenges for the corps were in the warehouses and airfields. The logistical and support morass overwhelmed Rowell's staff.

The Allies, for example, had to build an entire medical support train from scratch. Kienzle's fuzzy wuzzies might carry a severely wounded soldier down the trail to an evacuation station, but that was just the start. The Allies needed forward surgical teams, ambulances, and sufficient medical facilities at Port Moresby to deal with the casualties of the campaign. All that had to be organized while the fighting was under way.[4]

In frustration, on August 24, Rowell ordered what was left of the 39th Battalion withdrawn as soon as possible—that would free up more porters and supplies for Potts's brigade. He also held Potts's third battalion (2/27th Battalion) back at Port Moresby until the supply situation stabilized enough to support the whole brigade. Meanwhile, conditions at Myola improved with the renewal of airdrops and the assistance of an organized logistics team. "Prompt action was taken," Potts recalled, "to remove the existing staffs and replace them with efficient personnel." This was cold comfort. The delay had cost him four to five days. In addition, he would now be going into battle without one-third of his brigade.

What Potts did not know is that without these delays he might have beaten the Japanese to Isurava. He would have gotten there with superior numbers. He would have had a much more secure base of supply. He would have had every advantage. That, however, was not the hand Potts was dealt.

While Potts continued to bring up his force and sort out the logistics at Myola, the forward elements of the brigade made contact with the Maroubra Force. They reported the 39th Battalion looked to be in "shocking physical condition." No wonder—after weeks of harrowing jungle fighting. Having been routed at the battle of Kokoda (July 30), on August 8 during the lull in the Japanese offensive, the Maroubra Force had launched a counterattack and briefly regained the post (having time to find and bury Colonel Owen), before the Japanese again pushed them out. They retreated to Deniki. Forced out a few days later, they established a new defensive position at Isurava.

Potts's brigade not only made contact with the militia and a few natives and officers of Papuan Battalion as well as a handful of ANGAU patrol officers, they also made contact with the Japanese. The Japanese bombing raid on Port Moresby on August 17 was the seventy-eighth since the war began, but it proved to be one of the most consequential. The raid disrupted the logistics buildup at Myola, delaying the brigade's advance. When Potts reached Isurava, the enemy was already there. Horii had the initiative.

The brigade war diary reported the first engagements with the enemy on August 25. And, after that every day—fresh reports of Japanese patrolling activity, snipers, and mortar fire. The skirmishing reported in the war diary were the first signs of an offensive ordered by Horii.[5] While the movement of his own main force had been delayed by logistical challenges and harassment by Allied naval and air forces, he had still beaten the Australian regulars to the field of battle. Even as Potts's battalions were moving in, the commander of the South Seas Detachment had sketched out a scheme to encircle and annihilate the defenders at Isurava.

For the Japanese high command, completing a winning campaign as quickly as possible was more important than ever. The Japanese had expected an Allied counteroffensive, but the conventional wisdom was that the counterstrike would not come before 1943 at the earliest. Tokyo hoped to use that time to seal the outer ring of the empire's defenses. The Allies, however, looked to moving to the offensive in the autumn of 1942. There might be far less time and opportunity than Tokyo had hoped to consolidate gains, making the success of current operations an even more crucial imperative. They needed victory now.

Horii believed winning was possible. While his reinforcements had been maddeningly delayed, in addition to Colonel Yokoyama's advance force, for this fight Horii had fresh combat units from the 144th Regiment and the 41st Regiment that had been brought up to Kokoda. In total, he had about 3,000 men for the fight. While he would go into battle with a numerical advantage, Horii's lead in numbers has to be qualified. None of his units went into battle at full-strength not even the ones that had not engaged in battle since landing at Buna. Troops dropped out on the difficult march up the Owen Stanley Range. Fatigue and sickness took a toll as well. The official Japanese war history noted, that companies of "170–80 men" were reduced to "50–60."

Still, at the point of the spear, he had more men than the Australians. In addition to the ground troops, Horii's fire support had grown from one mountain gun to a full battalion of mountain artillery (though only three guns had so far made it to the front at Isurava). His forces were also backed by mortars and heavy machine guns.

Unlike the direct assault on Kokoda, Horii chose a scheme of maneuver that mimicked those the Japanese had used so successfully in the Malay campaign. Distract the enemy at the front and then sweep them up from behind. Horii brought up the 144th Regiment under the command of Colonel Masao Kusunose for the main assault. Horii's plan was to lead with an attack on August 26 down the trail coming from Kokoda and Deniki to pass through the Isurava village south to Alola.

The attack on the village was a feint. Horii planned to send forces around the high ground to either side through the dense jungle. The general anticipated that not only would they have the higher ground commanding the Australian position, they would circle around the position, cutting-off and annihilating the defenders. Meanwhile, Horii placed Colonel Kiyoshi Yazawa's 41st Regiment in reserve.

On August 26, following a morning barrage of mortar and artillery fire, the main force of the 1/144th under the command of Lieutenant Colonel Hatsuo Tsukamoto began the direct assault on the village. By nightfall they pushed against the enemy position in a driving rain, reaching the native garden west of the trail in front of the village. Colonel Kusunose concluded that "the enemy on this front are attacking with hearty spirit and are providing tenacious resistance." Further, he had difficulty communicating with flanking attacks on the high ground. They had made limited advances and seemed to have garnered no clear advantage. At 1 p.m., he directed units to "continue with their current responsibilities" and ordered the 3/144th to begin its advance forming the right wing of the attack with a mission to envelope the enemy from the west (right of the main trail but below the high ground) through an area of dense trees. At 3 a.m. on August 27, the 3/144th Battalion commanded by Lieutenant Colonel Gen'ichiro Kuwada began its attack.

Meanwhile, the 2/144th commanded by Major Koiwai Mitsuo continued its sweep around the eastern flank of the Australian position. The Japanese would move past Kaile south down the trail past Misima toward Abuari and the waterfall crossing.

Along the front, nothing went smoothly. From the start, maneuvers proved more difficult than Horii anticipated. The Japanese achieved no anticipated "advantage of height" in taking the high ground. The thick jungle offered no clear lines of sight over the enemy position, so the

Japanese could not effectively direct the fire of their mountain guns or mortars on the Australians.

Units got disoriented in the jungle. At times, they stumbled until they were "20–30 meters away" from the opposing lines, only learning they were near the enemy when the Australians started firing on them.

In some cases, confused Japanese units fired on each other. During the battle, Sergeant Imanishi found his platoon assigned to the frontal assault to fix the enemy's attention. Crawling laboriously down the slope toward the Australians to prepare for the attack, his platoon came under fire from behind. They were being shot at by another Japanese unit (likely the 3/144th) that had taken a nearby hilltop and mistook the troops on the slope for Australians.

It was no wonder that Horii had not been able to sweep the exhausted and depleted Australians from the field on the first day of the advance. The 39th Battalion had not picked bad ground to make their stand.

The terrain in Eora valley was very different from the highland plateau around Kokoda. Between the impenetrable jungle lowlands and high grasses of the central highlands was a different world. Beyond Kokoda, the track meanders along precipitous ridges down mountainous slopes. Densely matted rainforest and steep slippery muddy inclines dominated the countryside. Giant fallen trees became natural obstacles, not only difficult to traverse but offering cover and concealment to the enemy.

Isurava village sat high above the highlands plateau along one of the many ridges that had to be climbed and descended in the up-and-down trek to the coast. Sitting on a flat clearing in the Eora valley between two creeks, the village commanded the trail to Port Moresby with a clear line of sight on the enemy's route of advance. North of the village and east of the trail, dense forest gave way to a tilled garden area and a grassy expanse leading up to Isurava.

To the east of the village, Eora Creek ran along the bottom of a deep chasm, 1,500 feet below the village. A steep, heavily timbered slope bordered the side of the creek. Along the crest of the eastern ridge ran a trail linking four small villages (from north to south): Kaile, Misima, Asigari, and Abuari.

To the west, the high ground was covered with thick jungle and dense forest. A little over a quarter of mile behind the village, on high ground, a government "Rest House" (actually a collection of huts used by missionaries, government officials, and police patrols that had trafficked the Kokoda track before the war) held a commanding view of the valley.

Behind the Rest House, a mile farther down the track was the smaller village of Alola. From Alola, a trail led up the western escarpment past a log bridge and a plunging waterfall on a sheer rock face to Abuari and the trail north went to the other villages dotting the ridge. Alola was an important place to hold reserves in case the enemy broke through at Isurava. The village also provided a location to dispatch forces to the east or west to block the Japanese if the enemy tried to encircle the Australians' main defensive positions.

When Potts arrived on scene (now serving as overall commander), he would have to decide on how carry the battle. The brigadier had his two battalions of AIF troops from the 7th Division and the decimated 39th Battalion that was holding the front, as well as the 53rd Battalion at Alola.

The 53rd was another militia unit that had been hastily dispatched up the trail to join Maroubra Force. The battalion, coming up after the battles of Kokoda, had not yet engaged the Japanese in a major fight. Until now, the 53rd had been a backstop for the 39th protecting the main track to Port Moresby, conducting inclusive patrolling against the Japanese, and running a wire line back to headquarters. From what Potts knew and his brief personal observations he considered the poorly trained and untested 53rd battalion "sub-standard." As for the 39th Battalion, it was worn to the bone.

Potts, however, could only fight with the forces he had. The question was—what to do?

The brigade's orders were to concentrate at Isurava then take Kokoda. That was a command that made perfect sense when he had the order in hand ten days ago in Port Moresby. The situation looked far different now. With supply conditions still unsettled, a third of his force still back at Port Moresby, an enemy attacking to his front against Australian units already in contact, on ground he barely knew without a map worthy of the name, taking Kokoda was a bridge too far.

The initial plan was to defend. The 39th held good ground. It made no sense to yield it to the enemy. Holding the position made sense—but how? Potts had three options.

First, he could leave the 39th and 53th forward to slow the enemy while he concentrated his forces at Myola, holding the precious supply depot and preparing a more deliberate defense somewhere else.

Second, he could go all in. He could leave the 39th in place, not risking the precarious challenge of moving them in the middle of a battle. Potts could move up his 2/14th and 2/16th and put them on the high ground to the east and west of the village, creating a blocking position against any Japanese move down the Eora valley. He would then have the untested 53rd Battalion as his brigade reserve at Alola.

Third, he could pick a middle course. Potts could send one of his battalion's forward to replace the 39th (which in its current state could be little more than a speed bump to the advancing Japanese). He could backstop the defense with the 53rd and keep his second AIF battalion as a reserve. With this deployment, he wouldn't be fully committing himself. He could try to gain more intelligence about the enemy's intention, as well as safeguard his line of retreat in case the battle did not go well.

Potts dismissed option one as unrealistic. The 39th was in no shape to fight. He had little confidence in the 53rd.

He didn't think option two was feasible. Potts didn't feel he had sufficient supplies to support all four battalions forward at once.

Potts decided on option three. The 2/14th would replace the 39th. The 53rd would backstop the 2/14th. That would leave the 2/16th to guard Myola. Given the conditions as he knew them, Potts had not made a bad call.

The 21st Brigade commander chose the option that gave him the most flexibility and accounted for the supply situation. Potts's two battalions had about 550 men each. Plus he had the militia units, the untested 53rd, and less than 300 weary men of the 39th. In practical terms, it meant that the two sides would engage with a disadvantage in personnel numbers, but he was on the defensive holding ground that was not half bad.

In terms of the situation, the odds looked even. Both sides would be fighting with stretched supply lines. Both had to slog over mud and a mountain trail to get to the fight. Although the 21st Brigade had a difficult trek to reach the front, many of the Japanese had made a sixty-mile forced march from the beaches to get to the Alola Valley in time for the battle. Both sides suffered under the driving rain and chilling cold of the high mountain passes. Both sides depended on their infantry to carry the battle. Horii had an advantage in that he had a battalion of mountain artillery and mortars. The 39th had no fire support. The 2/14th had only mortars. The Japanese advantage in fire support was, however, offset a good bit by the fact that the terrain limited their ability to use indirect fires accurately against the Australians. Given the numbers and that the terrain favored the defender, Potts's chance of success was not beyond hope. Considering the helter-skelter manner the 21st Brigade had been thrown into battle, he could have expected worse.

On August 27, while Kusunose renewed his advance, Potts reported the 2/14th had begun the relief of the beleaguered 39th Battalion. The war diary of the 2/14th Battalion recorded that "it was quite evident at this stage that the enemy had received considerable reinforcements and had commenced a determined advance on our position."

The battle for Isurava was already well under way—and for the commander of the 21st Brigade it was beginning with one of the most complicated and potentially perilous operations that might be undertaken in combat, swapping out one unit for another in the middle of a running battle.

A "relief" is when one friendly force is brought in to replace another. This can be one of the most dangerous and harrowing military operations to undertake—even with experienced and trained forces. The confusion of moving and mixing forces from various commands might create opportunities for the enemy to exploit, and troops also had to worry about "friendly fire," the possibility of being mistaken for the enemy and engaged by your own troops. Under ideal conditions, the best time to conduct these operations was out of the presence of the enemy. These were not ideal conditions—they were among the worst. The 21st Brigade would have to relieve in place a worn-out militia unit while the Japanese were advancing to their front.

Though the standing doctrine of the time, *Infantry Training: Training and War 1937*, had scant guidance to offer on how to conduct this maneuver, the regulars and the militia managed the operation impressively well. Much credit that this movement did not result in a disaster goes to the spent men of the 39th Battalion who had held their own for two days as the Japanese attacked, suffering enemy breakthroughs and then fighting to restore their lines while waiting for the 2/14th to move up.

For their part, the 2/14th's movement was disciplined and professional, a notable accomplishment for their first jungle fight on terrain they did not know. Kienzle had delivered a brief to the units on the terrain and helped construct a model "sand table" to explain the layout of the ground, but there were no suitable maps and no time to practice the maneuver or fully scout out the terrain.

The passage of lines, with the 2/14th advancing to take the forward sector of the perimeter and the 39th withdrawing to take responsibility for the quieter rear-half, was accomplished even as fighting with the enemy continued that day and into the next. The entire 2/14th, with elements of the 39th engaged, continued to hold off the main assault from Kusunose's forces east of the trail through the forest and the native garden.

Meanwhile, after reports of the enemy moving to the high ground to the east, elements of the 53rd had been dispatched in the Abuari to hold the log bridge and the crossing at the waterfall, as well as to take back the village from the Japanese.

If the Japanese got their mountain guns on Abuari, they would be able to observe and range the brigade headquarters. When Potts received reports from the 53rd of Japanese moving along the trail on the high ground east of the creek, and with little faith that the 53rd would serve as an effective reserve or blocking force, he decided to adjust the plan. Potts was right about the 53rd. It was a poorly trained and poorly led outfit. At one point, in the middle of an advance on the eastern ridge, the troops broke and ran in panic. Conversely, the 39th—still holding their own at the front—had proven a more valuable asset than Potts anticipated. His adjustments to the battle plan accounted for both.

First, Potts needed to keep the 39th for now and send the 53rd back as soon possible. Second, he needed his third battalion. The general immediately requested the 2/27th be dispatched to the front. Potts also requested more bearers and additional airdrops at Myola. He was going into a big fight. They would go through the supplies on hand. They would need more. There would also be causalities. The brigade would need more carriers to evacuate the wounded. Still, what the brigadier needed most were troops that could fight. Potts worried more about being overrun than being chronically short of supplies if he brought his whole brigade forward.

His request to have the 2/27th sent up was denied. The Japanese had just landed at Milne Bay. Corps was worried that Port Moresby might also come under attack. The 2/27th might be needed to defend the beaches. Potts was on his own. The only option the brigadier had was bringing up the 2/16th to Alola, sending elements of the battalion to the trail on the high ground on the eastern ridge to protect his flank and relieve the 53rd. As soon as he could manage, Potts planned to also withdraw the 53rd. That would lessen supply needs.

For their part, when the Japanese renewed their offensive on August 28, they realized they were facing a dug-in enemy that been reinforced with fresh troops. The 3/144th, which tried to encircle the enemy to the west, got bogged down in skirmishing with the flank of the Australian 2/14th defensive position. Horii ordered them to regroup and move to the high ground, resuming the effort to circle around behind the village. At 2 a.m., the battalion moved out, struggling through the jungle out of the sight of the enemy. They would traipse through the jungle for the next two days before finding their way back to the fight.

Meanwhile, the advance of the 2/144th on the east encountered some resistance. Major Koiwai dispatched parties through the jungle looking for routes to bypass the enemy, not knowing the positions in front of them were only sparsely defended.

The plan for August 29 was to continue as before: fix the enemy at the front and envelope them on the flank. Horii decided, however, to reapportion the weight on the assault flank by shifting most of the troops from the push on Abuari to the assault on Isurava village.

The Japanese scheme of maneuver had not produced the sweeping results Horii had hoped for, with each day's fighting costing him men, ammunition, and rations he could scarcely afford given his own logistics difficulties. Still, he had fresh troops in reserve, and although overall the forces were numerically not that far apart, the Japanese had a clear numerical advantage at the point of attack, likely close to the three to one advantage often considered needed for an offensive succeeding against a defensive fighting force.

Potts not bringing up the full weight of the 2/16th or having his third battalion available on the most crucial day of battle had put the Australians at a disadvantage. With Potts's reduced forces in place and the enemy advancing on three fronts, and with rain pounding both sides through the night, the stage was set for the battle on August 29.

The Grim Face of Battle

The previous day, August 28, Lieutenant Colonel Arthur Key, who commanded the 2/14th Battalion, had taken control of the entire front. He was thirty-four years old on the day of the battle. He received a militia commission in 1927 and transferred to the AIF in 1939. He had commanded another battalion during the Middle East campaign, taking over the 2/14th in January 1942 right before the division was shipped back to Australia. Although he had not fought with the veterans of the 2/14th before, he had been with and trained with his troops for over six months.

Even before reaching the front, Key and his men knew from the rugged terrain they had crossed and the unforgiving weather—going from blistering heat to bitter cold and choking dust to slobbering mud, all punctuated by incessant rains—that this fighting would be little like what they had seen in the Middle East or trained for at the maneuver areas in New Queensland. In the midst of desperate jungle fighting, one of the first requests from the front was for more blankets to get through the bone-chilling sub-Alpine nights.

On August 28, Key's forces joined men from his A Company along with troops from the 39th in closing one of the breeches in the main line of defense. He saw firsthand the ferocity of the Japanese assaults. When he left his command post that night to check on conditions for himself, he only had to go a few yards to find his frontline troops and spy Japanese scurrying not far away in the dark. Key could only expect a renewed major offensive in the morning.

For the 39th, which had been holding and fighting for three days, the arrival of the 2/14th was a godsend. Gaunt, sick, hungry men in tattered uniforms gawked at the fresh troops that seemed like "Christ come down from the mountain." The 39th Battalion commander recalled, "There were already four times as many men holding our front and our flanks as there had been the previous day; and when A Company and part of Headquarters Company [the 2/14th] . . . arrived it was possible for the first time to provide a powerful reserve." Still, the two battalion commanders agreed that the plan to fully withdraw the militia while the Japanese were likely to renew the attack made no sense.

Key contacted Potts at the newly established brigade headquarters at Alola, who agreed that the 39th would remain in place for now. Potts notified division headquarters that he needed to keep the 39th. That request was approved.

At the front, Key had the battalion arrayed with an eye toward protecting the vital position in the main line of defense facing the trail to Deniki. Anchoring the eastern flank of the battalion was C Company of the 2/14th commanded by Captain Gerry Dickinson. On C Company's left on the other side of the trail was A. G. Cameron's D company. D Company's position was fronted by heavy trees that gave poor observation to their front, but also offered an obstacle for any massed Japanese assaults on their position. On the other side of D Company, anchoring the western flank of the battalion was C. C. P. Nye's B Company in a forward position they called the "cane field." B Company would have to carry the responsibility of blocking any effort to outflank the battalion by sweeping their position to the West below the ridgeline.

The battalion was backstopped by Captain S. H. Buckler's company in reserve, tucked in the middle between A Company, 39th Battalion on his left, and the rest of 39th Battalion on the right. This was how the diggers were arrayed when the enemy attacked again in force.

In addition to the firepower of the infantry, the battalion was fortunate to have some mortar support. *Infantry Training: Training and War 1937* reminded that "the battalion commander has in the mortar a powerful weapon" for the defense of a position. Mortars could serve as "reserve of fire . . . which may be used to supplement the fire plan at any point where it is proving to be ineffective, to break up enemy formations which have penetrated the defence." One proven tactic was to plan a line of final protective fire in front of defensive positions to block massed assaults or lob mortar shells in defilade or other concealed or covered (protected) positions where the enemy might be out of direct line of fire but able to bring machine gun or sniper fire on defensive positions. The battalion's single two-inch mortar and 39th Battalion's one three-inch mortar were in constant demand. After one day at the front, the battalion was already requesting resupply on mortar ammunition, even the single mortar proving immensely helpful for the defenders in holding off the Japanese.

Lieutenant Colonel Key had some modest cause for optimism after taking over the front. On the positive side, his company commanders had successfully concluded the relief of the 39th. His men were in position. He also had been able to arrange keeping the 39th in place to round out his defenses. Meanwhile, his men had already weathered a day and night of tough fighting, repelling human waves of enemy assault and causing the Japanese many casualities at the cost to the Australians of one officer and two men killed and only a dozen wounded. Having survived the night, all Key could do was wait to see what the dawn would bring.

Although the descriptions of battle in the pages of history often read like play-by-play reporting of sporting events, that is not how they transpire in real time. In between the assaults, retreats, and maneuvers that mark the progress of a battle, jungle warfare included harrowing patrolling at the front by both sides, sometimes blundering into enemy ambushes, enemies silently infiltrating through the bush, unexpected sniper fire, and harassment from lobs of artillery and mortar fire, a never-ending twenty-four-hour mish-mash in the always changing highlands weather from inky dark to driving rainstorms to bone-chilling dawns. Some small units were lost in the jungle, wandering around for days before regaining contact with their commands. Three of the 39th Battalion's platoons were unaccounted for when the battle began. Meanwhile the battle would wax and wane with frenzied firefights day and night broken by hours of eerie calm when troops would have to eat (throwing down a can of bully beef or fistful of rice), take a runny crap, or grab a fitful nap.

War did not come in discrete scenes and acts like an unfolding play. War was an endless, sleepless, exhausting feat of endurance. For the men at the front on both sides, for days, this was their miserable universe.

A Fateful Fight

The night of August 28 was clear and crisp. Then the decisive day of battle began. The 2/14th Battalion war diary reported the day broke "dull and overcast."

From dawn until about 8 a.m. on August 29, the Japanese peppered the front with fire. The morning was blanketed with a misty haze, mixing with the acrid stinking, sulfur-laced smoke of exploding artillery and mortar fire. The dismal weather provided good concealment for the enemy assault as the smoke from the exploding shells lay heavy on the valley floor. Out of the white, the enemy came; an estimated 100 screaming Japanese infantry stormed the position in front of Dickinson's company.

What in the end had cost the 39th in their defense of Kokoda on July 30 was an inability to hold or reestablish their line once the Japanese had broken through. If the enemy were willing to send attacks in waves against the Australians' position, there was always the possibility that sooner or later the enemy might find a spot to overrun the defenders. Once the enemy infantry were on them, the only course to prevent a rout was the timely commitment of the reserves.

If Key's companies were going to hold this position, they would have to do better.

The first breakthrough occurred before mid-morning, when a second wave of enemy stormed C Company's front. To make matters worse, D Company was also hard pressed with a frontal assault. Key decided he had to reinforce both. A Company sent a platoon to D Company and another to C Company.

The D Company fight was going so badly that Buckler, the A Company commander, brought forward a second platoon, using grenades and bayonets in close-quarter fighting to push the Japanese off the position.

C Company was in even more dire straits. The platoon from A Company that was sent forward to aid them immediately suffered heavy casualties and the platoon leader was killed, giving the Japanese their best opportunity for a decisive breakthrough, if they could continue to press the attacks before the diggers could recover the lost ground.

While the battalion had been timely in using its reinforcements, they just weren't enough. The battalion reserve had been virtually used up—and it wasn't even noon.

Farther down the track, remnants of the 39th Battalion were being evacuated. A mixed platoon of sick and wounded had reached the Isurava Rest House when a runner from the battalion requested volunteers to double back to the front as additional reinforcements. One digger remembered, "27 out of 30 went back. The three who stayed were minus a foot, a bullet in the throat and a forearm blown-off." They were led by an intrepid and determined Lieutenant Stewart Johnston, an AIF veteran who had been wounded earlier in the war, sent back to Australia, and later joined the militia to fight in Papua New Guinea. In addition to the sick parade of the 39th under Lieutenant Johnston, the brigade scrambled for every other available troop to reconstitute a fighting reserve.

Meanwhile at the front, though the reinforcements to C Company had failed to break the attack, they allowed time for the remnants of C Company platoon to regroup.

In close tactical combat it was not unusual in either the Australian or US armies to see informal leaders step forward and take action on their own initiative. This exercise of leadership is even more remarkable considering the conditions in which the practice often occurred—at the height of battle under a din of explosions, noise, and smoke. On this occasion, a handful of men, including a sergeant leading a small group of men from the battalion's headquarters company and three privates from one of the overrun platoons, organized their own counterattack.

One of the men leading the charge was twenty-four-year-old Private Bruce Steel Kingsbury from Preston, a small community near Melbourne, Australia. His father worked in real estate. Bruce hated the business. Unsatisfied, drifting from jobs on various farms and estates, he longed for a life of adventure. Kingsbury and his childhood friend Allen Avery joined the army in 1940. Later, Kingsbury volunteered to transfer to the infantry to join his mate in the 2/14th. Both were veterans of the fighting in the Middle East and the training in Queensland, but neither had ever assumed a position of any rank or responsibility.

Driven back from the front toward the battalion command post, leaderless, their platoon overrun and in disarray, Kingsbury, Avery, and another member of platoon decided on their own to joint the counterattack. When the deputy battalion commander saw them head back to the front he yelled out to Kingsbury, asking him where they were going. Kingsbury replied, "Just down the track skip." Kingsbury and Avery took off at a trot and then a dead run back toward their old platoon position.

The basic rifle Australian infantrymen carried was the Lee-Enfield Rifle, No. 4 Mk I, a short, bolt-action, magazine-fed weapon with ten rounds and spike bayonet the troops called a "pigsticker." Versions of the gun had been the staple arm in the British Empire since before World War I. While a sturdy, reliable weapon, an infantryman's Enfield was hardly daunting enough to repel a screaming mass of assaulting enemy.

Infantry units, however, were also equipped with light machine guns—the "Bren." This air-cooled machine gun was originally manufactured by the Brno Firm of Czechoslovakia. The design was later modified by the British arms manufacture Enfield. The weapon became known as the Bren, from "Brno" and "Enfield." Although the Bren fired the same standard .303 caliber ammunition as the infantry rifle, the machine gun had a thirty-round magazine that could fire in automatic or semiautomatic mode.

Before 1940, virtually no Australian units had been issued these weapons. Even a year later, many troops had never seen or trained on the Bren. That was unfortunate. For the close-quarters fighting in the New Guinea underbrush, the Bren and the US-supplied M1928 Thompson submachine guns were the weapons of choice.

The Thompson submachine gun was the most popular weapon among the soldiers during the campaign. They would usually pick up this weapon if they found one on the battlefield and throw away their issued M-1 rifle. While the Thompson weighed about the same as an American M-1 rifle or British Lee-Enfield, the submachine gun's firepower was an important advantage in close terrain.[6]

Like the Thompson, the Bren was exactly the kind of gun needed to blunt the assault of charging Japanese infantry. Kingsbury recovered his from another wounded member of the platoon, the weapon already burning hot from continuous firing. Brandishing the machine gun, and firing from the hip, he advanced. This was more than just wild bravado; firing from the hip was a technique the Australians had discovered was well-suited to jungle warfare and to breaking an unexpected charge of Japanese infantry.

Kingsbury and Avery (firing a Thompson) advanced, with the Bren blasting away. By reports, the firing was so forceful that in a few minutes it chopped away all the underbrush in front of their position. The entire incident last less than a minute—but it proved decisive.

The intensity of the counterattack killed several Japanese and forced others to take cover. More importantly, it provided the opportunity for the company to regain their positions and reestablish the company's defensive line.

That Kingsbury almost single-handedly could stop an enemy charge was not just the stuff of Hollywood movies. At the point Kingsbury arrived at the front, the enemy must have been nearly a spent force, exhausted, parched with thirst, and drained by having already beaten back one counterattack. They were clearly stunned and unprepared for a charge from an enemy that had seemed to be yielding the field to the attackers.

As others moved up and the Japanese withdrew, Avery turned as his mate collapsed, felled by a shot from a Japanese soldier firing from the woods. Avery briefly chased the enemy who had shot his friend, firing a fusillade from his Thompson into the tree line. He then quickly returned. Lifting Kingsbury in a fireman's carry, Avery ran to the aid station with his wounded friend. Kingsbury died.

Claims that Kingsbury changed the tide of the battle are over-exaggerated. Nevertheless, there was no question that his personal bravery had temporarily altered the course of battle and saved many lives, preventing the company and the battalion command post from being overrun. A year later Kingsbury's valor would be recognized by the Victoria Cross, the royal medal of bravery similar to the US Medal of Honor.

After Kingsbury's charge, the Japanese regrouped and pressed forward. Dickinson's company gave ground. Key was out of reserves. Potts ordered C Company of the 53rd Battalion forward to reinforce Dickinson, while two platoons of hungry, sick, and exhausted men of the 39th Battalion were reformed as a reserve for Key.

By 3 p.m., Cameron's D Company over the course of the day with the help of the A Company reserves had weathered eleven assaults on their position. The last one proved decisive, the company's front line pulled back, the Japanese pressed forward and swung around, attacking the now exposed flank of Nye's B Company from the rear. Key was forced to pull back along the entire front and try to reform the battalion's defensive positions. At 8:45 p.m., he reported the battalion could not hold the front anymore.

Potts brought up C and D Company of the 2/16th during the night and planned to use them in a counterattack in the morning to help restore the 2/14th front. Instead, they had to relieve the 2/14th, holding the front while during the night the 2/14th battalion withdrew to the high ground around the Rest House.

During the battle on August 29, the battalion reported losing 2 officers, 10 killed (including Kingsbury), 45 wounded, and 172 missing. Lieutenant Colonel Key was among the missing.

When the headquarters company had been cut off near the Isurava Rest House, Key ordered the men to break up into small groups and exfiltrate back to Australian lines. Key and four others were captured by the Japanese. The battalion also estimated inflicting 550 casualties on the enemy (the Japanese reported their official losses at 175). In the end, however, it wasn't a question of the number of casualties inflicted, the tide turned on the fact that the brigade lost control of the key ground that made defense of the position tenable.

While the battle continued the next day, the fight was over. The Japanese had not only advanced on the front, but to the high ground on the flanks. In addition, by the thirtieth, Horii had brought up five additional mountain guns. With eight guns of the battalion now in a better position, they could pound away at the Australians. The effective enemy fire contributed to Potts's decision that they couldn't continue to hold their ground for long.

If Potts did not withdraw, the whole command might be surrounded and annihilated, replaying some of the most crippling defeats in the Malay campaign. Potts led a fighting withdrawal, not only abandoning the position but, later, the key supply point at Myola as well.

Victory in Defeat

In their first major fight with the Japanese, the veterans of the AIF fared no better than the *chocos* at Kokoda. They lost for the same reason. That had less to do with the fighting quality of the troops, the state of supplies, or the jungle fighting tactics of the Australians. They lost because at the pointy end of the spear they lacked the firepower to hold off massed and determined Japanese assaults.

What might have made a difference in the tactical combat at Kokoda and Isurava was adequate fire support. That might have been provided by air support from fighters or indirect fires from artillery or mortars. The militia had none of that at Kokoda. The 2/14th had some mortar support at Isurava but limited ammunition, not much of a capacity to break the enemy with fire.

The other way to respond to massed assaults was with well-coordinated counterattacks. But even the bravest and best-led attack backed by grenades and bayonets in close-jungle fighting chewed through available manpower pretty quickly. In both battles (Kokoda and Isurava), the commanders lacked adequate reserves for the task.

The issues of reserves and firepower aside, Potts's decisions at Isurava are open to debate. The depleted and worn-out 39th and 53rd were just not adequate as reserves. Ham, in his history of the campaign, called using the 53rd to backstop the 2/14th as Potts's biggest mistake. Ham was likely right. There is an old maxim "quantity has a quality all its own." Potts did not have enough dependable troops forward to meet the enemy. With the 2/16th forward, he might have had the numbers to handle Horii's attack. Certainly, if the 2/27th had been there as well Potts could have stopped Horii cold.

Due to the supply situation, Potts decided on a more cautious course. That no doubt cost him the battle. In particular, the piecemeal approach to committing his counterattack forces was timid, reinforcing failure to stave-off little defeats, not leveraging his reserves to shape the course of the day. However, his dribs and drabs approach to feeding forces into the front ensured he would have enough troops to fight another day. Considering all he did not know when he reached the front—the fighting qualities of the militia battalions, the enemy's strength, the nature of the ground he would fight over, and the sturdiness of his supply lines—he had reason to be cautious.

Sometimes, trying to avoid risks is risky. If Horii had pressed the fight as he originally planned with strong flanking movements, he might have been able to sweep around the Australian position, particularly on the eastern flank. He decided, however, to shift additional forces away from the eastern flank along the trail from Kaile to Abuari to Alola. That decision ensured the frontal attack had the weight to break the Australian's front, but it cost Horii the opportunity to cut off and defeat three enemy battalions.

In retrospect, Horii's decision is also defensible. He had poor contact with the units on the flank and was unsure of their progress or the conditions they faced. He didn't have the bulk of mountain artillery in place to blast away at the enemy position until August 30. Further, the Australians appeared to have fresh reinforcements. Time was ticking. He could not afford to get bogged down in a protracted fight. So he made the decision to just press through. He needed a rigorous attack to either break through or fix the enemy while his other forces circled round. In the end, his troops did push the Australians off their strong defensive terrain and open the route to press the campaign toward Port Moresby.

Before the battle Horii had believed he could be in Port Moresby in five days. He expected friendly troops to be holding Milne Bay and that Japanese Army and Naval forces could threaten Port Moresby with attack from the sea. None of that happened.

The assault on Milne Bay had not gone well. The Japanese attacked with a battalion backed by armor expecting scant opposition, little knowing that the Allied garrison had been reinforced. The initial Japanese attack was thrown back. The Japanese renewed their offensive pushing back the Australian defenses, but eventually outnumbered, lacking supplies, and being pounded from Allied air strikes, the Japanese withdrew and by September the fighting had ended. Meanwhile, Horii's five days were up. He was not in Port Moresby. A defeated but still intact regular brigade of AIF forces blocked his path.

An engagement at the tactical level can ripple across the levels of war like dropping a pebble on the surface of pond. Horii had won a tactical victory, but operationally he was in deep trouble. Each battle cost him men, food, and ammunition, which had to be carried over the Owen Stanley Range. Each advance made supply more difficult. In contrast, each defeat pushed the enemy back, but conversely shortened their supply lines. And while Horii had defeated the enemy, they were still in the field, which meant he would have to fight them again to get to Port Moresby.

Each step forward was one step closer to the culminating point.

The Japanese war journalist Seizo Okada witnessed an illustration of the desperate situation Horii's troops had fallen into. When the first troops closed on Alola, they found a cache of food, weapons, and ammunition abandoned by the retreating Australians. The war stopped as the troops wildly plundered everything they could find. Okada joined in the feast, but marveling at the cases of corned beef, biscuits, and cans of butter, cheese, and milk in comparison to their meager rice rations, he later recalled, "Here in the Papuan mountains the standard of living was higher than in Japan! I saw something of the appalling power of Anglo-American civilization that Japan had so recklessly challenged."[7] He feared for the future.

To make matters worse, the failure at Milne Bay proved a double calamity. No longer fearing that threat of seaborne assault, the 7th Division released the third battalion of the Australian 21st Brigade to head up the Kokoda track to fight Horii. The Japanese would no longer be threatening the enemy from the sea, but they would also have to fight more diggers on the trail to Port Moresby.

On August 29, the war changed. Horii had won a battle, but he lost the campaign. Losing the campaign, coupled with the failure to break the US hold on Guadalcanal meant that the ability of the Japanese to hold their empire in the face of a determined Allied counteroffensive was in grave doubt.

On August 29, Potts lost a fight, failed in his assigned mission of driving the enemy back over the Owen Stanley Range, but he helped accomplish the vital strategic objective of greatly reducing the odds the enemy would ever set foot in Port Moresby. Despite the defeat, the delay imposed by the defense at Isurava had an outsized strategic and operational benefit.

If Horii had chosen a different course on August 28, if Bruce Kingsbury had not bought the battalion a couple of more hours of daylight on August 29, if any of the major fortunes of war had dramatically shifted the result, history might have had a different chapter.

But none of that happened.

Notes

1. Quoted in Kienzle, *The Architect of Kokoda*, p. 149.
2. Bischof and Dupont, *The Pacific War Revisited*, p. 27.
3. Ibid.

4. See Grogan, "The Operation of Forward Surgical Teams in the Kokoda-Buna Campaigns," pp. 68–73; Reed, "Endurance, Courage and Care."

5. Quotes and details of the Battle of Isurava (also called the Battle of Isurava–Abuari or the Battle of Isuraba) are from AWM52 2nd Australian Imperial Force and Commonwealth Military Forces Unit war diaries, 1939–45, 21 Infantry Brigade, August 1942, August 26–20, 1942; AWM52 2nd Australian Imperial Force and Commonwealth Military Forces Unit war diaries, 1939–45, 2/14 Infantry Battalion, August 1942, August 26–20, 1942; Collie and Marutani, *The Path of Infinite Sorrow*, pp. 85–90; Ham, *Kokoda*, pp. 166–176; Austin, *To Kokoda and Beyond*, pp. 146–160; McCarthy, *South-West Pacific Area*, pp. 199–211; FitzSimons, *Kokoda*, pp. 320–324; *Japanese Army Operations in the South Pacific Area*, pp. 161–163; Johnson, *Mud over Blood Revisited*, pp. 116–126; Edgar, *Warrior of Kokoda*, pp. 140–163.

6. Report of the Commanding General Buna Forces of the Buna Campaign, Dec. 1 1942–Jan. 25, 1942, pp. 68–69.

7. Quoted in Collie and Marutani, *The Path of Infinite Sorrow*, pp. 92–93.

9

Don't Come
Back Alive

WASHINGTON, DC, SEPTEMBER 16, 1942. *"I am pretty busy and have been unremittingly since I took over July 1st in 1939,"* confessed Army Chief of Staff George C. Marshall, *"as a matter of fact I have had about sixteen days' holiday in the period and have flown about 150,000 miles."*[1]

EVEN A STOIC ICON like George C. Marshall had to complain some-times—even if only in a private letter to an old friend. War stresses the limits of human endurance. When those limits are reached, it shows. War reveals the fragility of the mortal spirit—as well as how resilient humans can be, even in their darkest hour. The story of war often forgets these places, as if the warrior's world is akin to the quiet libraries, appointed offices, and comfy studies where historians write their histories. The truth is real war is a terrible and terrifying place. From the Pentagon to the front lines, people get tired and frustrated and err. On occasion, it is just human foibles bubbling to the top that account for some of the worst moments in military history.

History is catching up. Decades ago biographers such as Manchester, for example, tried to strip leaders like MacArthur of all human frailty. Today there is more recognition that unpacking the human dimension of war is crucial to truly knowing the ugly face of battle.

From the command post to the foxhole, humanity matters. Military organizations are designed in a vacuum with minimal key personnel and little redundancy, ignoring the fact that war goes on twenty-four hours a day in bone-chilling cold, driving rain, blinding snow, and airless swelter; that men still get flus, fevers, and colds. Yet, the notion of rotating

175

or resting commanders and staff was virtually unthinkable. It was not uncommon to find commanders and staffs as well as the men under their command on the edge of collapse after a harrowing tour of duty. Nowhere was that more true than in the major land campaigns of the Pacific War. They were a meat-grinder. As war in the jungle stretched into the autumn of 1942, both the Australians and Americans experienced the special suffering of fighting in the muck firsthand.

The Upside Down War

Brigadier Potts, whose 21st Brigade had arrived just in time to block the Japanese advance on Port Moresby, was in his own way a casualty of war. After withdrawing from Isurava, he decided to make a stand at Brigade Hill, a commanding position along a mountain ridge roughly halfway between Kokoda and Port Moresby. Though he was finally able to bring his 2/27th Battalion up in time for the fight, in a four-day battle starting September 6, the Australians were forced off the position.

A week later, Potts's forces tried to stop the enemy again at Ioribaiwa. The brigadier had less than half the Australians who had fought at Brigade Hill. Hard jungle fighting had taken its toll. The 2/14th and 2/16th had been reduced to a composite battalion.

Potts lost again. Despite the arrival of a fresh brigade from the 7th Division, the Australians were unable to hold their ground. They withdrew to Imita Ridge.

The two sides dug-in, facing one another, with the lights of Port Moresby at the Australians' backs. What next? The 7th Division steeled for the final defense of Port Moresby. In the town, service troops were warned that if the enemy came they'd have to battle for their lives.

Meanwhile, far away from the fighting, playing hide and seek with the enemy around Finschhafen, ANGAU officer Lloyd Purchase wrote his wife, "haven't heard whether the push over the Owen Stanley Range has been held up as I'm out of radio contact. Hope it is although I don't think Moresby can be worried unduly by such a threat."[2] He was right.

On October 2, the Japanese vanished. Australian patrols found the enemy trench lines on the Ioribaiwa Ridge deserted. When the 7th Division countermarched, they discovered a mostly empty, trampled trail littered with graves, excrement, and cast-aside enemy equipment. Advancing cautiously up the track, the Australians encountered the Japanese holding the ridge line over Eora Creek. It was a rear guard, a defense

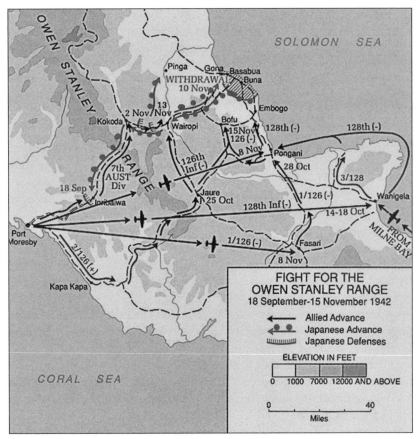

Engagement along the Kokoda Trail Campaign in New Guinea
Source: United States Army Center of Military History.

intended to allow time for the main body to withdraw back over the Owen Stanley Range to their foothold at Buna and Gona.

When the Aussies attacked, they got their first experience of how the enemy defended. The Japanese fortified and carefully camouflaged their positions. The diggers usually discovered enemy locations when the enemy opened fire on the cautiously advancing Australians. The Japanese also chose their ground well. That should not have come as a surprise. The South Seas Detachment was retreating over ground it knew well after months of jungle fighting. In contrast, many of the troops of the 7th Division were seeing this terrain for the first time. The defenders of the Kokoda trail would never forget the nightmares of an assault by masses of screaming enemy infantry or the constant fear of being outflanked in the dark. Those attacking up the trail learned another dangerous side of the Japanese—taking a prepared enemy defense was no easy task. It was a taste of things to come.

After a brisk fight, the enemy vanished again. The division probed farther down the trail.

Nothing. And then, the Aussies crested the highland plateau. The first troops walked back into Kokoda unopposed. The place was empty. The enemy was a ghost. Now there was no question, the Japanese were in full retreat. That meant the Australians had saved Port Moresby.

The Unsettled War

There was no sense of triumph on the Allied side. Having been shocked by the Japanese advance and a string of stinging defeats, the Australians remained anxious over what might be around the corner. One correspondent warned on October 2 (the day the Australians confirmed the enemy had abandoned their positions on Ioribaiwa Ridge) that "the threat of a Japanese invasion of Australia is now more real than it has ever been, and I think that within six months the people of Australia may know what the people of Russia feel like today."[3] Other press accounts offered more hopeful scenarios as the Australians picked their way up the meandering jungle trail past abandoned villages—a numbing patchwork of relentless marching, slipping, and climbing, punctuated by sharp fights with the Japanese rear guard.

Even when the Australians took the offensive, dispatches recounting the tales of the trail remained restrained and measured. "There is reason for optimism; but caution should not be discarded," reported the war correspondent for *The Telegraph*.[4] Other papers speculated that the Japanese maneuver might be some kind of ruse to draw the Allies into a trap. Much of the war reporting emphasized the difficulty of dealing with the weather and terrain, frustrating the prospects for a quick advance. News articles reflected the caution of the frontline troops advancing gingerly against a tenacious and dangerous enemy. The mood of the warlords reflected the conflicted reporting in the press. The successful defenses of Port Moresby and Milne Bay were virtually dismissed as cold comfort. As long as the main enemy force was present in Papua New Guinea the Japanese represented a grave threat.

At the same time, Japanese war reporting gave no clues to as to the enemy's intentions. Seizo Okada, who had been covering combat action with the 144th Regiment since the stirring fight at Isurava, was disgusted with the campaign and had long soured on the war. He recorded his thoughts in a personal memoir on the campaign, *Lost Troops* (1960). At the time, however, he couldn't put his frustrations in print. He could only overlook the searchlights at 7 Mile Drome on the outskirts of Port Moresby less than fifteen miles from the limit of the Japanese advance at Ioribaiwa Ridge and express his dismay at the immense sacrifice to get to that point—for nothing. He joined the regiment on the long torturous retreat back over the Owen Stanley Range.[5]

The Australians, however, were unaware of the enemy's desperate straits. An enemy still in Papua New Guinea in strength that had not been defeated by Australian troops in the field complicated Curtin's task of convincing Australians their nation was secure.

To MacArthur, the South Seas Force was an irritating obstacle frustrating his great offensive. Failing to annihilate the enemy during their attack over the Owen Stanley Range, MacArthur's men would now have to march back over the range and storm the defenses at Buna. That would cost him time, men, and resources—assets he would rather have used for his great counteroffensive.

Everyone found someone to blame. Curtin was frustrated that US troops were still on the sidelines. MacArthur doubted the fighting spirit of the Australians, as unimpressed by the AIF as the performance of the militia troops. General Blamey, the overall commander of land forces, was the man in the middle, pressed by both his prime minister and commander-in-chief to sort things out.

No War for Old Men

Blamey was fifty-eight years old when selected for command. Three years junior to MacArthur, the selection of both ran counter to the general belief that war was a young man's game.

In Australia, in March 1942, a triumvirate of younger Australian generals proposed that all general officers over fifty years of age be summarily retired. That move would have knocked out a dozen of the service's highest-ranking officers, all of them senior to the generals making the recommendation. The initiative, dubbed the "revolt of the generals," quickly faded when it was announced Blamey would be returning from the Middle East to assume the duties as commander-in-chief of Australian forces. Also, once the generals who made the proposal turned fifty, they lost interest in the idea.

A veteran of World War I, Blamey saw the horrors of the disastrous Gallipoli campaign firsthand. During World War II, he commanded the 2nd AIF in the Middle East, sparring as much with the British theater commanders as the enemy. In the autumn of 1942, he again stood with one foot in war and the other in the politics of high command, skirmishing with the warlords who were trying to run the war.

As the commander of SWPA's land forces, Blamey had to deal with the impatience of MacArthur and Curtin, on the one hand, and, on the other, with the frustration of his commanders for not standing up to the general and prime minister with their unrealistic expectations of what could humanly be accomplished on the ground with troops picking up the skills of jungle war as they went.

The pressure on Blamey continued to build. Regular AIF troops under combat-experienced leaders had been dispatched to the fight. MacArthur remained skeptical, even after the troops withstood the first Japanese assault at Milne Bay. He wrote Marshall, "I am not yet convinced of the efficiency of the Australian troops and do not attempt to forecast results."[6] Even after it was clear that Milne Bay was secure, MacArthur warned Marshall that "the enemys [*sic*] defeat . . . must not be accepted as a measure of relative fighting capacity of the troops involved."[7] MacArthur had convinced himself that the diggers could not match the Japanese in jungle fighting.

On September 15, at the height of the fighting at Ioribaiwa, Blamey delivered a national broadcast, declaring his confidence in Rowell, the corps commander directing the campaign on the ground, and the commanders under him, like Potts, as well as the fighting spirit of the Australian forces. "They have no qualms," Blamey declared, "about their ability to beat the Japanese."[8] If MacArthur could shape public opinion with his press operations, then Blamey hoped to do likewise with his authoritative voice as ground force commander.

The general's attempt to calm the public, however, had no impact on MacArthur, Curtin, or the Advisory War Council. Even after briefing the council on his personal inspection tour of the situation at Port Moresby, they were unmoved. All pushed Blamey to go back to the front, not just for a visit but to manage the campaign firsthand and shake things up.

Over the tempestuous weeks during the high-water mark of the Japanese advance and after, who can fairly unpack the many influences buffeting the senior commanders—from public pressure, to the demands

American GIs tend to wounded Aussie. (*Credit: Australian War Memorial, Reference 013953--2-*)

of their superiors, to personal slights and animosities—and justly judge performance in the field as well as assess how leaders were holding up to the rigors of leading men to their death. Out of this swirling maelstrom came a cascading series of decisions that would change who would lead the Allied fight for Papua New Guinea. The outcome and rationale for the decisions were debated hotly then—and the argument hasn't stopped to this day.

On September 28 Blamey and Rowell had a heated exchange. A few days later, Rowell was relieved. Blamey replaced Rowell with Lieutenant General Edmund Herring.

House cleaning didn't stop there. Rowell and General Allen, the 7th Division commander, had grilled Potts on his fighting withdrawal from Isurava and Brigade Hill, finding his conduct satisfactory. But, on October 22, Blamey visiting Potts's headquarters and had a row with him as well. Potts was relieved. Allen was relieved on October 29. A fresh team of Australian senior ground force commanders would carry the battle to the Japanese. And they would do so with the Americans by their side.

Ike's Trials

Leading the Aussie's American allies would be Robert L. Eichelberger. Eichelberger graduated from West Point in 1909, where he also picked up the nickname "Ike." He served in the Punitive Expeditionary Force into Mexico (1916–1917), his first experience with real combat. He saw more fighting with the American Expeditionary Forces in Siberia (1918–1920).

In both the Mexican and Russian operations, Eichelberger went out of his way to observe combat action and derided fellow officers who were content to remain at the command post. He later wrote,

> It became apparent that a very high percentage of officers were not suf-
> ficiently interested to make them leave their comfortable tents and card
> games. They passed up the chance to see troops in action when the risk
> was very small. . . . Most of these officers would advance into combat
> if properly led but I realize now that most of them would not have
> aroused the admiration and raised the morale of soldiers. There was a
> lot of timidity and a great deal of indifference and I have seen these
> qualities in later years on the long axis between Australia and Japan. [9]

Eichelberger believed the worst thing in the world was an officer who wouldn't share the privations, hardships, and dangers of the front.

When war came, Eichelberger was fifty-six years old (the same age as Blamey), an age when a soldier would normally be at the end of their career. Eichelberger proved to be a fanatical trainer and disciplinarian, good with soldiers, and in fine health and good physical condition for his age. In June 1942, six months after Pearl Harbor, Marshall appointed Ike as I Corps commander. Less than two months later while conducting troop training, Eichelberger received unexpected orders. His command was headed for Australia to reinforce MacArthur.

Eichelberger was not the first choice for command. After the outbreak of the war, Marshall sent Major Robert Charlwood Richardson Jr. to Australia to assess the situation. MacArthur offered Richardson, MacArthur's West Point classmate, the corps command. Richardson complained, however, about the plan to place the corps under the Australians. In the end, Marshall decided to send Eichelberger.[10]

On September 5, two US divisions were assigned to I Corps. For the counteroffensive MacArthur left the corps headquarters in Australia but ordered Eichelberger to select one division for the counteroffensive. Eichelberger sent the 32nd Infantry Division commanded by Major General Edwin F. Harding. Harding was Eichelberger's West Point classmate and friend. Harding's academy nicknames were "Frosty" and

"Venus." Harding's citation in his school yearbook is telling, written by a classmate extolling the virtues of "Mars" (a military career) over "Venus" (the promise of marriage and family), the passage invoked the image of a soldier consumed with visions of generalship, future wars, and selfless service—a good omen for a future warrior.

Allied intelligence reports concluded that the Japanese forces were few, poorly supplied, and demoralized. MacArthur's airman, General George C. Kenny, commander of the Allied Air Forces Southwest Pacific, had high hopes for Harding's success. On the eve of the Buna operation, Kenny wrote in his memoirs, "Harding was a nice guy. He was anxious to move and I believed with luck he would make good."[11] Everyone expected him to deliver.

There is little debate that the 32nd Division's preview in battle was a major disappointment. Early on November 19, 1942, after a month of offensive campaigning in New Guinea, elements of the division's 128th Infantry Regiment launched their first attack on the Japanese defenses in the Buna area. The assault failed. It was the first setback of many.

The US effort in the distant jungle gained global attention. It was difficult not to notice the United States was pouring fresh divisions into the fighting. FDR felt compelled to write Stalin, less the Soviet leader come to believe that the effort would detract from the US commitment to the cross-channel invasion. He wrote to Stalin, "I have a problem in persuading the people of Australia and New Zealand that the menace of Japan can be most effectively met by destroying the Nazis first. . . . [Y]ou, Churchill and I are in complete agreement on this." Stalin replied that he appreciated the need for the operations in Papua New Guinea to steady the theater and the Australian allies. It would, however, have been a great blow to US prestige if the GIs failed in the effort.[12]

On November 29, at 3 p.m., Eichelberger received a phone call from Brigadier General Stephen J. Chamberlin, the operations officer for General Headquarters, Southwest Pacific Area. MacArthur wanted Eichelberger in Papua New Guinea. Chamberlin called back at midnight; Eichelberger and his staff were to fly out at 7:30 a.m. That afternoon, Eichelberger conferred with MacArthur at his command post at Port Moresby and again over breakfast the following morning. From there Ike headed to the front and the real heart of darkness.

The general and his staff arrived at the 32nd Division command post on December 1 at 11 a.m. By December 5, Eichelberger found himself in a desperate battle to break through the Japanese defenses. In less than week he had gone from the soft life in Australia to the center of the maelstrom.

One early casualty in the campaign was the lingering animosity between the Australian and American commanders. Through 1944, the Australians under General Sir Thomas Blamey provided the majority of forces for the Papua New Guinea campaign and Lieutenant General Edmund F. Herring, commander of the Advance New Guinea Force, was technically Eichelberger's superior. In October, MacArthur declared in a public address, "No nation in the world is making a more supreme war effort than Australia. . . . It has unanimously and completely supported me in my military command, and the harmony and cooperation between Australians and Americans in this area are inspirational."[13] Privately, however, MacArthur was disappointed and suspicious. MacArthur believed the Australians failed to eject the Japanese from Papua New Guinea because they lacked sufficient determination. The Australians, in turn, had misgivings about the Americans. One US officer wrote, "I am damn disgusted with this whole mess and my close association with English and Australians during the past month doesn't make me like them any better—they would cut my throat."[14]

MacArthur directed Eichelberger to have nothing to do with the Australians and during the Buna campaign to take up issues directly with his staff, bypassing the Australian chain of command. The I Corps commander, however, worked well with Herring. Two days after Eichelberger arrived at Buna, he and Herring met for four and a half hours, conferring on the desperate situation at the front. After the war, the two generals remained on friendly terms. At the sharp end of war, Eichelberger came to believe, it really didn't matter much the color of your uniform. In retirement, Eichelberger was invited to visit Australia as a guest of the government. In turn, Herring and his wife visited the Eichelbergers in the United States.[15]

Eichelberger's relations with US commanders were far less sanguine. Although ordered to fire Harding, Ike hoped to improve the situation without relieving his West Point classmate. At the same time, Eichelberger fretted over his relationship with Major General Richard K. Sutherland, MacArthur's chief of staff. The two men intensely disliked each other. Eichelberger believed Sutherland was out for his job. If he didn't start firing people and showing progress, Eichelberger assumed that Sutherland, who had recommended Harding's relief, would come after him next.

Eichelberger was stunned when he appeared at the field headquarters. The I Corps commander found his old classmate tired, irritable, and unwilling to consider changes in the division leadership. At 9:30 a.m. on December 2, Eichelberger and Harding visited the front. The I Corps commander found the troops unshaven, sick, ragged, half-starved, and spiritless. Men cried at the thought of being ordered into battle. Eichelberger was dumbfounded and angered. After witnessing an unsuccessful attack on the front, he returned to the headquarters about 3 p.m. There is little question but that this tour of the battlefield proved decisive.[16]

Little more than twenty-four hours after reaching the front, Eichelberger dismissed almost all the division's senior leaders. Colonel John Mott, the division chief of staff (whom Eichelberger had nicknamed "Disaster Mott"), and the 128th Regiment's Colonel J. Tracy Hale Jr., who had served as the front commanders, were relieved as well.

Ike appointed the 32nd Division Artillery Commander, Brigadier General Albert W. Waldron, to command the division. The next day Eichelberger ordered the forces reorganized and an attack the following morning. The offensive was later postponed until December 5. This would be the first test of Eichelberger's combat leadership.

Weight of War

Eichelberger was no stranger to the human dimension of war and the frailty of men. Yet, there was no pressure cooker like this campaign. From the back-biting and second-guessing among the politicians and stars in Australia, to the heavy responsibilities of commanders at the front, to the trials of the skeletal men covered in mosquito welts and dripping with mud, war took its toll.

The signs of strain and the horrors of war were everywhere. Captain Hyman Samuelson and the first troops of the 96th Engineer Battalion (Colored) deployed to Port Moresby in April 1942. They ceaselessly worked on building up and maintain the airdromes. They prepared to defend the port during invasion scares like the Battle of the Coral Sea and the attack on Milne Bay. Still, in their months of toil they never came near the front. Though the troops might fret about being bombed or strafed by enemy planes, physical dangers never measured up to the perils at the front. And, even though they were far from the playground of Australia, there were still comforts behind the line. Samuelson recorded in his diary his disappointment because the officers' "party this evening was a fizzle. There was drinking, good food, and nurses; but every one seem tired." Yet, the shadow of war hung heavy. After months of deployment Samuelson wrote one officer "cracked up today. Wanted to kill himself and other people. He is being evacuated as insane. . . . Many enlisted men have also 'cracked' under the long strain."[17] War really could be hell.

If life at Port Moresby could be that trying, what the war at the front could do to any man—American, Australian, or Japanese—was the stuff of real nightmares. One soldier described Papua New Guinea as "an island of distress and sorrow. If there is a hell on earth it is New Guinea."[18]

A soldier in the 32nd Division recalled an officer who called his men "guinea pigs." They were anything but ready for the kind of fight they were thrown into. They lacked simple items like machetes to whack through the jungle, water purification tablets for the fetid ponds they drank from, and waterproof pouches to keep their salt tablets from melting away. They were issued fatigues, tie-dyed for jungle war, that bled out their colors with the first rain. In addition, as Brigadier Potts's brigade suffered at the Battle of Isurava, the troops at the front were limited by a logistical supply network that had to be built on the fly to support them. The Allies had to improvise and marshal every possible means from airlifts, portage, and sea-borne resupply to support them. A system that took many weeks to glue together.[19]

Things never got any better. Another US commander recalled after fighting for weeks on the stagnated front at Buna that "the prevailing wind in our faces continually carrying the stink of rotting bodies to us" produced as depressing and horrifying conditions as could be imagined.[20] Commanders didn't even have drugs to hand out to dull the stress and fatigue of battle.[21]

That the conditions of the Americans was desperate seems at odds with the image of the GIs as the army of plenty. The United States, however, was still building up its logistical backbone. At this point in the fighting they were not much better at covering the last miles to get supplies and support to the front than the Australians. Commanders had trouble communicating with forward troops, let alone meeting their needs. The Americans didn't have reliable logistical communications to the front until well into 1943.[22] Keeping the troops in the fight was as much a trial for the Americans at this point in the war as it had been for enemies and allies.

The Americans, like the Australian militia and the AIF troops before them, learned about jungle war the same way: by fighting in the jungle. And, they were learning how to survive the same way—by enduring. "Jungle toughness is only in part muscle toughness," wrote Osmar White, a journalist who had covered the fighting almost from the start. "Jungle toughness is primarily a condition of mind and of a bloodstream with antibodies in it."[23] The fighting sorted out who could cut it and who could not.

Sun Begins to Set

If Eichelberger thought his challenges were daunting, he could take comfort in the trials faced by his enemy. After the standoff at Ioribaiwa, on September 20, Horii dispatched a staff officer to personally brief the 17th Army Staff. This report would include the following, "The supply situation for the South Seas Force has already reached a crisis. The number of troops who are collapsing continues to rise. Allied pressure mounts daily with no improvement in sight." The detachment needed an immediate replenishment of supplies and reinforcements. To deliver the news, the officer walked back over the Owen Stanley Range, had to find transport to Rabaul, and report to headquarters. It would be seventeen days before he delivered his report—long after the future of the campaign was already determined.

On September 23, while Horii's men dug in after successfully wresting Imita Ridge from the Australians, General Hyakutake's staff was preparing a new order. The pressure of Allied attacks in the Solomons, a fruitless battle to regain Guadalcanal, the stagnated offensive over the Owen Stanley Range, and a failed assault on Milne Bay had left Hyakutake overstretched and underresourced. He had no immediate reinforcements for Horii. The army could do little to add to the air defenses against the incessant raids by Allied planes. Their supply lines were stretched beyond their limits. Their shipping was harassed. Intelligence indicated more enemy troops were on the way.

Seizing Port Moresby was no longer feasible. Leaving Horii's troops in place risked exposing his main force in Papua New Guinea to annihilation. What the command wanted to do was keep a foothold, retaining the option of advancing on Port Moresby later and holding down Allied troops who in turn would not be a threat elsewhere. Even more important was not to abandon the northern coast of Papua New Guinea to the Allies, ceding them a platform for threatening the strategic base at Rabaul.

Hyakutake ordered the commander of the South Seas Detachment to prepare to "assemble his main strength in the Isurava and Kokoda areas and secure these as a base for future operations. In addition, the defences in the Buna area will be strengthened." On September 30, Horii was ordered to begin his withdrawal.

Meanwhile, the 17th Army shifted its entire effort to the Solomons. Elements of the 38th Division, which arrived in Rabaul on October 6 and had been slated to reinforce Horii, were dispatched to the meatgrinder of Guadalcanal.

Horii experienced the full force of the dynamic called the culminating point, the point at which the attacker lost all his advantages. He had pushed his attack to the point that his vulnerabilities far outweighed his strengths. Not only was victory beyond his reach, he could not even hold the ground behind him.

Unlike the Allies, who were pushed backed toward a secure base of supply and reinforcements that actually made them stronger after retreat, Horii's men retreated on naked feet with open sores and empty stomachs back to a foothold that was still at the far end of a long, tenuous lifeline back to Rabaul. The physical and mental strain of war weighed as heavily on the Japanese as it did on the Allies.

The Japanese soldiers that retreated across the Owen Stanley Range were filthy, bearded, and sick—struggling through the jungle in tattered shreds clotted with mud and diarrhea. The uniforms of some had rotted away completely. They trudged the torturous muddy trails barefoot, clothed in the remnants of blankets and straw rice bags.

And they were starving. Horii had never been able to establish a dependable supply line to match the Allies. Having fought so hard to secure Kokoda, the Japanese could not hold it because they had never been able establish an air bridge and build up the station as a supply base. An occasional airdrop of rice or the intermittent trudging of supplies up the trail to the front was all that sustained the forward lines.

There is no question but that some Japanese troops also ate their enemy. "On the verge of starvation," write Collie and Marutani, "they dragged the bodies of Australians killed in recent skirmishes back to their dugouts. . . . They tore off the corpses clothing and cut strips of flesh from the thighs with knives or razor blades, then cooked it in their army-issue metal dixies."[24] The Allies also had reports of the enemy eating human flesh.[25] The Australian War Crimes section of the Tokyo tribunal also collected information and conducted interviews that document many cases of cannibalism practiced by Japanese forces in campaigns in the Asia Pacific.

There are no documented cases of cannibalism by the Australian or American troops on the Kokoda trail. But to write off Japanese cannibalism as a sign of the enemy's barbarity is wrong. While Allied troops could find themselves starving at the front, it was never to the point of famine and death faced by the Japanese soldiers during the campaign. Historian Karl James notes as the campaign progressed and the Japanese supply lines were hopelessly overextended, "more men succumbed to tropical diseases and exhaustion due to starvation and malnutrition."[26] Cannibalism, for the purposes of survival, is a documented action from the prehistoric to the modern world, found in many cultures including the West in experiences ranging from the Franklin Arctic expedition (1845) and the pioneers of the Donner Party in the American West (1846–1847) to the more recent case of a Uruguayan rugby team surviving an air crash in the Andes in 1972.[27] The fact that some Japanese soldiers practiced survival cannibalism suggests little in particular about the Japanese way of war, but it does reflect the desperate conditions that armies resort to when they venture far beyond their culminating point.[28] This is not to excuse criminal activity. Killing prisoners, let alone consuming their flesh, is clearly a war crime.

Japanese behavior in combat reflects some cultural elements but also the desperate material conditions they faced in the theater. The Japanese were not indifferent, for example, to casualties. Commanders recognized that prompt treatment of wounded might not only result in a soldier that could fight another day, but such practices improved morale.

During the fighting in China, the Japanese developed the concept of employing combat medics to treat battlefield wounds and shock.[29] Honorable medics were proficient and in high demand. Japanese medical doctrine was not radically different from Western medical practices. Nonambulatory patients were carried by stretcher to field-dressing (*hot-taijo*) and litter-clearing (*tanka kokanjo*) stations and from there sent to a field hospital. Invalids and amputees were evacuated to the homeland. In addition to battlefield treatment, the Japanese were particularly concerned about dysentery and gas gangrene, diseases that they frequently encountered. The problem for the Japanese Army was that under the strain of the campaign the medical system virtually collapsed. Basic sanitation practices were abandoned. If they were lucky, there were injections of morphine and camphor to help deal with the pain—until those supplies ran out.

Nothing illustrated the devastating impact of inadequate medical treatment more than the ravages of tropical diseases. The Japanese rate of infection far exceeded the Allies. Forty-five percent of the malaria patients died. Sixty percent of the dysentery patients died.[30]

The inability of Japanese medical support to keep up goes as well for the treatment of wounded and prisoners. The Japanese abandoned or shot their own injured if they lacked the capacity to care or transport them, reasoning both that the Allies would not take prisoners and surrendering was great dishonor. Indeed, few prisoners were taken on any side during the campaign. It was not uncommon for a soldier to be taken prisoner only because they were so ill they couldn't resist.[31]

In part, few Japanese prisoners were taken because they would rarely surrender. "When the plight of a unit became hopeless," an

American after-action report on the campaign summarized, "instructions would evidently be issued for the survivors to try to escape individually or in small groups."[32] Indeed, this practice is well documented from Japanese accounts.

The Japanese also felt the mental strain of battle and here cultural norms did affect how they dealt with the enormous stress of combat. The mountain guns that had proved such a vital advantage for the South Seas Detachment in their advance were a torturous burden on the retreat. Ordered to disable and bury the guns to keep them from falling into enemy hands, Lieutenant Yoshifumi Takagi complied with the order under protest—deeply humiliated at the thought of abandoning his guns, even for the purpose of freeing men to carry the wounded. After completing the detail, Takagi stood alone over the burial site—and blew his brains out. One soldier recalled, "I was so impressed by his officer spirit." As word of Takagi's suicide spread, his sacrifice lifted morale.[33] Both sides of the front at the Kokoda track lionized sacrifices—like Kingsbury, Templeton, and Owen for the Australians—Takagi for the Japanese. Mettle was a vital part of their war, part of the armor that protected them in the fear of battle and privations at the front. This cultural resilience did help sustain the Japanese in battle.

Horii knew, however, that spirit alone could not win battles. As best it could, the South Seas Force conducted a fighting withdrawal. Behind them, Japanese engineers and native laborers were constructing a mini–Maginot Line, a series of interlocking fortifications dug into the swampy lowlands that protected the Japanese beachhead. They were fortified with whatever could be found—palm trees, empty barrels filled with dirt, sometimes even poured concrete. When Horii's exhausted troops fell back they would find a modicum of wheat and rice to eat, but more importantly, defenses to defend. Horii, however, would not be with them. During the retreat, it was reported he drowned crossing a raging river, allegedly crying out "*Tenno Heika bonsai*," with his last breath.

In retreat, the South Seas Force matched the earlier Australian withdrawal over the Owen Stanley Range. They gave ground without ever being decisively defeated. But while the Australians had fallen back on bountiful supplies and reinforcements, the Japanese had a coral strewn reef and the ocean at their back, tacked to a very long flimsy lifeline. In November they were struggling to maintain their foothold with defenses centered around the villages of Buna and Gona, holding out against two Allied divisions.

By the time Eichelberger arrived at the front to fight, the Japanese chain of command had been completely revamped. The span of control of the 4th Fleet was reduced and in October 1942, Vice Admiral Inoue returned to Japan. The area of Papua New Guinea came under the 8th Fleet commanded by Vice Admiral Gunichi Mikawa. In December 1942, the fleet was under the authority of the Southeast Area fleet.

On the army side, the Japanese 8th Area Army under General Hitoshi Imamura assumed overall command of both Papua New Guinea and the Solomon Islands. The Japanese 18th Army under Lieutenant General Hatazō Adachi took over responsibilities for operations on mainland Papua New Guinea. Major General Kensaku Oda succeeded Horii in command of the South Seas Force. Major General Tsuyuo Yamagata commanded the troops in the area of Buna and Gora.

Battle for Buna

With their backs to the sea, the Japanese held two impregnable defensive positions on the swampy lowland along a narrow strip of the northeastern coast for weeks on end. The westernmost location included Buna Mission, the prewar government station, and Buna village, a half mile northwest of the station. Harding called this position the Urbana Front, named for Eichelberger's birthplace. Little more than a mile away to the east was Warren Front (after Harding's hometown), including the Duropa Plantation at Cape Endaiadere.[34]

Covering both positions were interlocking rings of fortified coconut log bunkers, fire trenches, and breastworks that blended perfectly into the surrounding jungle, swampy waterlogged lowlands of closely packed trees, tangles of roots, creepers, and underbrush. Meanwhile, the sea approaches were screened by treacherous coral reefs that stretch out twenty-five miles from land. The entire battlefield covered little more than sixteen square miles, a small but deadly jungle citadel.

Every assault took its toll up and down the US ranks. Three American generals fell in the fighting, including Brigadier General Hanford MacNider (one of the leaders of the America First movement who had volunteered to return to active service after the attack on Pearl Harbor). He was felled by a Japanese grenade.

The bloody standoff continued until the first week of December when the United States launched its most momentous attack of the campaign. For December 5, the assault on the Urbana Front was assigned to elements of the 2nd Battalion, 126th Infantry Regiment. For a period the regiment had been assigned to the 7th Australian Division. Though the battalion had been returned, the Australians retained the regimental commander and staff. Regiments were designed to operate as an integrated combined arms team, with the regimental headquarters coordinating the employment of the infantry battalions with mortars, artillery, and heavy machine guns. For the battle on the Urbana Front, the attack would be directed by a makeshift command.

Along with the 2nd Battalion, troops for the attack also included the Cannon Company, 128th Infantry Regiment. Among the many limitations of this force was that the Cannon Company had no cannons. After World War I, the infantry complained that they lacked accurate, responsive, close supporting fire. The army's solution was to add a cannon company to each regiment composed of four towed 105mm howitzers, crewed by infantrymen. For the Papua New Guinea campaign, however, the division left its guns in Australia. With limited visibility in the jungle and difficulty in accurately locating positions, the high command did not believe the employment of artillery was practical. In addition, moving the guns and artillery ammunition would have placed a great strain on the theater's limited transportation assets. If the infantry needed heavy fire support, it could be provided by aerial bombing. Supporting fires for infantry assaults would come from 37mm guns, mortars, and two small Australian pack howitzers. These were lighter and more manageable than standard artillery pieces. As for the Cannon Company, they fought as infantrymen.

The plan was simple. The assault would take place between the banks of the Girua River and Entrance Creek, which bounded the approach to Buna Village. Preceded by air attacks and mortar fire, the Cannon Company would attack in the west and the 2nd Battalion in the east with F Company, 2nd Battalion in reserve. The mission was to drive through the Japanese defenses and take the village. Army doctrine discouraged frontal assaults stating, "No decisive results can be expected from this plan of attack. The enemy's full strength is encountered simultaneously."[35] Yet, despite textbook admonitions, the terrain and disposition of the enemy forces seemed to offer no alternative. Before his relief, Mott had directed several reconnaissance patrols into the area and could find no open flank.

Colonel John E. Grosse, Eichelberger's inspector general, who had been in command of the Urbana Front for less than day, spent the early morning hours ensuring that the units were positioned to jump off. Satisfied, he returned to the command post to find Eichelberger, Waldron, and a covey of staff officers. After being briefed on the plan of attack, Eichelberger and Waldron headed forward to witness the assault.

At 10 a.m. nine B-25 bombers hit the target area followed by thirty minutes of mortar and gunfire. The acrid smoke of the gunfire clung to

Evacuating Australian wounded as Americans move up. *(Credit: Australian War Memorial, Reference 013849--2-)*

the thick foliage covering the enemy lines with bitter-smelling fog. In line, the Cannon Company, and E and G companies attacked into the wispy haze. H Company provided supporting fires with rifles and machine guns. The Cannon Company entered a large, open space south of the village and came under heavy fire in the tall grass. Though dry and slightly higher ground, the approach was well covered by fire that sliced across the open space. The advance made no progress.

Moving through the jungle, E Company came within fifty yards of the village but could not penetrate the Japanese main defensive line. It was not the first time the company failed to finish the job. During an attack against the village on December 1, E Company had abruptly withdrawn from the assault. A number of the men were found to be "considerably affected . . . crying and begging to go to the rear, and many were noticeably distressed." The attack on December 5 showed little better results. Waldron found the men "hugging the ground; you couldn't have put a finger between them and the ground."

G Company advance showed no more success. Troops would struggle forward noisily, slipping and straining through steaming mud, muck, and tangles of slippery vines, roots, and bushes, hugging the foliage for a shred of concealment. Exhausted, parched, feverish, ragged, loaded down with weapons and ammunition, small groups struggled forward. Every movement attracted waves of enemy fire, spits of shot leaping out of the jungle, each caliber with its own characteristic whine punctuated by ripping leaves and bark. Unable to see more than a few yards ahead, often leaderless and uncoordinated, surrounded by dead and wounded, the physical and mental will to drive on quickly evaporated. Casualties increased.

The young newlywed Arthur Kessenich was a member of G Company, but he was assigned to the supply section that had been left at Port Moresby. The days of lazy afternoon regimental baseball games and endless turns on the parade field were far behind his comrades. He was told the front was a "living hell on earth." When only 13 of the company's 180-man complement returned, he knew it was true. Many of these men fell in the December 5 battle.[36]

It was not difficult to sense that the Urbana Front's attack had spent its force. Eichelberger called Grosse forward from the command post. He wanted the reserve company, an additional eighty men, to move through E and G companies and continue the attack. Grosse disagreed; reserves were to reinforce success and they had yet to achieve even the promise of a breakthrough. He hoped to allow the battle to develop for a day or two so that it might open a weak spot on the flank of the position. Waldron wanted to continue the push toward the village. Eichelberger believed that the most promising course was to pressure the flank of the village between that position and the mission. The acting F Company commander, a lieutenant and one of only two officers left in the company, who had only taken over a few days earlier, was summoned to Eichelberger's observation post, briefed, and a short time later thrown into the line with orders to drive to the sea.

Eichelberger and Waldron each accompanied a platoon. Waldron "tried to show them that I didn't give a damn." He was hit in the shoulder by a bullet and knocked off his feet by an explosion. In minutes more than half the company was dead or wounded in foul pools of a blood red swamp. With Waldron down, for the remainder of the battle Eichelberger would serve both as the corps and division commander, and at times it seemed he acted like a company commander or even a squad leader. He was in the thick of the mud, blood, and sweat of war. In 1931, long before the war, when Winston Churchill wrote about future war he mused that generals most likely would be found "at their desks in their offices fifty or sixty miles from the front, anxiously listening to the trickle of the telephone for all the world as if they were speculators with large holdings when the market is disturbed."[37] Churchill never envisioned a combat general like Ike.

While Eichelberger pressed one small group of soldiers forward, Staff Sergeant Herman J. F. Bottcher, attached to G Company, was ordered to advance his platoon. Before he fell wounded, Waldron had watched the sergeant methodically prepare for the advance. Bottcher set up a machine gun position to clear the trees of snipers. Meanwhile, he called for demolition material to be brought up to blow the enemy breastworks that guarded the Japanese flank. An enemy round landed in the midst of the four men carrying the charges, killing two instantly. Bottcher was undeterred, deciding to root out the positions using his infantry alone. He led the remnants of the platoon forward, pausing to spot, outflank, and clear each enemy bunker that blocked his path.

Every time Bottcher's men wiped out an entrenched position they broke a link in the chain, opening up more and more room for the small group to advance without coming directly under the withering fire of the Japanese defenses. By the afternoon, Bottcher—with only about a dozen men left—drove all the way to the beach and dug in, splitting the Japanese position in two. Despite enemy counterattacks from the mission and the village, the position held. Buna village was locked in a stranglehold. The Japanese positions were isolated and could not reinforce one another. Though weeks of fighting remained, it was the beginning of the end of the battle for Buna.

Eichelberger, men like Bottcher, and a ragged band of Americans and Aussies won the day. MacArthur took the victory. On February 12, 1943, Churchill sent a note to the general and Prime Minister Curtin. "Sending you my most cordial congratulations upon the capture of Buna by American and Australian forces. . . . I should like to let you know how grateful we all feel throughout the British Empire that you stand guard over all these vital interests."[38] Defeat is an orphan. Victory has many fathers. MacArthur had his glory. Curtin had safeguarded his nation. Churchill clung to his empire. The reward for Eichelberger and his men would be more war.

Measure of Men

The successes and failures at Buna say a great deal about the capacity of the American spirit to prevail in war. Paramount to understanding the limitations of the 32nd Division is noting the physical obstacles that confronted the troops. There are perhaps a handful of places on earth so alien and inhospitable that the means and methods of modern war are totally unsuited. Papua New Guinea was one of them. Jungle sickness and disease alone almost wiped out the entire division. Dysentery and malaria were the most significant—not just because they were the most prevalent but because they could easily debilitate the most fit soldier. During the 1942 campaign, US troops in Papua New Guinea had about 1,598 combat fatalities. In contrast, records show over 6,000 malaria cases.[39]

When division veteran Clarence Jungwirth and his unit reached Buna in late December he was appalled by the conditions of the troops, barely recognizing men he lived and trained with for two years.[40] There were about 14,500 troops in the theater (most from the 32nd Division) and over 8,600 cases of malaria. It was not uncommon for every man in a company to go into battle feverish and dehydrated.

Even though both sides endured the same conditions, impossible terrain, insufferable heat, and debilitating disease, the jungle was not neutral. At the sharp edge of battle, an impenetrable jungle favors the defender. The attacker must haul his weapons, ammunition, food, and water to the front. The defender waits. The attacker blunders into battle. The defender picks where and when to employ his weapons to best effect. Where both sides are struggling on the edge of starvation and the limits of human endurance, such advantages, even if slight, are overwhelming.

Perhaps the greatest issue was underestimating the Japanese, not only in terms of the numbers and preparedness of the enemy defenses, but also in regard to the tenacity and skill of the individual soldier. The *Official Handbook of Japanese Military Forces* was no help whatsoever, based on a study of fighting methods designed for conventional conflict against Chinese or Russian forces on the Asian mainland. There was no discussion of the night attacks, snipers, or formidable field fortifications that compensated for the many inadequacies of the Japanese army and made their island defense so fearsome.[41] Even veterans of the theater before the war, including Eichelberger who had observed the enemy in China and their homeland of Japan, learned very little that would have prepared them for this kind of war.

There is little argument but that both sides conceptualized the war in terms of a fierce battle between their different worlds.[42] But separating cultural norms from the brutalizing conditions at the front is problematic. For sure, much propaganda and rhetoric was expended denigrating the humanity of the opposing sides. Nor is it difficult to find remembrances of brutality. "One of my first desires," Eichelberger remembered, "was to get Japanese prisoners. During the Buna fighting, an officer was captured but before I could interview him, he was killed by a fat slob of a cook who killed with a pistol butt in the rear areas." Eichelberger found one enemy soldier in the hospital already "out of it." Like many of the division veterans, when he saw the enemy up close it was difficult to imagine that these small, emaciated men could be such formidable foes.[43] The enemy, however, was not faceless. Combat was more than just fighting stereotypes.

The Americans did manage to capture a handful of Japanese soldiers. Below Buna Force Headquarters, each regimental headquarters had one Nisei, Japanese American soldiers who served as linguists and interpreters. These troops were far less storied than the Japanese American regiment that served in the Italian theater. One of the most decorated units in the US Army, the 442nd Regimental Combat Team even got its own movie, the 1951 feature *Go for Broke*. In contrast, the Nisei linguists were unheralded but in many ways more valuable than an infantryman. They were never allowed forward of regimental command posts, for had they been captured they undoubtedly would have been tortured and killed. Further, there was always the possibility they would be shot by their own troops. During the Buna campaign, a great deal of information was gained from captured documents and diaries, as well as the odd POW interview.[44]

Some of the observations from this intelligence are published in the official Buna after-action report. They record the frustrations and privations the enemy experienced as well as their determination and resilience. The Japanese were anything but a caricature.

In battle, the Americans respected and feared the fighting qualities of the Japanese soldier and with good reason; many of the enemy troops were combat veterans and experienced jungle fighters. A survey of division veterans from the campaign uniformly acknowledged the abilities of the enemy as individuals. Eichelberger concluded, "My own feeling now looking back is that the Japanese simple soldier was one of history's greatest. . . . We profited many times by the Japanese mistakes but never through their cowardice."[45] These troops were more than a match for the rookie 32nd Division.

Entering late in the war put the United States at a great disadvantage. Its leaders, doctrine, training, and weapons were untested. While the Americans learned the practice of war on the job, what often kept them in the fight was a wealth of material support available to the force including supplies, medical care, and transport. In Papua New Guinea, many of these advantages were denied.

Particularly critical was the lack of fire support, which could have been used to help destroy the enemy bunker system. There were operational reasons why more support was not provided. The coral reefs prevented ships within range to provide naval gun support. Lack of transport assets limited what could be shipped into theater. In addition, however, MacArthur clung to a belief that airpower could provide an adequate substitute. The command's dispatches made it appear as if airpower was playing a significant role in supporting the ground forces.[46] In reality, the services were totally unpracticed at coordinating ground and air forces and in precisely locating, targeting, and actually hitting small, hidden targets in the jungle. The B-25 strike on the morning of December 5 attack is a case in point. If the bombs had actually struck the Japanese defenses they would have virtually wiped out the enemy in a single stroke, but in fact, given the primitive nature of US air-ground operations they were an absolute waste of effort. Waldron recalled:

> One of the troubles on the Urbana Front on that day [December 5] was the fact that the front lines were so mixed that it was dangerous to do very much bombing. We couldn't fix a definite bombing line and do much effective bombing in front of it. Earlier in the campaign, a whole platoon had been practically wiped out because bombing had [fallen] too short, and we did not want to repeat a mistake like that.[47]

Eichelberger witnessed an air attack on Buna that resulted in ten friendly casualties. He wrote to Sutherland, "Tell George [Kenny] to give us an even break and not treat us worse than he does the Japs."[48] The bombing had much to say about the value of airpower in the jungle wars. Heavy bombers and close support aircraft had marginal utility in jungle battles.

That would be hard to know, listening to Kenny or MacArthur or Curtin for that matter. On January 19, 1943, Curtin penned a long report to FDR and Churchill on what they had learned in the Papua New Guinea campaign. "The outstanding military lesson of this operation," Curtin quoted MacArthur, "was the continuous calculated application of air power . . . employed in the most intimate tactical and logistical union with ground troops."[49] Curtin went on to ask for 2,000 additional aircraft for the Southwest Pacific.

There was no question that the warlords wanted more planes. There was no question to the value of land-based air power in extending the sustainable footprint that the Allies could control.[50] Every airbase created the potential of another 500-mile radius of air and ground that SWPA could establish air supremacy over. But arguing that the planes tipped the balance in ground combat—well, that was just a made-up excuse to argue for more airplanes.

The mortars and light howitzers available to the troops proved equally useless at striking fortified positions. Nor were the troops skilled at employing them. The normal practice was to begin with a barrage of mortar fire on suspected positions followed by an infantry assault. The explosions did little damage and alerted the Japanese of an impending assault.

The decision not to make a major effort to get heavier artillery to the front had been a serious error. When Brigadier General James F. Collins, the I Corps Artillery commander, arrived in Australia he found that the high command had ordered artillery and mortar men trained as infantry since it didn't think such weapons would be needed for jungle warfare. On its own initiative the I Corps artillery staff disassembled and shipped a 105mm howitzer to the front. This piece proved very effective at bunker busting and discredited the belief that artillery could not be manhandled and supported in jungle terrain or that targets couldn't be accurately located and struck with indirect fire. The lack of proper fire support was another shortfall that could be marked up to inexperience. Even Eichelberger admitted that if they had brought up more guns and moved more deliberately that Buna could have been taken at less cost.[51]

Inadequate fire support as well as poor armor and air support were serious defects. In the Normandy campaign, for example, armor, artillery, and close air support, as well as mountains of logistical and medical support, kept the US army in the fight while it learned from its mistakes and soldiers gained the skills and knowledge required to succeed in battle. The men fighting the jungle war had none of these advantages.

It is difficult to criticize the performance of National Guard divisions such as the 32nd Division. The divisions were in active federal service for two years before they went into battle. The division was reorganized, prepared for war in Europe, and sent to the Pacific. Key leadership was changed. Troops were unprepared for jungle warfare. In the rush to get men into the battle it is remarkable that commanders expected anything more than a mediocre first effort. In the end, the US learning curve on jungle warfare proved not much different from the Australians.

It is part of the mythology of war that national character and experience count for much. Few expect the average citizen to pick up a palette and paint with grace and authority, lacking years of lessons and practice. Yet, so many accept as a matter of faith that the resilience and

Eichelberger (*center*) and Blamey (*left*) at captured Buna Mission. *(Credit: Australian War Memorial, Reference 014101-1- [1])*

strength of spirit will persevere in battle. The achievement of Sergeant Bottcher was a case in point.

Bottcher was not a typical soldier or an average American by any measure. When he got excited his guttural German accent made him barely intelligible. He had fought in the Spanish Civil War under the Abraham Lincoln Brigade. Decorated for bravery and promoted on the battlefield to the rank of captain, Bottcher had a thorough education in the misery and the skills of battle. Though his US citizenship was revoked, he was allowed to enlist in the US Army with about six hundred other veterans of the Republican cause. On Papua New Guinea whether Bottcher was a fellow traveler of the Comintern was of less concern than his fighting qualities. Devoid of officers, Bottcher was selected to lead the platoon because he was a natural leader, one of the few who were physically and mentally prepared for the rigors of war. On December 5, he demonstrated the acme of mettle, the wherewithal to take out a prepared defensive position with nothing more than a handful of infantrymen. In 1942, he was an exception.[52]

Harding, in fact, summed up the issue well when he wrote MacArthur requesting reconsideration of his relief.

> There has been criticism of the conduct of the troops in battle. Certainly they did not fight as skillfully as they must learn to fight. There was poor leadership as well as good. A few officers had to be relieved of command of their units and assigned to jobs behind the lines. Some men broke under the strain, others succumbed to exhaustion. The process of separating the men from the boys in the ordeal by battle worked as it always does.[53]

Eichelberger, in fact, agreed with this assessment. As the campaign waned he wrote MacArthur, "I now have more time for reflection and I realize that our men whom I found in the Buna area were half-starved. . . . A few weeks of that diet coupled with fever and the Japanese could have finished them off with clubs." In contrast, he noted the corps' other division would be coming into combat not only better prepared for such harsh conditions but trained and tested for months in the skills of jungle fighting, scouting, patrolling, individual and squad combat—all the preparations that the 32nd Division had lacked.[54]

During the campaign, Eichelberger observed a squad assault a Japanese bunker, but when greeted by a curtain of withering fire, they quickly withdrew. A short time later, he found the same Americans laughing, relaxing, and smoking. They were men full of spirit; all they needed was the training and support to do the job. Their failures were physical not moral, social, or cultural. At Buna and in subsequent fighting, soldiers and marines learned the skills that allowed them to persevere, and earn the distinction of being men of mettle. Surviving the battlefields of the Pacific was an affirmation of the US soldier. Not to say the Japanese and Australians didn't fight well. They did. Maybe the Americans were not better, but they were every damn bit as good.

Notes

1. Letter to Major General King, September 16, 1942, *Papers of George C. Marshall*, vol. 3, p. 359.
2. Letter "Dear Cele," dated 16 Sept [1942], MS 3752 Papers of Lloyd Purchase.
3. "Sidelights from Sydney," *Cessnock Eagle and South Maitland Recorder*, October, 2, 1942, National Library of Australia p. 2.
4. "Japs Retreating in Haste," *The Telegraph*, October 2, 1942, National Library of Australia p. 2.
5. See also AWM54 492/4/62, "Lost Troops."
6. From: CINC SWPA To: Chief of Staff, No. 382, August 30, 1942, National Security Archive Project, George C. Marshall Museum.
7. From: CINC SWPA To: Chief of Staff, No. C 436, September 6, 1942, National Security Archive Project, George C. Marshall Museum.
8. "Tough Men, Tough Task," *The Argus*, September 16, 1942, National Library of Australia, p. 2.
9. Eichelberger Papers, box 2, p. III-21. See also pp. II-25–II-26, III-51, III-53.
10. See correspondence: War Department, signed Richardson, July 8, 1942, National Security Archive Project, George C. Marshall Museum; Memorandum for the Chief of Staff, subject: Organization of the Corps in Australia, July 22, 1942, National Security Archive Project, George C. Marshall Museum; Memorandum for the Chief of Staff, subject: Command of the American Ground Troops in Australia, July 28, 1942, National Security Archive Project, George C. Marshall Museum; Memorandum for the War Department Classified Message Center, subject: Corps Commander for Australia, August 2, 1942, National Security Archive Project, George C. Marshall Museum; Memorandum for the Chief of Staff, subject: Command of the American Ground Troops in Australia, August 3, 1942, National Security Archive Project, George C. Marshall Museum.
11. Kenney, *General Kenney Reports*, pp. 122–123.
12. "Roosevelt to Stalin, sent 19 November 1942, received 21 November 1942," in Reynolds and Pechatnov, *The Kremlin Letters*, p. 177.
13. *Army and Navy Journal*, Oct 31, 1942, p. 242.
14. Letter to Chamberlin, 30 September 1942, Stephen J. Chamberlin Papers.
15. Dictation II, Eichelberger Papers, box 2, pp. 37, 54.
16. Harding's Diary, box 279, RG 319, National Archives and Records Administration p. 12–14; Colonel Mott's Statement, 10 December 1942, box 280, RG 319, National Archives and Records Administration, p. 8.
17. Samuelson, *Love, War and the 96th Engineers (Colored)*, pp. 138–139.
18. Toler, *Disillusionment at Age 21*, p. 181.
19. See Desrosiers, "Operational Logistics in a Maritime Theater of Operations."
20. Stoelb, *Time in Hell*, p. 35.

21. Over the course of the war, the US military, following British practices, issued stimulants to deal with stress and fatigue. The use of amphetamines in this theater, however, was not widespread before 1943. See Rasmussen, "Medical Science and the Military," p. 226.

22. Thompson and Harris, *The Signal Corps*, pp. 247–254.

23. White, *Green Armour*, p. 145.

24. Collie and Marutani, *The Path of Infinite Sorrow*, p. 164.

25. See, for example, AWM52, 8/2/25 25th Brigade War Diary, September–October 1942, entry October 15, 1942.

26. Karl James, "On Australia's Doorstep, Kokoda and Milne Bay," in Dean, *Australia 1942*, p. 212.

27. Rautman and Fenton, "A Case of Historic Cannibalism in the American West," pp. 321–341.

28. See Tanaka, *Hidden Horrors*, pp. 126–127; Rees, *Horror in the East*, pp. 93–97.

29. See Pennington, *Casualties of History*, pp. 65–75. See also Collie and Marutani, *The Path of Infinite Sorrow*, pp. 146–147, 194.

30. Joy, "Malaria in American Troops in the South Southwest Pacific," p. 196.

31. In Pike, *Hirohito's War*, p. 408, the author wrote, "Remarkably in the New Guinea Campaign not a single Australian soldier survived capture by the Japanese." However, according to Damien Fenton at the Australian War Memorial, at least one survived capture in New Guinea after 1942. Further, of the Australians who were captured on New Britain in 1941, in June 1942 the 1,054 survivors (178 noncommissioned officers, 667 soldiers, and 209 civilians)—according to the National Archives of Australia and documents received from the Japanese government in 2012—left Rabaul on a freighter requisitioned by the Japanese Navy, the *Montevideo Maru*. On July 1, the vessel (not marked as carrying prisoners of war) was sunk by the USS *Sturgeon*. All died. Aldrich, *The Faraway War*, features accounts by Australian and American soldiers claiming that Japanese prisoners were also killed. An estimated 350 Japanese prisoners were taken by the Australians and Americans over the course of the campaign. Accounts of Japanese cannibalism of prisoners are given in Rees, *Horror in the East*.

32. "Report of the Commanding General Buna Forces of the Buna Campaign," p. 66.

33. Quoted in Collie and Marutani, *The Path of Infinite Sorrow*, p. 185.

34. Unless noted otherwise, information and quotes on the Battle of Buna are from Colonel Mott's Statement, 10 December 1942, box 280, RG 319, National Archives and Records Administration, pp. 2–3, 6; interview with Major General A. W. Waldron, March 1944, OCMH Waldron, 11 Files, US Army Heritage and Education Center, pp. 1–2; Milner, *Victory in Papua*, pp. 234–251.

35. Cockrell, "Brown Shoes and Mortar Boards," pp. 216–217.

36. Kessenich, "This Is Your Life."

37. Arnn, *Churchill's Trial*, p. 44

38. Gilbert and Arnn, *The Churchill Documents*, vol. 18, p. 417.

39. Joy, "Malaria in American Troops in the South Southwest Pacific," p. 197.

40. Information on Clarence Jungwirth from Jungwirth, "Diary of a National Guardsman in World War II."

41. *Handbook on Japanese Forces*. This manual superseded TM 30-480, September 21, 1942, which provided similar information.

42. See also Rose, *Myth and the Greatest Generation*, pp. 24–26.

43 Letter to Sutherland, December 11, 1942, box 280, RG 319, National Archives and Records Group.

44. Linguist operations are described in James McNaughton, "Training Linguists for the Pacific War, 1941–1942," and James McNaughton, "Nisei Linguists and the New Perspectives on the Pacific War: Intelligence, Race, and Continuity," in Bellafaire, *The U.S. Army in World War II*, pp. 129–146; 371–382.

45. Eichelberger Papers, box 2, p. IV-12.

46. *Army and Navy Journal*, November 28, 1942, p. 374; *Army and Navy Journal*, December 12, 1942, p. 429.

47. Interview with Major General A. W. Waldron, 1944, OCMH Waldron, 11 Files, p. 3.

48. Letter, Eichelberger to Sutherland, box, 280, RG 319, National Archives and Records Administration.

49. Letter, Dear Mr. President/Dear Mr. Churchill, January 19, 1943, in Gilbert and Arnn, *The Churchill Documents*, vol. 18, p. 159.

50. The value of air operation in the theater are analyzed in Joe Gray Taylor, "Air Superiority in the Southwest Pacific," in Cooling, *Case Studies in the Achievement of Air Superiority*, pp. 383–453; Null, "Weapon of Denial, Air Power and the Battle for New Guinea," pp. 1–32.

51. Interview with Major General A. W. Waldron, March 1944, OCMH Waldron, 11 Files, p. 2; Stephen J. Chamberlin Papers, pp. 17–18; Eichelberger Interview November 21, 1942, Eichelberger Papers. See also Headquarters, Army Ground Forces, Subject: Extracts from the Buna Campaign Report, July 15, 1943, Reel 302, #4585, National Security Archive Project, George C. Marshall Museum.

52. Landis, *The Abraham Lincoln Brigade*, p. xix.

53. Appendix, letter to MacArthur, December 7, 1942, box, 280, RG 319, National Archives and Records Administration.

54. Letter, Eichelberger to MacArthur, January 12, 1943, Eichelberger Papers, box 2.

10

An Unfair Fight

SANANANDA, JANUARY 12, 1943. *"No, just go without me. I am tired. Besides, it feels good lying on the warm grass like this, so I don't mind dying here."*[1]

A JAPANESE LIEUTENANT'S last recorded words, whispered in shallow breaths as he lay, sword resting across his chest, could serve as a metaphor for the Imperial Japanese Army's war effort. It was six months after the first troops of the South Seas Force had touched the gentle sands at Buna. Now, the footholds at Buna and Gona and the logistical base at Giruwa had been lost. Food resupply became more sporadic. Then there were no supplies at all. What was left of the 11,000 men securing the Buna beachhead area and about 4,000 at Giruwa—riddled with malaria, stricken with dripping chronic diarrhea, and starving to near madness—withdrew from Japan's strategic foothold in Papua New Guinea. They were evacuated in barges or moved by forced march through the jungle, escaping to Salamaua and Lae (which the Japanese had held since the first months of the war).

Staff Sergeant Sadashige Imanishi—who after surviving the grueling campaign charging over the Owen Stanley Range, then backtracking in the humiliating retreat, and finally enduring the futile last-ditch defense of Buna, Gona, and Giruwa—missed the barge evacuations. He had to walk out. Imanishi stumbled through the jungle for miles to get safely beyond the advancing Allied lines. On the retreat, he became so sick, hungry, and desperate that Imanishi admitted to digging up bodies for food. Otherwise, he knew he would die.

Lieutenant Colonel Tsukamoto, who had first led the assault over the Owen Stanley Range to Kokoda, had 240 exhausted, sick, and wounded men left with little ammunition and no food. He decided to retreat. It took over a week to walk to Giruwa where he found the situation equally desperate. He and his men resumed their grueling march to escape the Allies.

Colonel Yokoyama, who had led the advance force at Buna, reverted to his duties as the head of engineers. His main duties were evacuating causalities. One night he commandeered two barges and loaded them with the worst of the sick, feverish men. Later he learned the barges had been designated for the evacuation of the general and his staff. Thanklessly, Yokoyama was threatened with courts-martial for his initiative.

Seizo Okada, the war journalist who hated the war and had covered the campaign since the heady days of the advance at Kokodan, escaped after the defeat at Buna on a transport ship. That ship was sunk by enemy planes. Rescued by another ship, he made it back to Rabaul where he attended a press briefing that included Colonel Tsuji, the Imperial staff officer who had pressed for the campaign to begin with. When Tsuji was asked about the operation, Okada recalled the colonel stood up, spat out "a blunder," and left.

For the Imperial Japanese Army, the loss of the beachhead on the northeast coast of Papua New Guinea was not the only disaster. In November, the army had shifted 7,000 troops from the 38th Infantry Division that were to reinforce Horii's South Seas Force in Papua New Guinea in a desperate effort to wrest back Guadalcanal. There the Imperial troops fared little better. Despite the reinforcements and a furious naval and air campaign, the Japanese not only failed to drive the US Marines into the sea, the Americans reinforced their defenses with army divisions and launched a strong counteroffensive. By December, the high command seriously began considering withdrawing from the island. While the remnants of desperate Japanese troops were fleeing in Papua New Guinea, plans for the evacuation at Guadalcanal were well under way. During the first week of February, the last Japanese troops sailed away.

The twin Allied victories at Papua New Guinea and the Solomon Islands left no cause for optimism. The enemy had punched holes in the defensive ring of the Japanese Empire that couldn't be sealed. Whenever, if ever, the Allies decide to turn their main effort from the west to defeat Hitler back to the east, the path was open for a march to the foot of the Imperial throne. For the Japanese high command, the challenge of defending both the Southwest Pacific and Central Pacific approaches had become near impossible.

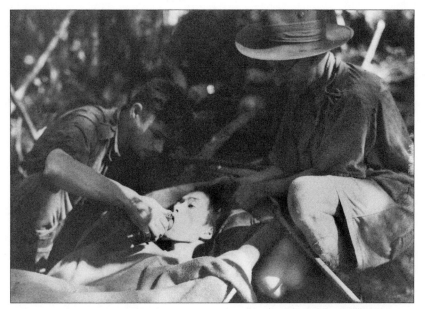

Caring for a Japanese POW. *(Credit: Australian War Memorial, Reference 026839--1)*

Operation Cartwheel

The question for Allied Indo-Pacific strategy now was—what next? How to keep the pressure up until the decisive blow was brought?

At this point in the conflict, it would be wrong to conclude, as some have done, that the Allies just pounded the enemy into submission by brute force. The Allies used their advantages to expand their options for bringing the enemy to heel. The strength and resilience of the Allies opened up more opportunities as the door swung the other way for the Axis powers. In January 1943, while the tide turned decisively in Papua New Guinea and Guadalcanal, the Allied leaders met at Casablanca in North Africa. Casablanca was another crucial turning point in adjusting Allied strategy (though the Allies continued to operate along the principles established during the Anglo-American talks in December 1941). Although the timing of the Allied invasion of Europe continued to be in dispute, the cross-channel invasion remained the top priority.

For the Pacific, Churchill and FDR reaffirmed an earlier decision to support both MacArthur and Nimitz, who each planned an axis of advance toward the Japanese mainland. "In the end," historian Ron Spector sums up in his history of the Pacific War, "the Casablanca talks produced no concrete plan for the defeat of Germany or Japan—and no ironclad commitment to devote a greater percentage of resources to the Pacific."[2] What the Casablanca meeting did accomplish, however, was a reaffirmation of support for continued offensive operations in the Southwest Pacific.

As the year wore on, the debate over the balance of Asia-Pacific strategy intensified—like an unending sibling rivalry. Curtin continued to protest the "Germany First" strategy to Churchill and FDR. In particular, Curtin peppered them with requests for more resources, particularly aircraft.[3] But his argument was losing its potency. The advance in the Southwest Pacific had been sold as crucial to protecting Australia and its lines of communications. That imperative seemed accomplished.

For his part, King continued to favor shifting efforts to the Central Pacific and placing Nimitz in overall command.[4] Meanwhile, MacArthur had plans of his own. He pitched a scheme aimed at taking back Rabaul. His original outline called for seven additional divisions (that would have almost doubled the size of his ground troops), requirements that irked the Combined Chiefs of Staff, as they wanted to husband US ground forces for the war in the west. In July 1942, the JCS approved the Rabaul operation—with the caveat that the offensive employ forces that were already in or scheduled to be deployed to the theater. The campaign was code-named Operation Cartwheel.[5]

Operation Cartwheel was a pincer movement, with MacArthur driving from Papua New Guinea and Nimitz directing an advance through the Solomon Islands that would encircle Rabaul, leaving the base isolated and vulnerable to invasion. Although on paper MacArthur had overall command of the operation, in practice the wing of the offensive in the Solomons, by agreement, operated independent of his control. It wasn't just that the navy loathed ceding any authority to MacArthur (though the animosity between King and MacArthur was well known) the expanse of the theater made it unrealistic for MacArthur to manage both wings of the offensive. If there was a need of confirmation of the wisdom of this decision, note that the Japanese tried to group the command of their ground forces in Papua New Guinea and the Solomons under a single headquarters. Their effort failed miserably.

As the year progressed, Operation Cartwheel moved at a more tentative pace than expected. After the hard-won victories at Buna, over the months ahead MacArthur's men turned their attention first to recapturing Lae, Salamaua, and Finschhafen on the Huon Peninsula.

Meanwhile, after the victory at Guadalcanal, Nimitz spent the year driving up the island chain from New Georgia to Vella Lavella to Bougainville. It was slow, tough going. King questioned if it was all worth it (even though he had pressed for the attack on the Solomons to begin with). King increasingly turned his attention toward the drive in the Central Pacific, which he saw as the key to finishing it all.

Objective Rabaul became even less crucial as it became evident that Australia and the lines of communication were secure. Further, supporting the punishing land campaign in Papua New Guinea had heavily taxed Rabaul's air and naval assets. In the Battle of the Bismarck Sea (March 1943), Allied planes pummeled a naval convoy attempting to reinforce the remaining Japanese positions on the Huon Peninsula. Further, an August air raid wiped out what was left of most Japanese aviation assets on the peninsula. Remaining combat aviation forces were dispatched to the defense of Hollandia up the coast. There were no major combat naval and air forces left at Rabaul. Over the course of the year, the mighty fortress was reduced mostly to a garrison, albeit one with an estimated 60,000 men, mostly the bone-thin, bedraggled men who had withdrawn from Papua New Guinea and a disparate collection of service troops. There was a question, King rightly argued, if the trapped and isolated garrison was still a prize worth having.

In August 1943 at the Quadrant Conference in Quebec, FDR and Churchill formally agreed to set Operation Cartwheel aside. They intended to increasingly shift the weight of Allied effort to Europe. For Churchill and FDR, Europe became even more of an imperative. A year earlier, in 1942, the commitment to a second front was a critical promise for keeping the Russians in the war. Even the mere threat of invasion kept Hitler from pressing the full weight of his military force on the Eastern Front. Hitler felt compelled to build an "Atlantic Wall" against Western invasion on the coast of France. Now, over a year later, FDR and Churchill were worried less about a Soviet collapse than that Stalin, now in a more favorable military position, might cut a separate peace or that the Soviets would advance to such an extent that Stalin might dominate postwar Europe. As a result, the Anglo-American warlords intended to press forward with both an invasion of Italy and then a cross-channel invasion in 1944.[6] That meant pouring additional resources into the Pacific War had to stop.

While the Combined Chiefs of Staff soured on the prospects for invading Rabaul, MacArthur managed to preserve the independence of his command and continued to develop a rationale for sustained operations in the Papua New Guinea theater that would place him in a position to liberate the Philippines. The intense disagreement over Pacific strategy (that continued through the spring of 1944) was at the time, and after, often described as interservice squabbling, or a titanic struggle between the egos of MacArthur and King. There was certainly plenty of that. But in fairness, each had a case to make. Neither option was without its benefits and drawbacks. Further, progress in the war didn't settle the matter. In fact, it did the opposite. Each could point to enough advances to claim all they needed was a few more forces to press the battle home.

In practice, the dual offensives served one another. Nimitz relied on the progress of the Papua New Guinea and Solomon Islands campaigns to cover his flank, as well as draw off enemy resources. In addition, the dual offense kept up maximum pressure on the Japanese. That was important to the Joint Chiefs who were looking for ways to shorten the war. They fretted about the burdens of the global crusade on a supportive but war-weary public. The dual offensive pressed the enemy on several fronts, making the prospects for a major enemy setback more likely.

Much of the debate over the discord of Pacific strategy is in fact overblown. Steve Reardon argues in his history of the Joint Chiefs of Staff, "In contrast to other aspects of the war, there were relatively few sharp disagreements among the JCS over the merits of one course of strategy in the Pacific over another."[7] He is right. True, Marshall and King had to frequently referee debates with MacArthur. True, the course of the strategy shifted as the campaign progressed. But compared to disputes over other strategic matters (like decisions on the timing of the second front), the squabbles of the Pacific War were lesser frictions that didn't hamstring the overall effort.

Historian John A. Adams argues (and he is not alone) that King's view of appointing a single overall commander in the Pacific would have resolved many of these issues. A single commander could "balance Japanese threats in other areas against actions in the southwest Pacific," Adams concludes.[8] Putting aside the challenge of managing MacArthur, there is reason to question this conclusion. After all, the Western theater didn't have an overall commander. Duties were split between the Mediterranean (MTO) and European theater of operations (ETO). They were related but separate campaigns. Arguably, geographical differences, the span of control, and types of missions in the Pacific were disparate enough to merit separate commanders as well. The Central Pacific war was, after all, a war of fleets. MacArthur's campaigns were not. True, there was a need for balancing the efforts of theaters. But, that was the job of the JCS. It is not clear how outsourcing the responsibility to a single commander over a theater that covered more than a quarter of the planet would have made difficult choices any easier. Arguably, shouldering one leader with the job would have made the burdens of the field commander greater and more overwhelming.

Further, it would be wrong to call the US strategy at this point in the war "ad hoc" or indecisive.[9] A better description of the Allied effort would be flexible and adaptive. Good strategy in a prolonged conflict can never be precisely linear. Commanders must react and adapt to match the enemy's moves. The abandonment of Operation Cartwheel is a case in point. Rather than inflexible strategy, the Allies maneuvered their strategy just like they did their forces.

In 1943, the United States and the Allies had options. The enemy less so. The crack in the Japanese outer ring had left Japan with a Hobson's choice. To defend in the Central Pacific, the Japanese needed ships and planes. Shoring up that front meant their defenses in the Southwest Pacific would be deprived of air cover and naval support to resupply, reposition, and reinforce their ground forces. But to hold the Southwest Pacific, the Imperial Japanese Army needed men—which would then be unavailable to reinforce the garrisons holding the vital strong points in the Central Pacific.

If nothing else, the JCS reasoned, MacArthur's operations in the Southwest Pacific tied down enemy forces that otherwise might be shifted elsewhere. On this matter their judgment was spot on. Over the year, the Japanese diverted one division to shore-up the defense of Papua New Guinea. In the months that followed, they tried to send three more. One was redirected elsewhere. The other two deployed but took heavy losses from US submarine attacks on the troop carriers. These actions illustrated that forces tied down or lost in the Papua New Guinea theater were soldiers that were not free to fight elsewhere.

For now, the Joint Chiefs decided to underwrite MacArthur's war. The upshot was MacArthur received support for planning additional offensive operations in theater. Meanwhile, US forces (though never reaching the levels he hoped) continued to build. His troops were more experienced. His leaders were more proven and tested. At the height of the campaign he would have almost 1.4 million men under arms including eight US divisions.

After months of strategic squabbling MacArthur had support for operations aimed at the China-Formosa-Luzon area, which the JCS considered an active option for basing the final assault on Japan. This operation could, MacArthur reasoned, put SWPA forces in position to liberate the Philippines. The challenge for MacArthur was to get there before Nimitz could pull off a decisive drive through the Central Pacific. MacArthur had get there with the ground, air, and amphibious forces he had on hand. What that required was a speedy and successful conclusion to the Papua New Guinea campaign against an enemy still determined not to yield the imperial outreaches—an enemy becoming more rapacious, desperate, determined, and resolute with each defeat.

Setting Sun

The fate of common men, like Sadashige Imanishi, serving at the furthest reaches of the empire were tethered back to the core of the imperium in the halls of the royal palace in Tokyo. The conventional narrative—that Emperor Hirohito's influence was crucial in the decision to go to war but that he played a less significant role in determining the conduct of the conflict—was challenged in Herbert Bix's biography, *Hirohito and the Making of Modern Japan* (2000). In particular, Hirohito closely followed operations in the Southwest Pacific. The emperor was loath to abandon efforts to retake Guadalcanal, mollified only with the promise to "take the offensive in New Guinea and restore the morale of the troops."[10] Hirohito continued to press for a strategy that did not abandon the outer ring defense of the empire, even as the Allied advances made that strategy untenable.

In late 1942, General Hitoshi Imamura was given command over the 8th Army area in the Southwest Pacific. This included the 17th Army, which had been campaigning in both Papua New Guinea and the Solomon Islands. Hereafter, Lieutenant General Haruyoshi Hyakutake's 17th Army would be primarily responsible for the defense of Bougainville. Meanwhile, the newly formed 18th Army under the command of Lieutenant General Hatazō Adachi would take charge of operations in Papua New Guinea. Adachi's command included three fresh divisions, one of which was almost completely wiped out before it got to the battlefield when eight transports were sunk at the Battle of the Bismarck Sea (March 2–4, 1943). Despite the losses, in Lae on the north side of the Huon Gulf (175 miles from Buna), Hatazō didn't stay on the defensive, launching an assault on Kanga Force (the ANGAU unit that had harried the Japanese forces for months) and trying to seize their airstrip at Wau.[11] The foray and the effort to consolidate defenses made perfect sense. But was it enough to hold against the major enemy offensive that was headed his way?

Sinews of War

For the Allies, the urge to take the battle to the enemy compelled a passion for innovation and risk-taking, a rationale not too different from the Japanese initial enthusiasm for the raid on Pearl Harbor. This resulted in a battle far different from the previous clashes of the campaign. Rather than fights carried by Australian militias, regulars, or ground infantry, the next step included an operation that combined all these together in combination with air and naval forces. This was an example of war at the graduate level.

As the Americans poured more into the campaign, those resources brought new capabilities and practices that were not available during the first phase of the jungle war. The Americans began to exploit the full potential of the forces they could bring to the front. For example, initially field artillery had been discounted as an asset for jungle fighting. There was a presumption that jungle wars were all about infantry and there was little or no use for combined arms like artillery and tanks. That assumption proved wrong—even in some of the most impossible terrain in Papua New Guinea.

The most obvious way to bring fire on the enemy was from above. Fly above the jungle, mountains, swift flowing rivers, swamps, and seas of mud and just drop a bomb or strafe an enemy position. Close air support, however, had limited value in jungle fighting because of the difficulty of specifically locating and identifying targets as well as the danger of using bombs in close proximity of friendly ground troops. Anything less than 1,000 meters was dangerous; 500 meters was near suicidal and as likely to result in killing friendly troops as the enemy. On the one hand, 500 meters was far too huge a distance for troops to cross in attacking the enemy without covering fire.[12] On the other hand, accurate artillery support could be brought within 50 meters. Troops could get much closer to enemy lines before fire would have to be shifted away. That was an important advantage in jungle fighting.

Getting the guns to the front, however, was the problem. But, the Allies soon learned that could be solved in part by using light, portable artillery but also by using engineers to help improve transport conditions and air resupply to deliver ammunition so heavier artillery could be moved closer to the front.

A bigger problem was seeing the target. Typically, the US military employed a forward observer, a soldier assigned to identify the target, relay the information to the guns, and direct the fire on to the enemy. In defensive situations, the Japanese were really good at concealing their positions. That combined with the limited line of sight in the jungle meant that the observers usually had to get really close to the enemy to see them, definitely close enough to get shot. The Japanese were also smart enough to figure out to shoot as a priority anyone with binoculars, a radio, or a field phone—presuming they were part of the enemy command and control or an artillery observer.

Aerial observers were better suited to the task of directing artillery in the jungle. In the Buna campaign, the Americans used the Wirraway, a single-engine fixed wing propeller Royal Australian Air Force aircraft for the aerial observer mission. The planes were not purposely suited to the task. In fact, the Wirraway was not purposely suited for anything. The plane was originally built for general training, but the Australians wound up building several hundred planes, using them for everything from aerial observersation, to bombers and fighters and distributing propaganda leaflets. One Wirraway was even credited with downing a Zero near Gona. But the real value of the craft to the Americans was as an aerial observer.

The US after-action report concluded that "air observation, thanks to virtual control of the air by our forces and the superb work of the Australian air observers using Wirraways, established numerous registered points in enemy territory and adjusted fire on many targets of opportunity."[13] The report added, "The fearless and consistently fine work of the Wirraways was extremely helpful. . . . The Wirraway observers were thoroughly familiar with the terrain, were personally briefed by ground force officials who knew what information was important and why, and were flown in a manner by which the specific information they were after could be best obtained." Although they were a genuine asset, the problem was that the planes could not fly low and slow enough to be really effective aerial observers. The planes also required a prepared airfield for takeoff and landing, restricting their range. Further, the planes did not belong to the ground commander. All these factors limited their utility and responsiveness. The army had to figure out how to do better than the Wirraways.

The Americans had the answer; they had started using light artillery air spotter planes in 1941. By the time the divisions went to war, the spotter planes were organic to the ground forces. But, they did not fly in Papua New Guinea until 1943. Duncan Doolittle, pilot and air artillery observer, was assigned to the 41st Division, which had been fighting in Buna. He recalled the Americans' first task was to convince the Papua New Guinea veterans that they weren't "buying a Brooklyn Bridge." By the time the spotter planes arrived, "they had been in the jungle fighting for six months or so and their observations—they hadn't been able to see anything except from some kind of a bomber, a navy bomber, flying around with an observer, and that wasn't very adequate. So we had to show them what the planes could do and how to do it."[14] The push up the coast offered a great opportunity to showcase how the air observers could benefit both reconnaissance and directing artillery fire.

The rugged planes were ideal for taking off and landing on short unimproved strips. Their small 65-horsepower motors sipped gas, allowing the planes to loiter over the battlefield for up to three hours. The planes were unarmed, but since the Japanese air force had been largely driven from the skies, the planes could circle at 1,000 feet—out of range from the enemy small arms fire, but close enough to observe the ground in detail. The planes could be dissembled, moved along the coast by ship, and reassembled and ready to fly the same day.

All the Allies' new capabilities came together during the coastal campaign, not just with more effective air-observer-artillery teams, but in the employment of fire support overall. Paired with more available artillery, "the Ramu-Markham and Lae Finschhafen campaigns saw many of the lessons of this training period come to fruition" concluded one historian; "most notable was the much closer coordination of infantry, artillery and engineering units, which was required in jungle warfare as forward observation officers moved up with the foremost infantry companies, and engineers assisted the artillery troops in moving their guns forward."[15] All the pieces of the army's combined arms team were coming together. It was not just men fighting with bayonets, grenades, and tommy guns anymore. The close fight was becoming much more unfair to the Japanese.

Ogawa Masatsugu, who fought at Finschhafen, experienced the shifting nature of fighting firsthand. "If we fired one shell, hundreds came back at us. 'Please don't fire at them,' we'd pray to our guns from our trenches."[16] The influence of fire support was reflected in prisoners of war interviews and captured documents. According to one action report, "The enemy feared our mortars first, our artillery second and our aerial strafing and bombing third."[17]

The Lifeblood of War

The Allies were also greatly aided in their task by more air and naval support than had ever been available before in the campaign. There was no obstacle to bringing Allied air, logistical, and naval power forward to the northern Papua New Guinea coast. That, combined with an American-led Army, gave MacArthur all he needed to take the war to the enemy. In part, MacArthur was also ready to go because of the capacity to extend the lines of communication that had been built over the last half of 1942 and into 1943.[18] This infrastructure stood in contrast to logistical lines built over the first six months of the campaign, which were made up as the war went along. There was no US theater command in the Pacific before the war. All the military commands overseas operated pretty much independently. As a result, there was no joint logistical command structure when the war started. Nor had the army and navy developed any real capabilities or doctrine to support expeditionary warfare.

For the navy, Base Force Headquarters in Pearl Harbor was responsible for supporting operations in the Pacific. There were not, however, sufficient assets in Hawaii to support building up overseas bases, nor did it make sense to route requests through Pearl Harbor to support operations in the Southwest Pacific. Support had to be coordinated directly from logistical commands in the continental United States and shipped through ports on the West Coast. In addition, the navy had to coordinate with the army who had the lion's share of responsibility for airfields and supply depots in the theater. Then there was the biggest challenge of allocating sufficient merchant marine assets to support the needs of all the theaters—a daunting challenge in that there was never adequate shipping to meet the demands of all the theater commanders. None of the integrated operational capability to manage these tasks existed when the war started.

In 1943, King and Marshall signed a joint directive, "Basic Logistical Plan for Command Areas Involving Both Army and Navy Operations." While the plan set up a coordinating framework, it hardly solved all the problems that had to be worked out on the ground half a world away. The effort to sort things out, however, was well under way. In truth until this point in the campaign, MacArthur's troops did fight on a shoestring. The Allies could not efficiently get supplies to the front. Further, it is fair to criticize the Allies for the often haphazard manner in which SWPA rushed troops forward before establishing a logistical base adequate to support them. Nevertheless, by 1943 the Americans overcame the challenge of building a logistical pipeline to sustain their armed forces over the vast distances of the Pacific theater. With Australia as a major staging base, MacArthur began to spread logistical nodes connecting to the forward forces in places like Milne Bay, Buna, and Finschhafen, building up facilities with airfields and floating dry docks, expanding repair and maintenance facilities into floating bases, and setting up mobile logistics in places that had virtually no infrastructure. The Allies also vastly improved their capabilities for marine salvage, clearing ports and waterways of wrecks and damage, recovering cargo, and ensuring continuity of operations. Logistical operations in the Southwest Pacific never looked like textbook affairs. SWPA staging operations could still be chaotic, balancing MacArthur's demands for swifter movement with the need for methodical planning. Still, they got the job done.

And it wasn't just having warehouses full of supplies. The Allies had also greatly improved task force operations, grouping ships with all they needed for combat operations and building a fleet of purpose-built amphibious ships and boats (the so-called Gator Navy), a family of landing ships that provided everything from rocket fire support to hospital ships. The day after Pearl Harbor, the US Navy did not have one ship that could discharge a tank, truck, or heavy equipment on to beach. They had scant capacity to deliver anything to foreign shores that lacked fixed docks, cranes, trucks, and rail cars to unload men and supplies and move them where they were needed. All that changed over the next two years as services built out the Gator Navy fleets of assault, landing, and transport ships that could conduct logistics over the shores, carrying men and material from the fleet right up to the beach without the aid of established port facilities.

While the Allies were building out their infrastructure, they were also expanding their capacity to interdict the enemy's supply lines. The contributions of the submarine fleet after the disaster at Pearl Harbor were little known to most Americans in the early days of the war. The first Hollywood films like *Crash Dive* did not begin to appear on screens until 1943. The stories of men on desperate missions in cramped quarters made for popular combat dramas. Unlike stories of land fighting, these films gave a better flavor of what life in the war was really like.

The privations of undersea warfare were nothing compared with what men in the jungle endured—but life was no picnic either. Ships were built for tropic operations—including having air conditioning. There was, however, no guarantee the air conditioning worked. It often did not. Life for a few dozen sailors cramped in a submarine while they were at sea was sweaty, foul-smelling, and exhausting. Yet, the food was good. Duty on shore in Australia was pleasant (including more than a few wartime marriages). Still when they were in the heat of battle, undersea warfare could be a harrowing experience.[19]

The Australian Navy did not operate any submarines during World War II. Submarine Forces, Southwest Pacific Area, operated US boats out of Fremantle, Western Australia, and Brisbane, Queensland. In 1942, US submarines were still a relatively new threat in theater. The first US submarines did not start patrolling out of Fremantle until March 31, 1942. Their operational area was also huge—covering over 3 million square miles—with about two dozen subs that also had to balance their ship-hunting missions with intelligence gathering tasks, search and rescue, and special operations (mostly supporting guerrilla operations in the Philippines), chores that MacArthur often gave higher priority than the interdiction of shipping.

By the second half of 1943, however, the submarines operating out of Fremantle were ravaging Japanese shipping. They sunk fifty enemy ships, effectively cutting the line of supplies coming out of Indonesia through the South China Sea. Overall, the impact of submarine warfare was significant. The Japanese started the war with 6 million tons of cargo carrying capacity. That number would actually go down not up as the war expanded. By the end of 1943, the Japanese would have only 5 million tons of capacity. More than half the losses came from submarine attacks.

In addition to the submarines, the Americans built out their naval fleet with patrol torpedo (PT) boats, like the ones immortalized in the John Wayne movie *They Were Expendable* (1945) or featured in the TV sitcom *McHale's Navy* (1962). They did not start operating in the waters of Papua New Guinea until December 1942. This fleet wasn't really built out until 1943. But, once operational, the boats mostly concentrated on hunting barges that were used to resupply the Japanese.[20]

The expanding capabilities of the Allies stood in sharp contrast to the capacity of the Japanese to conduct over the shore resupply. Not only were US submarines savaging the Japanese maritime fleet, the Imperial Japanese force was utterly strained in its ability to conduct expeditionary logistics. At Guadalcanal they were reduced to throwing supplies overboard in waterproof barrels and hoping they would drift ashore.

The balance of pumping the lifeblood of war, logistics, had clearly swung to the Allies. Some historians have concluded that the overwhelming advantages the Americans amassed accounts for why they won and negated all the Allies' strategic missteps. "Because of its material superiority," writes historian Ron Spector repeating a conclusion made by many others, "the United States could afford such expensive— and occasionally dangerous—luxuries as divided command and the lack of an overall strategy in its war against Japan."[21] This judgment, however, lacks a sense of proportionality. The measure of victories is what the warlords achieve with their advantages. The Japanese achieved gains beyond measure in the early campaigns of 1942, all squandered in the years that followed. When MacArthur had the advantage, he made good use of it. This was illustrated well by one of the most unusual battles of the campaign—the unfair fight from above.

War from the Clouds

While MacArthur pondered his broader offensive toward the Japanese homeland, he also pressed Blamey to wrap up the conquest of the northeast coast of Papua New Guinea, wiping out the enemy garrisons in the Lae-Salamaua area, strong points the enemy had held since the lightning campaign in the spring of 1942. Much had changed over the year. Blamey now held every material advantage in trying to take these territories back. The problem was getting there. Marching over the Owen Stanley Range was no picnic. Advancing in the lowland littorals along the northern Papua New Guinea coast wasn't much better. There were no real serviceable roads that could sustain a modern army. Nor was there any place to put one. Numerous rivers crisscrossed disease-causing, swampy, jungle-filled patches and isolated valleys. Picking up the pace of the campaign demanded looking for ways to avoid protracted, debilitating jungle fighting. The imperative for launching swift operations was looking for ways to bypass long, tedious marches through the interior that culminated in butting head-on against prepared enemy positions.

To accomplish that end, Blamey planned a double envelopment to encircle and destroy the remaining Japanese foothold. One wing would be an amphibious operation landing the 9th Division that would move on Lae, and the 7th Division would advance overland from the west, blocking any efforts to reinforce Lae. Meanwhile, the 3rd Division and the US 41st Infantry Division would advance on Salamaua. By threatening both enemy garrisons at the same time, Blamey hoped to prevent the Japanese from shifting forces in one area to support another, or throwing up impenetrable defensive lines like the ones the Allies had faced at Buna and Gona.

The first surprise Blamey encountered in his effort to mount a swift campaign was that part of the operation went swifter than expected. Enemy opposition at Salamaua melted away. Meanwhile, mounting the Lae operation proved frustratingly slow. As a result, the Japanese forces withdrew from Salamaua and reinforced Lae, with the 51st Division commanded by General Hidemitsu Nakano (which had deployed to Papua New Guinea to fight under General Hatazō Adachi's 18th Army). After Buna, the Japanese had had the opportunity to consolidate and offer one solid front—at a place that wasn't easy to get to over land. This was exactly what Blamey didn't want.

Further complicating the challenge was that one wing of the Australian offensive was to be carried by one tired division. After the fight at Buna-Gona, the 7th Division was a spent force. It had to be packed up, transported back to Port Moresby, rested, refit, then transported to the mouth of the Lakekamu River and up the river, where they would march to the Markham River—then cross the swift-flowing waters to set up a blocking position to trap the Japanese at Lae. Weeks had already been lost managing the movement of the division. More time would be eaten up making the difficult overland march to the Markham River crossing and building up the ground logistical tail to sustain the troops. Blamey pondered trying something else.

The Allies had an increasing advantage over the Japanese as the war progressed because they had more options for moving forces by land, sea, and air—and the enemy had less. While the Allies could maneuver in all three dimensions of war at the same time, it would be difficult, if not impossible, for the Japanese to match them. For the Lae operation, the Allies had a new option they had yet to employ. To speed up the campaign, MacArthur allocated one battalion of the US 503rd Parachute Infantry Regiment to seize an airfield on the other side of the river and aid the 7th Division's river crossing.

Until now, the airborne regiment, which had arrived at their camp in Australia in December 1942 (a year after the attack on Pearl Harbor), had seen nothing of war. Their battles had been in Sydney bars. A US fighter pilot recalled one episode when he walked into a dance hall brawl with the 503rd's airborne troops. He heard an Australian girl exclaim as the fist-swinging began, "I just don't understand all this. Aren't all of you on the same side? I can't tell a pilot from a paratrooper." On this occasion, the fight gave way to drunken champagne toasts with the paratroopers toasting the skill of the US Army Air Corps and the pilots attesting to the men who "fearlessly jump down into enemy territory. We look down from above and admire your courage and valor."[22]

In August 1943, the party was over. The regiment deployed to Port Moresby in anticipation of being called up for the advance on the Huon Peninsula. They would be the pioneers of airborne operations in the Pacific theater. Airborne forces, like the navy's aircraft carriers were one of the true innovations of combat in World War II. Troops and even some large equipment like jeeps and light artillery to could be parachuted or inserted by gliders into remote locations—delivering an attacking force to where the enemy was least prepared to counter them.

The conditions needed for a successful airborne assault limited their utility. Adequate weather was needed for transporting and inserting forces. Airborne units had limited fire support and supplies, so the attacker either needed to be able to have a secure air bridge to deliver supplies, reinforcements, and fire support, or the attacker needed to quickly link up with a ground force that could provide that kind of support.

Airborne operations had a checkered history during the war. On the one hand, there was the incredibly successful German airborne assault in Crete (May 1941). On the other, there was the near disastrous, American attack in Sicily (July 1943) when US naval ships mistakenly opened fire on the transports carrying the airborne troops.

In SWPA, where air assets were always in scarce supply, diverting planes for an airborne operation was never an easy decision. Of course, airborne troops could always be thrown into the line like regular infantry. The US Army in Europe would be pressed on occasion to do just that, like at the Battle of the Bulge (December 16, 1944, to January 25, 1945). But committing specially trained forces in that manner was a bad option to be avoided. It was best to find a tactical situation in which the airborne troops could be employed in a manner best suited to their training and capabilities—where the rewards were worth the hazard.

Sometimes in battle the best way to reduce risks is to take more risks. As the complicated plan to get the 7th Division to its objective unfolded, Major General George Alan Vasey, the division commander, labeled the whole scheme a "dog's breakfast." It would be a long, tough march. The overland supply route to support the troops would have to be cut out of the jungle. With the addition of the airborne assault, however, there was the possibility of shortcutting the ground march altogether. Vasey proposed expanding the plan to seize the airfield. Instead of adding a river crossing after an exhausting march, he wanted to airland most of the division after the airborne forces seized an aerial bridgehead, as well as resupplying his troops by air until the overload route was established.

Taking an airfield and preparing it to airland a whole division, however, was a much bigger task than just temporarily holding a drop zone to secure the far side of a river crossing. The plan had to be expanded to employ the whole 503rd Parachute Infantry Regiment supported by elements of Australian 2/4th Field Artillery Regiment. In the end, for the task of taking the drop zone, Colonel Kenneth H. Kinsler, the regimental commander, would have 1,700 of his troops plus the fifty-four Australian gunners for the task.

Empty Skies

There was only one reason why the Americans could even think about pulling off this operation: the Japanese air forces were increasingly spent. After the losses at Buna and Guadalcanal the Imperial staffs pressed for closer cooperation in the field.[23] One area of particular criticism was the lack of integration between the army and navy (which each independently controlled air forces) in achieving air control. The concerns started in the halls of the Imperial quarters and rippled across the Pacific. In response, Admiral Yamamoto organized a massive air counteroffensive—Operation I-Go. From April 1–16, 1943, the Japanese navy aerial units launched massed fighter/bomber raids from bases at Rabaul, Bougainville, and the Shortland Islands. Targets included Guadalcanal and the Solomons and Port Moresby, Oro Bay, and Milne Bay in Papua New Guinea.

The attacks got the Allies' attention. Captain Samuelson recorded on April 13 a raid on Port Moresby that was estimated at 100 bombers. "The escort was heavy," he wrote, "that even with all our fighters in the air, we were hopelessly out numbered." But then, like a passing storm, the attacks were over—and the dromes got back to business. He mused that the Japanese might be able to still get to Port Moresby, but they would have to hammer all the airdromes, including the ones at Milne Bay before they could even try. Even then he wrote, "there are thousands of Engineer troops scattered throughout Papua, thousands of natives who could help, thousands of other troops who could work on the dromes in an emergency. Yes, it could be done, but it would cost the Japs more than they can [afford] at present."[24] He was right.

Operation I-Go was the last great hurrah of Japanese air power in the Southwest Pacific. In 1942, the Allies would have not risked conducting sustained ground operations out of the range of land-based air cover, but over the course of months of combat the Japanese lost hundreds of planes and experienced pilots that were not replaced. As Michael W. Myers notes in his study of Japan's shortfalls, "The Japanese realized that a major problem in their prosecution of the war in the Solomons and New Guinea was lack of control of the airspace over the battlefields."[25] They realized their error far too late to do anything about it.

The problem was far deeper than the lack of interservice cooperation or combat losses. The development of the Japanese air arm that took place before the war produced some superb designs, like the Japanese Zero, but with the outbreak of the war, the industry lost contact with Western manufacturing developments, and almost immediately the Japanese fell behind in the pace of aircraft design and innovation. In addition, Japanese maintenance, repair, and ground support were extremely poor compared to the Allies. Poor readiness, combined with lagging aircraft innovation and the losses of planes and pilots increasingly left the Allies alone in the clouds.[26]

The Americans had freedom to maneuver their airborne forces. All they needed was a target. The target they found was Nadzab.[27] The village of Nadzab, about twenty-five miles southeast of the port city of Lae on the Markham River, seemed like an ideal objective for the operation. Nadzab had a small airstrip that before the war had been used for emergency landings. The field was long since overgrown, but with engineer support could be made serviceable in short order.

The target was also far enough from the enemy forces that a counterattack couldn't be swiftly mounted against the airborne troops. That was vital. On a drop zone, it always took some time to gather forces together that would likely be widely scattered during the drop. Airborne troops were most vulnerable when they first landed before they had a chance to organize into units and prepare their defenses.

Another advantage of the target was its location in the wide open expanse of the valley floor. At some points the Markham Valley was twenty-five miles wide, bounded by jungles and mountains. Airborne troops needed to drop onto flat ground. Trees and rocky terrain could cause death and injuries. If the terrain was swampy or too close to a water feature, troops might drown.

The Allies not only had the right ground, they had the right mix of forces for the job. Airborne missions, like amphibious operations, were always joint (including forces of more than one service) and inherently more difficult to coordinate. Success was dependent on each component doing its part. In this operation, the role of the 5th Air Force, who would have responsibility for ferrying the airborne troops, was as crucial as the task of the men who would have to fight and hold the ground.

Although this was the first combat drop in the South Pacific, it was not the Americans' first airborne combat experience of the war. In particular, they could draw on the lessons of airborne operations in the Mediterranean, specifically the airborne assault in Sicily. One key lesson learned was the importance of practice. On September 2, the 5th Air Force started three days of practice runs on an abandoned airstrip west of Port Moresby. The crews from the 54th Troop Carrier Wing, commanded by Colonel Paul H. Prentiss, practiced formation flying, hitting aerial checkpoints, and verifying the forward and trailing edges of the paratroopers' drop zones and runs on the drop zone. These practices were crucial. An airborne operation was like a vast aerial ballet, with masses of different planes conducting different parts of the mission crisscrossing in the sky.

Another important contribution was MacArthur's intelligence team, in particular their maturing capability to decode Japanese tactical radio traffic. The Allies were confident that the enemy would not mount any significant air or ground defense against the airborne assault. The Allies were also confident of their capacity to detect a

Japanese air attack and mount a powerful defense using both naval aviation and ground-based airpower.

Even with the strong intelligence, Kenney assigned 100 fighters to escort the air armada and bombers to pummel the drop zone before the troops landed—just in case. The Allies after all had not completely cleaned the skies of enemy planes. In fact, during their assault on Lae, Australian troops complained about being strafed by Japanese Zeros.[28]

With the amphibious assault of the 9th Division set for September 4, the airborne assault on Nadzab was scheduled the following day. The theater air forces commander, General Kenney, assembled an air fleet of over 300 planes for the forty-five-minute flight over the Owen Stanley Range to the target.

It was remarkable to think that after a year of bitter fighting on the ground the Allies were still less than an hour's flight from the place they started. The air armada, taking off from eight different airdromes at Port Moresby, included bombers to neutralize the drop zone, transports to carry the airborne troopers, fighters to protect the bombers and the transports, and seven specially outfitted planes to lay down a smoke screen. The air component of the fight for Nadzab was a remarkable testament to how far SWPA's air capabilities had evolved over the year. The Allies had scraped to find two planes to airland reinforcements at Kokoda. Now, they could flood the skies with planes if they had to support an operation. And the skies they flew were virtually devoid of Japanese Zeros.

The best manner to implement "access" operations (to put forces in the theater where the enemy doesn't want them) is always to put them where the enemy is not. In 1942, the South Seas Force had made its spectacular initial advances in Papua New Guinea, in large part, because they faced scant opposition during their landings at Buna. In contrast, the Americans discovered, as they took the offensive against the Japanese, that finding spots where they did not have to fight their way in grew increasingly scarce. The goal of this operation was to attack, for once, where the enemy wasn't.

Colonel Kinsler's plan for the assault reflected that he expected scant opposition. Kinsler planned to drop Lieutenant Colonel John Britten's 1st Battalion directly onto the Nadzab airstrip. They would clear the airfield of enemy troops and start to prepare the field for airland operations until the Australian engineers arrived to take up the task. The 2nd Battalion commanded by Lieutenant Colonel George M. Jones would drop north of the 1st Battalion and secure Gabsonkek, a small village. From there his troops would cover the flank of the airstrip. The

3rd Battalion commanded by Lieutenant Colonel John J. Tolson would drop east of the airstrip, taking over Gabmatzung mission, a cluster of buildings run by a group of German Lutheran missionaries. If any Japanese did attack, Tolson's battalion would be in place to block their advance. Kinsler, however, counted on intelligence reports and air reconnaissance that indicated little activity in the area. He also expected the simultaneous attack by the Australian 9th Division, which had begun the day before, would hold the enemy's attention.

Zero Hour

For the paratroopers it was a long uncomfortable day even before they reached the target. The troops were mustered at 3 a.m. for breakfast before being assembled and trucked to the field for loading. The morning started with a light rain, so most of the troops boarded the transports soaking wet.

Soon the sky flooded with planes. Captain Samuelson watch the armada form up over the harbor before heading inland. "The huge formations of transport carrying the paratroopers to the other side of the island made a beautiful spectacle this morning," he wrote his wife.[29]

Packed in the planes for hours, the nervous, sweaty, smelly troopers had gone from shivering temperatures as the planes crested the Owen Stanley Range at 9,000 feet to hot muggy weather of the valley floor. Then the red warning lights in the planes began to flash.

Time for action. Because the Allies expected little enemy air activity, air defense fire, or large enemy units on the ground, the drop did not have to occur at night to conceal the airborne assault. Parachuting in daylight would, they expected, make it much easier to consolidate the troops on the ground and organize them into fighting formations. Daylight flying also reduced the likelihood on an aerial accident among the dense formation of planes over the drop zone.

At least that was the plan.

Green light was the signal to jump. Under the direction of a jumpmaster, each paratrooper hooked up to a static line, a cable fixed to the aircraft. As they jumped out in the fetal position, the backwash of the plane's engines tossed them like a ball. Before they could feel the pull of gravity and the sensation of plummeting to earth, they felt a massive jerk as their break cord (which was hooked into the static line) reached its full extent. The break cord ripped off the entire back piece of the parachute pack tray, the canopy unfurled, and the soldiers watched as the ground rushed up to meet them. At a little after 10 a.m., parachutes began blossoming, dots across the sky.

The C-47 transports came over in waves of six planes, thirty seconds apart. Each plane dropped a "stick" of airborne troops over the drop zone. All three battalions were dropped on the field without any enemy interference. While there was no enemy, parachuting operations revealed how dangerous they could be. Three troopers were killed. Two died when their parachutes failed to deploy. Another trooper drifted out of the drop zone, hit a tree, and fell to his death. Thirty-three others were injured in the drop.

The challenge quickly shifted from consolidating the defense of the drop zone into preparing the airfield for the arrival of additional troops and supplies and building up a capable, sustainable fighting force before the enemy could interfere. The biggest obstacle turned out not to be the enemy but the pit-pit and kunai grasses and huge craters left by the B-17 bomb run on the drop zone.

Before the assault, Colonel Kinsler, his battalion commanders, and several regimental staff officers made a high altitude reconnaissance flight over the target. Although they gained an appreciation for the lay of the land, from several thousand feet in the air, they really couldn't gauge the conditions they would face on the ground,

From jump altitude between 400 and 500 feet (out of the range of enemy small arms fire), the drop zone looked smooth and flat. The troopers thought they were jumping into knee-high grass.

That was wrong. As the ground loomed closer into view the paratroopers saw they were dropping onto anything but flat open terrain. The valley floor was covered in tall pit-pit grass (which resembled sugar cane with long broad leaves) and kunai grass, which ranged from six to ten feet high and stood as dense as a woven mat. Walking was difficult through the tangled roots and impenetrable stalks of high grass. Visibility was zero. It was a blistering hot day. Each trooper jumped with eighty pounds of gear that had to be humped through the high grass. It took two hours to assemble the units before they were ready to move out and begin operations.

Firepower at the Front

The difficulty in sorting out the men and getting them to their objectives wasn't the only problem. The artillery support didn't work out at all as planned. Over the months of bitter jungle fighting, the Allies had learned the value of having readily available fire support for the ground troops. Airborne operations, however, created a special challenge. The Allies lacked the means to airland larger artillery pieces. That wasn't much of an issue for the regiment. It didn't have any organic artillery.

Recognizing the need for more robust and immediate fire support on the drop zone, adding the Australian gunners to the jump made perfect sense. The fact that the regiment had never tried anything like that before didn't seem an overwhelming obstacle. The Australian Field Artillery battalion planned to dismantle four short-barrel 25lbs guns (twenty-five pounds was the weight of the shell fired by the gun), drop them in parts, and then assemble them on the airfield. The Australian 25lbs was a 75mm pack howitzer (not much different from the mountain guns the Japanese used during the Kokoda campaign). The only problem with the plan was that it had never been tried before. A test drop suggested the plan should work. The other problem was the artillerymen had never jumped out of an airplane before.

An officer from the 1st Battalion was detailed to train the gunners in the basics of jumping out of a plane. There was even time for one practice jump. That ought to serve. Everyone thought.

That simple plan proved more complicated than it sounded. By the time for the kickoff of the operation, the battalion had only been able to field two operational guns. Fielding serviceable artillery, not worn out from heavy use in jungle fighting, proved to be only the first problem.

Nothing quite went right. The winds in the Markham Valley could be strong. They also shifted over the course of the day. The 5th Air Force timed their arrival exactly right for the regiment's drop over the objective. But the gunners were dropped three hours after the airborne troops. And by then, the wind had shifted. A strong gust through the valley combined with the pilots' mistake of overflying the drop zone deposited the gunners far to the west. Some landed in the trees. One broke his shoulder.

Undaunted, the gunners assembled their crews and set to the task of collecting the parts of the two howitzers, assembling them, and getting ready to provide support to the regiment. Fortunately, there was no enemy to fight so they did not have to try to complete the task under fire.

After arriving on the drop zone, one gun was ready within hours. But since there was no enemy activity and wanting to maintain the element of surprise, the artillerymen decided not to fire any rounds, not even to register the guns (a process of firing to account for the accuracy of artillery by judging where rounds actually land in relation to a fixed known point). As a result, that gun was not even brought into action until the next day. Meanwhile, it took three days to find the parts for the second gun. They were lost in the tall pit-pit and kunai grasses. In addition, the guns were also dropped with 192 boxes of powder and ammunition, but some of the ammunition was lost when the boxes tore away from their chutes. So the battalion had to worry about husbanding its ammunition until resupply.

Problems with the gunners aside, while the Americans organized the defense of the field and patrols, a detachment of engineers and signalers, a company of a Papuan Infantry, and 800 native bearers marched overland and forded the river to link up with the Americans and help prepare the airstrip for landing the Australian forces.

The engineers were an important addition—maybe the most important addition. While troops could wade across most of the channels in the winding river, the main channel was 15 feet deep and over 200 feet wide. The water rushed by at over seven knots. One engineer drowned making the crossing. Without a boating and bridging capability, the regiment would have never been able to safely cross the river. After crossing in small folding boats and rubber rafts, the engineers constructed a small bridge using the floating boats. The link with the Americans occurred a little after noon, just as the first US troops were getting ready to move out. The bridge was in place by 3 p.m.

More unexpected problems complicated the effort to rapidly expand the base of operations. The airstrip was in god-awful shape. The troops set fire to the kunai grass to clear the drop zone and the air strip. The engineers got to work making the field serviceable.

The next day, units from the Australian 7th Division began airlanding at the Nadzab airfield, but the build-up of forces went slower than Kinsler had hoped. Nevertheless, the Allies had enough forces on the ground to go on the offensive. While the 7th Division proceeded with the offensive toward Lae, the regiment continued with its mission of securing the surrounding area and protecting the airstrip.

Over the next days, troops from the airfield had sporadic contact with the enemy. Intelligence estimates suggested there were thousands of enemy troops at Lae. Where were they? The textbook response to an enemy airborne attack is to conduct a counterattack as quickly as possible—before the enemy has an opportunity to reorganize and resupply. That the Allies had only encountered disorganized resistance was a sign that the enemy was still unprepared for the assault from the sky—even though the attackers had been at Nadzab for several days.

When the airborne resumed the offensive on September 16, they encountered mostly sick enemy troops who were in no condition to do much fighting. In the end, the Allies marched into Lae unopposed—the enemy had withdrawn. In fact, the airborne attack had been more disconcerting than the Allies anticipated. In response to frantic request for air support, Rabaul dispatched an air armada of some eighty fighters and bombers. These were intercepted by Allied air defenses. Barely any enemy planes got through. When General Nakano reported the extent of the landing at Nadzab, he was ordered a retreat to escape the Allies' pincer envelopment. The command decided to consolidate their forces to try to hold the more strategically important position at Finschhafen. The last troops left Lae on September 15.

As a result, the airborne landing facilitated capturing a key objective without a slug-out battle as in Buna. However, because the operation had moved slower than anticipated, a sizable Japanese force escaped to fight another day. Of Nakano's estimated force of 11,000 about 9,000 successfully evacuated the peninsula.

On September 17, the 503rd Regiment's job was done. The sweaty, tired airborne troopers reassembled to be transported back to Port Moresby. Mission complete.

Airborne operations are rated among the most hazardous operations a military can conduct. The seizure of Nadzab and the advance on Lae bore the hallmarks of all that could go wrong—from delays due to bad weather to the somewhat inept effort to parachute artillery support into the drop zone. Yet, the action was a remarkable success. The regiment suffered only a handful of causalities, losing more men in a tragic plane crash and fire on the Nadzab airfield (killing fifty-nine and wounding ninety-two in addition to the deaths of the eleven-man aircrew) than they did in combat with the enemy.

The small, but successful, engagement illustrated how to extend the jungle war beyond slogging through the torturous trails of the Owen Stanley Range—bypass the terrain and the enemy whenever possible— and take the ground that mattered.

The operation also demonstrated the increasing sophistication of the Allies in marshalling and managing all the combat assets at their disposal. While Japanese commanders continued to squabble over interservice cooperation, the Allies had made significant strides in orchestrating what General George Patton once called "the musicians of Mars."

In contrast, the next phase of the campaign proved far more protracted and difficult. The Allied assault on Finschhafen began on September 22, 1943, and lasted a month. Nevertheless, consolidating Allied control over the Huon Peninsula allowed the US forces to bring forward aircraft and supplies as a base for the next phase of MacArthur's offensive. In the months ahead, Nadzab would be expanded with the construction of four all-weather airfields, eventually becoming the main Allied airbase in Papua New Guinea. After the liberation of Finschhafen, it was turned into one of largest Allied support bases in the Southwest Pacific with airfields, fuel dumps, and port facilities. In many ways, seizing locations that could be developed into major support bases for moving the campaign forward was more of an accomplishment than defeating the enemy in the field.

The liberation of Finschhafen brought to a close the great campaign that started on the Buna beaches, crossed the Owen Stanley Range to Port Moresby skyline, back over the mountains to Buna and up the coast. Over the course of the campaign the Japanese lost between 12,000 and 13,000 troops out of a total estimated force of about 20,000. The Australians lost 2,000; the Americans about 600. The disparity in casualties resulted from the same reasons the Japanese lost the campaign—paying the great price of fighting a sustained jungle campaign long past the culminating point of victory.

Notes

1. Quotes and information on Japanese military activities in this section are from Collie and Marutani, *The Path of Infinite Sorrow*, pp. 208, 263, 270–271.

2. Spector, *Eagle Against the Sun*, p. 222.

3. John Curtin to Winston Churchill, March 30, 1943, No. 62, in Gilbert and Arnn, *The Churchill Documents*, vol. 18, pp. 858–861.

4. Memorandum for General Marshall, Subject: Offensive Operations in the Solomons–New Guinea Area," March 19, 1943, National Security Archives Project, George C. Marshall Museum; Memorandum for the Chief of Staff, Subject: Conference on Operations in the Pacific, March 16, 1943, National Security Archives Project, George C. Marshall Museum; Minutes, Pacific Military Conference, PMC 5th Meeting, March 17, 1943, National Security Archives Project, George C. Marshall Museum.

5. The JCS Elkton Plan was codenamed "Cartwheel." See "The Elkton (Cartwheel) Plan, February 28, 1943," in Ross, *U.S. War Plans, 1938–1945*, pp. 271–277.

6. Stoler, *Allies in War*, p. 126.

7. Reardon, *Council of War*, p. 32.

8. Adams, *If Mahan Ran the Great Pacific War*, p. 193.

9. Quoted in Reardon, *Council of War*, p. 32.

10. Quoted in Bix, *Hirohito and the Making of Modern Japan*, p. 461.

11. Operations at Wau are described in Bradley, *The Battle for Wau*.

12. Threlfall, *Jungle Warriors*, pp. 170–171.

13. "Report of the Commanding General Buna Forces on the Buna Campaign," p. 75.

14. Doolittle, Oral History, p. 19.

15. Threlfall, *Jungle Warriors*, p. 200.

16. Quoted in Cook and Cook, *Japan at War*, p. 271.

17. "Report of the Commanding General Buna Forces on the Buna Campaign," p. 61.

18. Information on the logistics buildup from Carter, *Beans, Bullets and Black Oil*, pp. 63–68; Ballantine, *U.S. Naval Logistics in the Second World War*, pp. 101–131; Director of the Service, Supply and Procurement Staff, Department of War, "Logistics in World War II, Final Report of the Army Service Forces," pp. 48–51; Anthony W. Gray Jr., "Joint Logistics in the Pacific Theater," in Gropman, *The Big L*, pp. 301–324.

19. Information on submarine operations are taken from Symonds, "For Want of a Nail," p. 666. See Cairns, *Secret Fleets*, p. 114 and pp. 137–152. See also Benere, "A Critical Examination of the U.S. Navy's Use of Unrestricted Submarine Warfare in the Pacific Theater During World War II"; O'Connell, *Submarine Operational Effectiveness in the 20th Century*, pp. 21–218; COMINCH to CINCPAC, COMZAC, War Plans, CINPAC Files, Subject: Running Estimate and Summary, December 7, 1941, to August 31, 1942, US Naval War College.

20. On PT operations, see, for example, Bulkley, *At Close Quarters*.

21. Spector, *Eagle Against the Sun*, p. 560.

22. Rothgeb, *New Guinea Skies*, pp. 181, 183.

23. Operation I-Go described in Gamble, *Fortress Rabaul*, pp. 316–327.

24. Samuelson, *Love, War and the 96th Engineers (Colored)*, pp. 172, 177.

25. Myers, *The Pacific War and Contingent Victory*, p. 100. See also Harries and Harries, *Soldiers of the Sun*, pp. 363–366; Wolfe, *The 5th Fighter Command in World War II*, p. 1255.

26. See Joe Gray Taylor, "Air Superiority in the Southwest Pacific," in Franklin, *Case Studies in the Achievement of Air Superiority*, pp. 366–369.

27. Accounts of the Battle of Nadzab are based on Riseley, "Adjutant's Journal"; Dexter, *The New Guinea Offensives*, pp. 344–346; Rems, *South Pacific Cauldron*, pp. 69–71; Dilley, *Behind the Lines*, pp. 126–131; Greene Jr., "Canopies of Blue," pp. 30–38; Lowe, "Nadzab (1943)"; Duffey, *War at the End of the World*, pp. 238–241.

28. Guard, *The Pacific War Uncensored*, p. 179.

29. Samuelson, *Love, War and the 96th Engineers (Colored)*, p. 226.

11

Aftermath

JULY 1944, AUSTRALIA. *"Caught by the Japs, I would have my head chopped off immediately," recalled Charles Lindbergh.*

AFTER THE ATTACK on Pearl Harbor, Lindbergh threw himself into the war effort, volunteering to serve as a consultant for a number of aviation companies. In 1943, he persuaded United Aircraft to send him to the Pacific theater as technical representative, examining the performance of war planes under combat conditions. He did not do that. Instead, he used the consulting as an excuse to fight in the war. On May 21, 1944, Lindbergh led a raid on Rabaul. He flew his maiden combat flight—out of the field at Nadzab (the one captured by the US airborne forces).

In July, it looked like Lucky Lindy's luck ran out. He flew back to Australia to meet with US high command. General Kenney, the senior US air officer, was appalled to learn Lindbergh was flying in combat. "He went on to tell me," Lindbergh wrote in his diary, "that were I caught by the Japs, I would have my head chopped off immediately if they found out I was flying combat as a civilian." Kenney fretted about how many army regulations Lindbergh might have violated in his zeal to get into the fight. Kenney passed Lindbergh on to General Sutherland, MacArthur's No. 2. Sutherland suggested a work-around. He put Lindbergh on "observer status," which, Lindbergh recalled, "put me in a position to do about anything I wanted to."[1] Lindbergh went back to battle. The man who opposed the war, in the end, played a small but significant role in helping win the jungle campaign. He flew fifty combat missions. His days of battle were just one of many footnotes in a deep and complex historical legacy that the war bequeathed us.

Ending the Never-Ending War

By 1944, MacArthur had the war he wanted. His political victories were as substantive as his military ones. As the war lengthened, coalition relations with the Australians proved anything but frictionless. Still, assessing the essence of his leadership, as well as the other American and Australian warlords that prosecuted the war, requires looking past the squabbles, misjudgments, misunderstandings, subterfuges, and differences that plague every coalition relationship and asking the important question: Did the partners get what they really needed? In this case, the answer is yes. The Australians were committed to the defense of Australia and its place in the postwar world. The Americans were committed to victory against Japan. The Australian-American alliance from 1942 to 1943 helped accomplished both. MacArthur delivered. At the same time, on the battlefield, MacArthur had the forces and strategic position he needed to drive to the Philippines and press toward the Japanese homeland.

While the Americans prepared to press on, the inevitability of defeat was whispered in the halls of Japan's imperial palace. Prince Konoe joined private conversations with the Lord Privy Seal, Marquis Kido, and Mamou Shigemitsu in the Foreign Office over how Japan might get out of the war despite the continued resolve of the emperor, the prime minister, and the imperial staff to fight on. At the same time, with the emperor's consent, Tojo drastically reorganized the senior command structure. He forced out the sitting army chief of staff and took the position himself in addition to his dual roles of army minister and prime minister. The positions of navy minister and navy chief of staff were also consolidated. As a result, Tojo had a tighter grip on both operational military command and administration.

The government's hold on Japanese society was equally unshakable. Wartime cinema, for instance, was heavily regulated by the Home Ministry. Though audiences craved entertainment films that distracted from the daily grind of life (in the same way the popularity of movies in the United States and Australia skyrocketed during the Great Depression), the ministry insisted studios also produce films of "national policy," including contemporary war stories. A typical production was the 1943 film *Ano Hata o ute* (Tear Down the Stars and Stripes), which tells the story of the Japanese victory at the Battle of Corregidor, depicting courageous troops liberating Asian peoples from Western aggression. Not released in theaters until February 1944 when the war fortunes had clearly turned against the Japanese, the film nevertheless reflected the government's insistence on emphasizing the just nature of the national effort, validation that every privation, every sacrifice, every excess was acceptable in the name of national virtue.

Japanese literature carried similar messages of the eternal commitment to struggle and sacrifice. In a survey of wartime writings, Donald Keene argues contemporary writers "urged redoubled efforts when the ominous signs of reverses appeared."[2] Literature critical of the regime and the war effort was, not surprisingly, hard to come by. With the prospects for the great empire worsening, the government attempted to harness the people. "No slackening of effort can be tolerated," Prime Minister Tojo declared in a radio address to the nation. "The time has come for the Japanese people to adapt themselves to the present war situation and a determined battle front will be established at home and measures taken to ensure an epoch-making increase in war output."[3] The age limit for work was abolished, as were pleasures like teahouses and geishas. For a nation already burdened by years of war, the worst suffering was yet to come. The men at the top so dominated the military and people that they could force the nation to fight to the point of national suicide—and absurdity. In March 1943, even as the war turned against them, the government declared National Smile Week.

The regime's treatment of society was reflected in Japanese fighting strategy as well. Although many conceded that the war was unwinnable after the fateful defeats at Guadalcanal and Papua New Guinea, strategy devolved into an exercise in fatalism—they would fight on until the end, not just out of a sense of warped martial virtue, but because they could do so without retrospection. Now, with his grip on Japanese strategy unshakable, Tojo continued to demand a defense of the empire. After the reversals in Papua New Guinea, the Imperial Headquarters began to map out a plan for an "absolute defense line," to hold the empire. The planning acknowledged abandoning support for the remaining forces at Rabaul and in eastern New Guinea. Nevertheless, the Japanese persisted in developing a scheme for holding the Southwest Pacific.

Meanwhile, on February 29, 1944, four months before the cross-channel invasion in Normandy and the campaign that began the Allied liberation of Europe, MacArthur launched his crusade to liberate Asia. MacArthur's men began their assault on the Admiralties, a small island chain north of mainland Papua New Guinea and New Britain. The success of this operation would have a double benefit. First, holding the Admiralties would complete the encirclement of Rabaul, essentially accomplishing the objective of Operation Cartwheel. Trapped on Rabaul, the remaining Japanese garrison could do little more than tend their garden patches until the empire surrendered. Second, the ports and airfields in the Admiralties offered the Allies a base of support to advance up the littorals of the northern coast and also reach the Mandate Islands. The occupation of the Admiralties would set up operations for a swing to the west toward the JCS objective of Luzon-Formosa-China.

After seizing the Admiralties, MacArthur was ready to start his famous "island hopping" campaign. Hollandia was halfway up the Papua New Guinea coast. Both sides recognized its value. To the Japanese, absent holding Port Moresby, Hollandia was seen as the last key terrain they believed suitable for maintaining the empire's outer ring. With control of the Admiralties, Hollandia was now within reach. Operation Reckless, the conquest of Hollandia, took place in April 1944. The ground forces were led by I Corps under Eichelberger. Hollandia was a major step in the seven-month campaign that allowed MacArthur's forces to leap frog up the New Guinea littorals from the Admiralty Islands to Hollandia and from there to Wakde-Sarmi, Biak, Noemfoor, Sansapor-Mar, and Morotai, until they were at the shores of Leyte Gulf and the foot of the Philippines.

If not for the success of this campaign, MacArthur would have lost the argument that his wing of Pacific operations could deliver strategic results and liberate the Philippines before 1945. At this point there was little question but that it just made sense for MacArthur to continue on the offensive. The United States had poured men and material into the Southwest Pacific, not just to safeguard Australia, but to create a breach in the empire's defenses that could never be closed—this was the rationale for the offensive on Guadalcanal and Papua New Guinea. Having put an invading army in place it was now impractical to take it away; repositioning all those forces to the Central Pacific would have taken a massive logistical effort—as massive as the offensive campaign itself. Much like the Allied campaign in the Mediterranean theater of operations, fighting its way up the Italian boot, it would not have made much sense to turn off a campaign that was well under way. After all, at the very least MacArthur's operations tied down a significant number of enemy forces

MacArthur achieved success after success. On October 20, 1944, his forces began the invasion of the Philippines. He waded ashore with the troops. In a subsequent radio address he declared, "I have returned." The last Japanese forces were ordered to surrender on August 15, 1945, after the United States dropped two atomic bombs on the Japanese mainland and Russia declared war on Japan. On September 2, 1945, the Japanese signed the instrument of surrender in the presence of MacArthur. World War II ended.

Fog of History

The Japanese surrender was anything but the end of this story. The never-ending effort to get to the truth of what happened was just at its beginning. Nothing illustrates the fight for the last word in history better than the battle at Buna. MacArthur's war for ownership of the campaign's legacy began long before the final victory. Throughout the fighting, press releases were slanted to favor the Americans—and MacArthur. His decision to move his forward headquarters to Port Moresby (November 1942) made it appear as if he was personally directing the fighting, yet throughout the campaign he was as removed from the front as he would have been if he had remained at his residence in the Lennons Hotel in Brisbane.

MacArthur never saw the Buna front. Rather, he relied on brief visits by Southerland. Eichelberger felt that MacArthur had little appreciation for the true nature of jungle fighting. He did not know the "minutiae of soldiering,"[4] Ike argued. War looked very different knee deep in mud and mosquitos. "He [MacArthur] could have learned many things," Eichelberger recalled, "if he had taken a 40 minute plane ride to Dobradura near Buna."[5] Ike fumed, "Instead of realizing that the defeat of the Japanese at Buna was a miracle, he resented the delay in the extinction of the Japanese troops."[6] No one would ever convince Eichelberger that MacArthur understood Eichelberger's war.

Eichelberger and his staff prepared an official history of the campaign. The general wrote in the preface, "the purpose of this report is to aid those who fight under similar circumstances in the future. Its value may be judged by the Allied lives it saves . . . and the enemy it kills." But even as the staff clerks pecked out the report there were some who were ready to dispute its conclusions. Not all the division veterans were enthused with Eichelberger's relentless pursuit of victory and willingness to accept high casualties.

Some derided "Bobby the Butcher" and labeled the temporary cemetery at Buna "Eichelberger Square."[7] Nevertheless, the report was forwarded to the War Department, which at Marshall's direction was preparing a series called *American Forces in Action*, designed primarily for wounded soldiers in hospitals as a portrait of their experiences, sacrifices, and achievements. Responsibility for preparing and reviewing the manuscripts went to a newly created Historical Division that handled publication. In an odd twist of fate, the man in charge was Major General Edwin Harding, the man Eichelberger had relieved at Buna.[8]

Harding, who never received another combat command, took the opportunity to even an old score. An article in the *Saturday Evening Post* at Harding's instigation suggested that an unnamed general exacerbated the losses at Buna by ordering direct attacks on fortified bunkers. The same officer ran away at the sound of Japanese mortars. The article seemed a veiled criticism of Eichelberger. When Brigadier General Albert W. Waldron was asked about the accuracy of the piece, he replied he respected Eichelberger but "the only other general I can think they were referring to would be Gen. Eichelberger. I have high regard for Gen. Harding." The interviewer added in his notes, "By tone, Gen. Waldron seemed to be damming Gen. Eichelberger with faint praise."[9] The official monograph, *Papuan Campaign: The Buna-Sanananda Operation, 16 November 1942–23 January 1943*, published under Harding's supervision, barely addressed Eichelberger's role in the campaign.

In frustration, Eichelberger wrote to officials in Washington to counter Harding's campaign to restore Harding's own reputation at what Eichelberger believed was his expense. If Harding had a dispute with anyone, Eichelberger believed it should have been with MacArthur for ordering unprepared American troops into battle. When Harding reported to MacArthur after he was relieved of his command, the supreme commander claimed he didn't know why Harding had been replaced. Eichelberger believed MacArthur feigned ignorance because he wanted to deflect any possible criticism onto Eichelberger.

One of Eichelberger's traits many admired was the general's steady humility, but, in truth, Eichelberger was not without fault here. He was fragile, jealously guarding his victory with almost pathological obsession. Over the years many aspects of the campaign rankled the hero of Buna. After the war, while serving under MacArthur in the occupation force in Japan, Eichelberger announced that he would take up an offer from the *Saturday Evening Post* to write a war memoir. He felt the forces under his command had never gotten the credit they deserved. A spate of wartime books written by combat journalists and MacArthur sycophants, such as Pat Robinson's *The Fight for New Guinea: General Douglas MacArthur's First Offensive* (1943) and *MacArthur and the War Against Japan* by Frazier Hunt (1944), barely mentioned Eichelberger or his efforts in the fight for Buna. As the titles suggest, they are tributes to the strategic genius of MacArthur.

Eichelberger wanted his say. Eichelberger's version was serialized in the magazine and published in 1949 as a book under the title *Our Jungle Road to Tokyo*. Among the tales it told, one peaked a number of reader eyebrows. MacArthur allegedly told Eichelberger, "time is of the essence. Take Buna or don't come back alive." A lively debate about the incident ensued. Some questioned whether MacArthur had ever issued such an order. Kenney's narrative, which was published the same year, claimed MacArthur said, "Bob, that is the job I'm giving you—go get Buna. Now, Bob I have no illusions about your personal courage, but remember that you are of no use to me—dead."[10] Nor did Kenney confirm Eichelberger's claim that he had been specifically ordered to relieve Harding.

The differing accounts did not go unnoticed. The division's historical association commissioned a record of its service in World War II, written by division veteran H. W. Blakely. Blakely, whose account is more sympathetic to Harding than Eichelberger, noted the divergent recollections implying that Eichelberger exaggerated his own importance.[11] Eichelberger was deeply offended when he read a draft of Blakely's manuscript.

In particular, Eichelberger was rankled at the notion he had made up MacArthur's dictum. He wrote to Samuel Milner, with whom he had kept up an active correspondence while Milner worked on his volume for the Center of Military History, that he had proof that his version was correct. Frazier Hunt had recorded the incident in *MacArthur and the War Against Japan* (1944). Eichelberger wrote Hunt to find out where he had gotten his version of the fateful November 30 meeting. Hunt claimed MacArthur had dictated the account to him. Eichelberger was so anxious about the issue, he kept Hunt's reply in his bank box.[12] There is other evidence to corroborate the story, including contemporary accounts. James F. Collins on the I Corps artillery staff heard the story directly from Eichelberger, as did Harding.[13]

Other witnesses recall that MacArthur's remarks as recorded by Kenney did occur, but at a breakfast meeting the following morning before Eichelberger left for the Buna front. In short, it appears that MacArthur made both remarks. Such would be in keeping with his character. The first reflected the general's flair for the dramatic. It is not even surprising that he would have encouraged that the story be spread throughout the command. Major General William H. Gill, who assumed command of the division after the Buna operation, recalled hearing the story shortly after arriving in Australia.[14] It was already part of the MacArthur legend.

Kenney's version appears to have been deliberately misleading, conflating the evening and morning sessions into a single meeting. Eichelberger believed the misrepresentation was intentional, conjecturing the ever-loyal Kenney was trying to protect MacArthur's reputation. "Don't come back alive" may have carried cachet in wartime, and indeed, MacArthur might have encouraged talk about the order to sharpen his image as a hard driving combat leader, but such talk in a postwar reminiscence might have perhaps seemed unduly harsh.[15]

Eichelberger, for his part, claims he was shaken by the command to take Buna or not come back alive and also took to heart MacArthur's imperative to win the campaign as quickly as possible regardless of the cost. "It was in my mind constantly," he recalled, "and was without a doubt responsible for the fact that I exposed myself far too much in the presence of the enemy."[16] After the campaign MacArthur laughed at the order, recalling he had been a given a similar direction during World War I. At the same time, MacArthur's dispatches veiled the desperate nature of the campaign. Eichelberger found this particularly upsetting. "I did resent," he recalled, "when I returned from Buna, that the word was given out that I exposed myself too much. It was a matter of common gossip around his staff."[17] The staff presumed that Eichelberger braved danger because he was a show-off rather than, as he saw himself, a leader risking danger to accomplish a desperate mission.

Eichelberger believed, in part, MacArthur pushed for an early success in the theater out of competition with the war in Europe. If he couldn't show progress he would lose the fight for resources. Before the battle for Buna began, MacArthur fretted the Marshall men had already stolen a headline on him. On November 14, 1942, the *Army and Navy Journal* declared, "Editors Elated as American Forces Launch Sweeping Offensive in Africa." On November 21 the journal reported that the president had sent a congratulatory letter to Eisenhower on the success of the North African campaign. The *New York Times* declared Eisenhower's offensive might well be the "turning point in the war." When MacArthur heard about the victory, he told Eichelberger, "Well, no one can touch him now."[18]

Eichelberger also suspected that he had been tainted by what he called MacArthur's "vivid hatreds." Eichelberger, for one, believed the story that during the interwar years MacArthur had consigned Marshall to an Illinois National Guard assignment to end his career. While serving on MacArthur's staff at the War Department, Eichelberger recalled the general declared, "Marshall is the most over-rated man in the United States Army. He will never be a general officer while I am Chief of Staff."[19] Eichelberger often heard the general disparage Marshall and his protégés. In turn, MacArthur used to needle Eichelberger by referring to "your friend General Marshall."[20] As the war progressed, Eichelberger never received his fourth star. MacArthur blamed the lack of promotion on the "European gang," but Eichelberger always blamed MacArthur: "I believe I would have been promoted within two days if he had recommended me."[21]

Over the years, Eichelberger's animosity toward MacArthur became legend. Anxious for the publication of Milner's official history, Eichelberger assumed delays were the result of MacArthur's influence. Although there is no evidence MacArthur directly interfered with the project, many of the participants, including MacArthur's loyal lieutenants, peppered Milner with their own interpretation of events. Southerland wrote, "The historian [Milner] should examine with a critical eye some of the cited letters from General Eichelberger. . . . [T]hey also contain a considerable amount of propaganda which was recognized at the time, designed to enhance the reputation of General Eichelberger at GHQ. . . . [H]e is not particularly modest in recording his activities."[22] In fact, reading the Sutherland-Eichelberger correspondence does evoke comparisons to the dispatches prepared by nineteenth-century generals that were read to parliaments and press, designed more as a political narrative of the campaign to influence politicians and popular opinion than an exchange of military information. Indeed, Eichelberger's letters with their occasional rhetorical flourishes of how he loved the sound of the guns and the smell of battle are reminiscent of MacArthur's own highly embellished dispatches. Today, one would call it spin.

The war for reputations aside, the issue of Eichelberger's generalship has never been fully resolved. His career has attracted little interest. Jay Luvaas, a well-known and respected military historian who concentrated on the nineteenth century, was drawn to the subject because Eichelberger was a friend. Luvaas's student John Shortal, a US Army officer and professor at West Point, was drawn to the topic by Luvaas's encouragement and Eichelberger's apparent reputation for sterling, unselfish combat leadership, an appealing and refreshing subject for a young officer writing in the disillusioning wake of the disasters of Vietnam. Both historians for the most part treated Eichelberger the way Manchester treated MacArthur.

In contrast, another serious treatment, Paul Chwialkowski's biography, *In Caesar's Shadow*, is damming.

> Eichelberger placed his troops in needless jeopardy and suffered unnecessary losses. . . . He exaggerated his own victories and, in a burst of grandiosity, shamelessly sought publicity and medals. . . . His preoccupation with publicity and problems with MacArthur dominated his thoughts. . . . Unable to tame these unresolved conflicts, Eichelberger spent the last years of his life with unhappy memories, inner turmoil, and angry vendettas.[23]

In regard to Buna, Chwialkowski largely accepted Harding's criticism of Eichelberger and drew selectively on the official history to bolster his case.

In Caesar's Shadow, however, is deeply flawed. There is an evident command of the secondary literature and conspicuous effort to demonstrate that all the relevant archives had been consulted, as well as the concerted effort to appear controversial and turn the view of Luvaas and Shortal on their head. Chwialkowski's analysis, however, lacks an understanding of the real nature of battle. During the Papua New Guinea campaign Eichelberger did not always act like a general, but Buna was not a battle for generals. What was needed on this small, isolated, and personal battlefield were squad leaders and frontline commanders. Those were sorely lacking. If Ike occasionally played these roles, he did so with good effect, not only making the difference in some battles (like ordering in the reserves on the December 5 attack), but perhaps more importantly gaining an appreciation for what combat was really like, what men could and could not accomplish, and what was needed to provide the margin of victory.

Harding's relief, Eichelberger's attrition tactics, and the problematic relations with MacArthur are interesting academic questions, but they amount to little more than second-guessing the past. It is a simple matter for historians to point to the most efficient and bloodless course of the campaign armed with a bookcase of evidence and after-the-fact knowledge, but in a horrifying, debilitating jungle war—where cool logic and thoughtful contemplation were in short supply—the way forward was far less clear. All three leaders deserve more charitable assessments.

In the case of Eichelberger, the proper measure of leadership is not whether he made perfect choices, but whether he made suitable decisions given the conditions at hand. Mud, sweat, death, fear, uncertainty, hate, anger, sickness, disease, and suffering do make a difference. It is difficult to argue that Eichelberger did not measure up. In the end, the reputational squabbling and academic debates over generalship were mostly distractions from history.

Getting past the politics was no less difficult for the official military historians. In 1957, the US Army's Center of Military History published its official history of the campaign, *Victory in Papua* by Samuel Milner. Like all the official army World War II histories, the manuscript was subjected to a rigorous review process supervised by the army's chief historian at the time, Kent Roberts Greenfield. Milner's book was not his favorite. Greenfield complained that Milner ignored the larger strategic questions. "The Question is one that this book must face and deal with," he chided, "if it is to attempt an evaluation of the importance of this campaign."[24] Milner, however, skirted any deep analysis of MacArthur's strategic choices. He gave MacArthur a pass. In large part, this was likely due to the fact that MacArthur's formidable former chief of staff, General Sutherland, was among those reviewing the manuscript. If there had been a whiff of criticism, Sutherland would have no doubt ensured the book would have never seen a bookshelf.

Bloody Buna (1974) was authored by Lida Mayo, who also had a long career as an official army historian and served as Milner's assistant. Mayo never thought the official history gave the trials of the soldiers slugging through the mud their due. She had long worked on a manuscript on the campaign. Her work was completed and published after retiring. Mayo's book was popular in the United States and a bestseller in Australia (probably because it at least mentioned Australians were there). Still, she did little to diminish MacArthur's shadow over the campaign. The book starts out this way. "The battle for Buna in New Guinea, won by General Douglas MacArthur," Mayo writes, as if there was no one else on the battlefield.[25]

Over three decades later, history professor Stephen R. Taaffe, bridged the difference between Mayo and Milner, on the one hand, and Falk and many other MacArthur critics on the other. Taaffe delivers a balanced but critical assessment of the campaign. In *MacArthur's Jungle War* (1998), he argues victory resulted from more than just the general's strategic genius. In fact, MacArthur had made his share of mistakes—and dedicated no small effort to covering them up. Taaffe, however, concludes that MacArthur successfully fought and won an important campaign. In 2016, the military writer James Duffy also delivered a balanced overview of the campaign, *War at the End of the World*, and came down in much the same place.

Remembering War

If any lesson can be learned from Papua New Guinea, it is that success and failure in war is anything but a game of generals. Others squabbled over their piece of history. The fight for remembering was a bitter one among the men who fought at the front. War veterans had no common view. That's not surprising. It was a global war. They could have indeed been fighting in different wars. Nothing illustrated the cacophony of memory more than officers recalling their wartime experience—to other officers.

Following VJ Day (victory against Japan), the army dispatched many field-grade officers (the ranks of major and lieutenant colonel) to the former dusty cavalry post of Fort Leavenworth to study the practice of combined arms warfare, the coordinated employment of infantry, armor, and artillery as well other supporting arms and airpower. The school played an influential and important role preparing regular army commanders and staff officers for World War II. As the war ranks swelled, however, there was not time or space for every qualified mid-grade officer to attend Leavenworth, so they were sent after—after many of them had learned the art of war on the job in hell holes like Papua New Guinea and the dead zones of the Normandy beachhead. After they smelled rotting corpses, survived withering artillery fire, and saw men bleed out in a trench, they were sent to school to learn about fighting.

When the war ended, the army had a huge backlog of officers eligible to attend the college. These students were older, had much more combat experience and rank than the classes that came through before the conflict. The army sent them to school anyway.

Regardless of how grizzled the student body was, the school taught in much the same way as it had before Pearl Harbor. Leavenworth had long practiced teaching the "school solution," preparing instructors with standardized answers used to guide grading the solutions officers proposed to solve tactical problems assigned in class. As one observer noted, instructing was "a platform performance with kind of a capital P."[26] They taught war by the numbers.

Invariably, however, when presented the school solution, veterans of the European campaign would respond with a dismissive criticism, such as, that was not how you are supposed to do it, and then would describe their own wartime experiences. Then, veterans of the Pacific campaigns would also throw up their hands, railing against the school solution, but arguing that those European Joes did not know what they were talking about and go on to describe the tactics used in the theater they fought.

Everybody described the war they knew—a reminder that there was more than one way to manage combined arms warfare (the integrated employment of arms like infantry, tanks, and artillery). Such stories underscore one of the most bedrock realities of combat. A Papua New Guinea veteran for instance would be appalled to hear how an infantry company fought in France. They would be dead in minutes if they tried to maneuver like that against a Japanese position in Buna.

Veterans of the Southwest Pacific were perhaps the most frustrated of all, feeling they never got their fair share of attention, other than the postwar fascination with Tiki bars. Even to other veterans, the protracted land campaigns in the Pacific, such as the remote operations in Papua New Guinea, seemed obscure. Today, Europe still dominates the remembrance of war. One academic survey, written almost half a century after the Battle

of Buna, found that less than 20 percent of the books and articles published about World War II dealt with the Pacific theater.

There are a number of explanations for this. Perhaps the simplest
is most persuasive. By one estimate toward the end of the conflict only
about 15 percent of the men and material deployed around the world
were engaged in the battle against Japan. The generation that shaped the
postwar memories and myths of war largely had their eyes turned
toward Europe where most American fathers, husbands, and sons saw
the sharp edge of combat.[27]

Many readers were stunned in 1981 when they read Eugene
Sledge's memoirs of the marines fighting on Peleliu and Okinawa and
his vivid descriptions of the appalling suffering and privations of frontline combat in the Pacific. Sledge had kept notes of his experience
tucked away in a pocket Bible, but it took him years to again face the
daunting experiences of men in battle and put them together in *With the
Old Breed*. The experiences of the soldiers at Buna were just as jarring.

In recent years some have stepped forward to round out the story of
the epic struggle in the Southwest Pacific, not just retelling the tale of
the jungle fighting, but all the parts of the battle they contributed to victory. Some heroes flew over the battlefield. The air campaign, for
instance, is described in Bruce Gamble's *Fortress Rabaul: The Battle
for the Southwest Pacific, January 1942–April 1943* (2010).[28] Some
skimmed above the waves or slithered silently below them. Ian W. Toll
delivers a riveting account of the naval campaign in *Pacific Crucible:
War at Sea in the Pacific, 1941–1942* (2012). And then, of course, there
were those that fought in the mud and slop at the front, a tale well told
by James Campbell in *The Ghost Mountain Boys* (2008).

There are, however, many other narratives left incomplete by
those who didn't make it or veterans who left their war in the jungle.
Sergeant Herman Bottcher never told his story. He was later killed in
action during the Philippines campaign. He is buried in Manila. Colonel
Kenneth H. Kinsler who led the airborne drop committed suicide a
month later. He was forty-two years old. He is buried at the military
cemetery in Hawaii.

Others worked far behind the lines, patching up broken bodies,
stringing wire, or serving up powdered eggs. No one really wrote their
story. So many voices of men and women, great and modest, are still
absent from this history. The experiences of Black soldiers in Papua
New Guinea is a case in point. It is still parsed in pieces. The US presence in Australia introduced Aussies to the state of US race relations.
On occasion, race riots between Black and White US soldiers and

Australians broke out in Brisbane, Melbourne, and other cities and towns. When Captain Hyman Samuelson, who commanded Black troops, was stationed in Australia before being deployed to Papua New Guinea, dealing with race relations was a constant distraction. "The Australians are wonderfully tolerant," he wrote his wife, "but the Americans, especially the Southern boys are a problem."[29] At one point after a fight, a hundred of his men were rousted out of town by White solders burnishing bayonets. To keep the two sides apart, the colored troops were banned from town.

Race followed the troops into war. Along with the all-White combat forces, many all-Black units, like the engineer troops commanded by Captain Samuelson, were sent to Papua New Guinea where they built and ran the infrastructure that won the campaign. Arguably, victory in Papua New Guinea is as much theirs as anyone's. Yet, while White American soldiers were not uniformly racists, disparaging attitudes toward African American soldiers was not uncommon in the combat zone. Young US combat surgeon George Sharpe, who deployed to Papua New Guinea, recalled, "There was a great deal of anti-black bias that, for those of us who had more enlightened views, was very discouraging. Most of all the work on the base that was really physical was done by blacks. . . . Every effort was made to malign them."[30] Inequality was an endemic problem.

Nor was the shabby treatment of Black soldiers a problem limited to the Southwest Pacific. They never got their due. During the war, the army attempted to improve the image of African American servicemen. In 1943, they requested Frank Capra make a documentary on the subject. *The Negro Soldier* was released in 1944. Originally intended to buck up the morale of Black soldiers, eventually the documentary was screened for a wider military audience and later released to the public. The film actually proved popular in the military. Surveys of White soldiers overwhelmingly recommended showing the film to White and Black audiences. George Sharpe remembered hearing about the film and asked his commanders to screen it. That didn't happen. Most screenings took place at stateside military posts.

Although they were American brothers in arms, there were many who did not consider Black soldiers their brothers or equals, but there were also many in uniform and Americans across the country who did. Some like Captain Sharpe bore no ill-will toward men of color. Others like Captain Hyman Samuelson through serving with Black troops learned to respect and admire their service and sacrifice. In Papua New Guinea, Black soldiers made substantive contributions to the campaign that were never adequately recognized. Then, and to this day, the story of their trials and contributions is unfinished work.

War and Popular Culture

The war Americans back home knew was another distraction from grasping the realities of battling in the muck and mud. In popular culture a different set of truths shaped the American image of wartime in the Pacific. The first big movie on the jungle war was *Guadalcanal Diary* (it debuted in 1943, six years before the most famous film on the Pacific War, *The Sands of Iwo Jima*—in 1949 with John Wayne in the starring role). Rushed into production, *Guadalcanal Diary* had no real star, rather it was mostly filled with stock players whose faces and characters were familiar to most moviegoers. Playing to packed theaters across the country, the film bore all the elements of great Hollywood war movies and bad history, setting the model for a steady stream of productions that continued to the end of the decade.

Although the film fixed the popular interpretation of the Pacific War, the images it presented were not accurate nor were the experiences of the first marines on Guadalcanal typical. The regiment's landing was unopposed. After securing the airfield and bringing in reinforcements, the marines cautiously expanded operations. Thus, while it was their first campaign, they had an opportunity to gradually become accustomed to conditions before taking on the Japanese in pitched battles. In fact, in the film, which stays fairly true to the chronology of the campaign, the first major combat scene appears very late in the movie. Some of the most horrific and desperate fighting came later in the campaign. In this film, there is little evidence of suffering and hardship. The actors looked well-fed, maybe they seemed they could have used a shave or a change of clothes. The movie was filmed near Oceanside, California. Neither the place nor the men had the desperate, ghastly gaunt look of war. This was nothing like the fight for Buna. In the movie, the marines talk about home a lot, moon about the girl left behind, the newborn baby, the old neighborhood, food, and their obsession with baseball, leaving the impression that is what occupied their war, along with an occasional battle. Charles McDonald (a veteran of the European campaigns) in his memoir of commanding a company during the war angrily recalled when a reporter asked what he wanted most from home. "I've got something to say. Tell them it's too damned serious over here to be talking about hot dogs and baked beans and the things we're missing. Tell them it's hell . . . there're men getting killed and wounded every minute, and they're miserable and they're suffering." *Guadalcanal Diary* was far removed from what veterans like McDonald and the survivors of the fight for Buna experienced.

In fairness, Robert Brent Toplin argues in *Reel History: A Defense of Hollywood* (2002), it is unfair to expect historical films, like war movies—whether they are contemporary movies, such as *Guadalcanal Diary*, or cinema created long after the fact, such as *Saving Private Ryan*—to accurately portray history. In the end, moviemakers have to deliver a clear and compelling narrative, not record history. The medium has significant limitations as a history teacher. Conversely, that doesn't mean film has no historical worth. "Audiences receive a modicum of information about broad historical events," writes Toplin, and they are "emotionally and conceptually rewarded . . . [when] memorable films address important questions about the past and attach viewers' emotions to the debates about them."[31] That was certainly true in the case of *Guadalcanal Diary*. The film connected its American audience to their fighting men in the far-off Pacific, even if it did not convey the brutal reality of ground war in a faraway place.

It was unrealistic to expect movies to get the real substance of the combat experience. In postwar popular culture, the novel was the only hope for finding a place in the public imagination for the true-life experiences of battle. But, that proved a long time in coming. The most notable work centered on Guadalcanal, James Jones's *The Thin Red Line*. Jones was without question the most important, widely read, and influential writer of that generation who probed the effects of the war on the individual soldier.

Jones was an infantryman wounded at Guadalcanal (though he actually spent less than two days in battle before he was hit in the head by a mortar fragment). After the war he turned to writing full-time. *The Thin Red Line* (1962) was the second of a trilogy on the war, including *Here to Eternity* (1951) and *Whistle* (1978). Jones's work was path-breaking stuff, demonstrating that the World War II version of the lost generation novel could be both commercially and artistically successful. Historian Gerald Linderman was so taken with Jones's description of life in the Pacific that he cites liberally from the novel in *The World Within War: America's Combat Experiences in World War* (1997). Indeed, Jones's descriptions of the grizzly horrors of close-quarters combat rival and perhaps surpass many other war novels and memoirs of jungle war.

Jones also shared the sentiment of many postwar novelists, a revulsion of war as a wasteful, obscene act, while nevertheless admiring the sacrifices and bravery of the individual soldier. The novelist Anton Myrer, a Pacific combat veteran who wrote a novelized version of the battle of Buna in *Once an Eagle* (1968), noted that he had emerged from World War II "in a state of great turmoil, at the core of which was an angry awareness of war as the most vicious and fraudulent self-deception man had ever had."[32] Conversely, his adoration for the individual soldier was almost mythic. Late in life, Myrer wrote:

> What has happened? What's become of the yeoman, the backbone of the Republic—the quiet, competent countryman who could sow and reap his own grain, build his home and barns, cut and split his firewood, prune his fruit trees, butcher his hogs, and even spin flax on winter evenings right along with his wife? This same yeoman who could, when the need arose, march astonishing distances with full pack and rifle, hit what he aimed at, live in large part off the country—and with sufficient training could match the British grenadier at his own game? Are these such negligible skills? The infantryman, it seems to me, follows in the old yeoman tradition: the complete man, able to turn his hand at a hundred-and-one crafts and duties—the unassuming individual soldier without whose humble presence all the laser bombs and time-fire shells and tank columns are less than worthless.[33]

Jones and Myrer followed in a long tradition of postwar writers who exalted the individual even as they sometimes despised the cause, the machines of war, and the generals who commanded them. Myrer, in particular, had a deep antipathy toward MacArthur. He deeply admired Eichelberger, however, as the model of a "G.I. general" that empathized with his men. Myrer patterned the hero of his novel in part on Eichelberger.

   The Thin Red Line and *Once an Eagle* with their singular visions of combat came out more than a quarter of a century after the battles of Buna and Guadalcanal, after thousands of screenings and TV reruns of *Guadalcanal Diary*, after generations of school children had learned about the venerable feats of Douglas MacArthur, and all but a handful of veterans and military historians had forgotten about Robert Eichelberger. These intervening decades did as much, perhaps more, to fashion the image of the American soldier than the war itself.

   After Reagan and the resurgence of US power following the lethargy of the 1970s, Americans fell in love with World War II again, nostalgia that continued through the angry years of the Iraq and Afghanistan wars. One reflection of this fascination was the ten-part miniseries *The Pacific* (2010), based on the accounts of marines who served in the theater (including their experiences at Guadalcanal). Even today, after decades of the longest war against transnational terrorism and the emergence of a new era of great power competition, our reverence for the last of the greatest generation remains strong—as does our interest in the controversies and contradictions of their great struggle.

Reclaiming the Other

At the same time, Americans are as unsettled and divided today as ever over how they feel about their martial legacy. The injustice to African American soldiers is one issue. There are others. John Dower's deeply influential book, *War Without Mercy: Race and Power in the Pacific War* (1987) drew attention to other racial animosity that surrounded the conflict. Dower sought to remind readers that the divisions between the peoples that fought were real and raw. "Dower notes," summed up Michael L. Krenn in a survey of race and US foreign relations, that the Pacific War was "infused with racist perceptions on both sides."[34] This reality can't be denied.

Conversely, there was a difference between race in war and a race war. It is notable (despite the hostilities expressed during World War II), after the armistice, the conflict did not continue as a race war. Krenn points out that "once the Japanese were no longer a threat, the United States came to view them as errant children who now needed remedial education in the areas of democracy, government, and civilization." This was clearly reflected by both US policies during the occupation of Japan and attitudes back in the United States. "Americans' anger toward the people of Japan," Krenn writes, "did not disappear overnight, of course, but once the heat of war abated they became more willing to view the actions of the Japanese as what, unfortunately, occurred when an inferior people broke free from the constraints of Western civilization and power."[35] This, in practice, was not much different from the attitude Americans took toward a "White" Germany and Austria after World War II.

The argument could be made that the United States put its race hatred aside because it needed new allies to fight the Cold War. US occupation policies, however, were put in place years before Washington recognized it was in an intractable standoff with Moscow. The fact that both Americans and Australians so easily shed the worst extremes of racial animosity expressed during the war was such that hatreds were not the taproot defining relations between peoples. Indeed, the emphasis on the racial divides during World War II faded quickly in the official histories. In the United States, it was only after the divisions of the Civil Rights Movement in the 1960s and the bitterness of the Vietnam War in the 1970s that historians reenergized the theme of race war in America's past. And it took a while for this new appreciation for race and war to take hold. Dower's book came after the Vietnam War and on the heels of an upswing of anti-Japanese attitudes in the United States in the 1980s when Japan emerged as a major economic competitor, particularly for the US auto industry. *War Without Mercy* recovered what was in the decades after the great conflict an increasingly buried part of the war's history. In truth, the "good war" was suffused with much blind hate. But race hate did not define everything about why they fought. Perhaps that is why, when Japan faded as a major economic competitor, so did the compulsion of historians to focus myopically on the hatred of the other.

Global Conflict

For historians, the US war was, of course, not America's war alone. History proliferation gripped the world after war. No one attempted to dominate the debate more than Churchill, who carpet-bombed history with his magisterial multivolume account of the global conflict. Churchill tried to win the war for history before the other sides even armed themselves. His six-volume work was published between 1948 and 1964. The result was an admixture of his own idiosyncratic view of the war, settling old scores, postwar politics and concern about the outbreak of the Cold War, as well as the demands of publishers and the demands he put on himself and his writing and research team.

The volume covering 1942, the crucial year of the war and the decisive phase in Papua New Guinea, was the fourth and longest volume in the series. *The Hinge of Fate* ran to a thousand pages in the US edition.[36] Churchill's view of events played well in the United States. Veteran CBS broadcaster Edward R. Murrow proclaimed, "No other man of the century has made and written such history."[37] There was more skepticism down under. Two major newspapers serialized parts of the book. One was followed by a blunt critique of the many disagreements between Churchill and Curtin.[38]

No one came close to getting Churchill's say, Curtin least of all. John Curtin died on July 5, 1945. He never had an opportunity to tell his side of the story. Others did. As in the United States and England, participants in the conflict wrote their memoirs or were subjects of

studies, refighting the controversies of the days from their own perspective. In 1949, the widow of Major General George Alan Vasey (who
commanded the 7th Division in Papua New Guinea) made news by
sharing a letter her husband had written claiming that Blamey had fired
Rowell, the corps commander, not for having a defeatist attitude but for
personal reasons. "It was with reluctance, but a grave sense of responsibility," the article noted that she disclosed the truth.[39] She wanted to
set history right or, at least get her say. Many others felt the same.

Others never got the chance to lay their claim to history's truths.
There were many, many voices that never joined the chorus of the story.
One of them was Lloyd Purchase. On December 11, 1944, the headmas-
ter of the Canberra Grammar School reported, "It grieves me to have to
record the death of six more Old Boys, bringing the total to 21. Captain
Purchase (ANGAU) was No. 2 on the roll when the school opened in
1929." Purchase was killed in action, guiding a group of AEF regulars.
All that reminds us now of his service and sacrifice is the collection of
letters to "Dear Cele." I am not sure before this writing that his story has
ever seen the light of day. Such stories deserve not to be forgotten.

The first official Australian history of the campaign, *South-West
Pacific Area–First Year: Kokoda to Wau,* came out in 1959. Dudley
McCarthy, who had served in Papua New Guinea before and during the
war, summed up his feeling about the story he had been asked to com-
pile. He wrote:

> In it [the book] there is none of the wild, heart-thrilling drama of great
> bodies of men meeting on wide battlefields in the shocks of massed
> encounter. Instead, for the most part, it is the story of small groups of
> men, infinitesimally small against the mountains in which they fought,
> who killed one another in stealthy and isolated encounters beside the
> tracks which were life to all of them; of warfare in which men first
> conquered the country and then allied themselves with it and then
> killed or died in the midst of a great loneliness.[40]

McCarthy came at his task with the sensibilities of a journalist. At the
time the government had a tradition for outsourcing the writing of official histories to writers with a reporter's background. McCarthy had a
turn at freelance journalism before the war and there is some of that
character in his work. After the war he walked the trails and battlefields
to gain a reporter's eye of the ground. And, like a journalist, he didn't
avoid controversy or refrain from issuing terse judgements on the commanders and units that fought Australia's biggest jungle war.

With unrestricted access to official records, McCarthy had a real advantage over other chroniclers. That was just as well. "The official war history was probably the only history, or at least the only comprehensive and detailed history, that most members of the public ever expected to see," noted one director of the government's official military history program, "the government supported official histories because it was simply inconceivable anyone else would."[41] McCarthy, however, did not come close to getting the last word. The Australian appetite for the history of their war (despite the official government historian's view) has only grown over time.

A number of studies on the US side of the campaign have been matched with works by Aussie historians on their people's contribution—including Phillip Bradley's *Hell's Battlefield: The Australians in New Guinea in World War II* (2012). More recently, Lachlan Grant, a historian at the Australian War Memorial, contributed *Australian Soldiers in Asia-Pacific in World War II* (2014). History refuses to be set in stone. More is added, seemingly every day.

No nation struggles with its history of the great war more than Japan. The Japanese have authored the most comprehensive official history of the war—102 volumes. That said, this official effort has come with much criticism. These are not great histories. Often the context of operations is filled in using Western historical sources that dilute the Japanese perspective. Further, there is little self-reflection in the effort. As historical interpretation, it is very unsatisfying.

In postwar Japan, the past haunted every aspect of Japanese life from national identity to foreign policy. The impulse, however, was to suppress the experience. In an anthropological assessment of Japanese culture intended to guide the postwar occupation, Ruth Benedict concluded on an optimistic note. "Japan's real strength which she can use in remaking herself into a peaceful nation," she summed up, "lies in her ability to say of [a] course of action, 'That failed' and throw her energies into other channels."[42] That was pretty much what the Japanese did. The past was left unexamined.

The impulse to revisit the bygone conflict could not, however, be suppressed forever. The controversial historian Saburō Ienaga's *The Pacific War, 1931–1945* (1968) was meant to force the Japanese people to confront the worst of Japan's behavior. Rather than gloss over the history or focus on Japan as victim (the target of the 1945 nuclear attacks on Hiroshima and Nagasaki), he wrote to spark deep reflection and self-criticism. He also cautioned that he saw in America's war in

Vietnam and the Japanese support for the war a reflection of the militarist past that drove Japan to fifteen years of disastrous war decades earlier. This was perhaps the high-water mark of revisionist Japanese history in the struggle to account for the worst of the wartime excesses.

More sober, less politicized histories followed. The Japanese narrative has been the subject of notable attention in recent works such as Craig Collie and Hajime Marutani, *The Path of Infinite Sorrow: The Japanese on the Kokoda Track* (2009). Such books tend to paint the great land battles of the Pacific, as one noted Japanese historian remarked, like the US battle of Gettysburg, divorcing the fighting from the grander geopolitics that divided the armies, the virulent racism, and inexcusable atrocities, focusing instead on the nobility and trials of soldiering. Walking a tightrope between reconciliation and revisionism, Japanese military historians continue to bring forth their side of the story.

In the course of building a future, Japan struggled to shape its past. Unquestionably, there were excesses in the war that could not just be excused as the fortunes or frictions of war. They were intentional. In the Papua New Guinea theater, one egregious policy that still opens old wounds was the implementation of forced prostitution, the "comfort women." The Japanese shipped Chinese and South Korean women to Rabaul where they were forced to work in brothels.[43] Such abuses can't be ignored. Forgiving can be done without forgetting.

Today, Japan remains locked in the cycle of history—finding fault, taking responsibility, forgiving, understanding, and outrage. The passage of time does nothing to curb the cycle; it only adds contemporary concerns, perceptions, and prejudices.[44] Yet, it is a cycle that present-day Japan seems determined to break, unmooring itself from the constraints of dealing with its wartime legacy.[45] How the nation masters that effort to forge its place in today's Asia may, in part, hinge more than ever on making peace with the past.

No one on Papua New Guinea was left unaffected by the great jungle fight. There was no question but that as the presence of outsiders expanded, they had a transformative impact on local society. In the wild highlands, for example, where Whites were barely seen before the battle of Kokoda, everything changed. The gradual transformation "as a result of the people's interaction with the newcomers was abruptly accelerated in 1943," concluded one study. On the one hand, the war brought

> some positive effects, including paradoxically, the almost total cessation of tribal fighting, the construction of an all-weather airstrip at Goroka which ensured its future as a town and administrative and commercial

centre, and the compulsory growing of vegetables, coffee, etc, which laid the foundations for a cash economy and material prosperity.[46]

On the other hand, the foreign armies also brought death, disruption, and ravaged the landscape. The only unanimous conclusion of the war's impact was that the great island would never be the same.

When the jungle war ended, the world moved on and mostly forgot about the faraway land. On reflection, the impact of the war is still debated, along with the rest of the long legacy of how outsiders changed the people and the place—for better and worse. Today, Papua New Guinea remains one of the poorest and most poorly governed places on earth.

These are the voices of the Indigenous, Japanese, Australian, and American peoples. We must never stop listening to them. We may never fully know the objective truth of what happened in the heart of darkness, but to make military history useful for those who understand conflict will long be part of the human experience, we must try.

Notes

1. Quotes on Lindbergh's conversations in Australia are from Lindbergh, *The Wartime Journals*, pp. 870–874. Kenney's account is in Kenney, *General Kenney Reports*, pp. 411–414. MacArthur was even more pleased with meeting Lindbergh, when the aviator explained he had developed techniques that would allow P-38 fighters to extend their combat range to 700 miles. MacArthur knew that was "a gift from heaven." Anything that greatly extended the range of land-based attack aircraft also greatly extended their reach so they could support ground operations, harass enemy shipping, and conduct bomber escort. If the price of that expertise was allowing Lindbergh to strafe enemy positions and dogfight with Zeros—so be it.

2. Keene, "Japanese Writers and the Greater East Asia War," p. 209.

3. Browne, *Tojo*, p. 170.

4. Eichelberger Papers, box 2, I-42.

5. Ibid., p. I-37

6. Ibid., p. I-42

7. Chwialkowski, *In Caesar's Shadow*, p. 66.

8. Report of the Commanding General Buna Forces of the Buna Campaign, December 1 1942–January 25, 1943.

9. Chwialkowski, *In Caesar's Shadow*, p. 66; Kahn Jr., "Terrible Days of Company E," *Saturday Evening Post*; interview with Major General A. W. Waldron, March 1944, OCMH Waldron, 11 Files, p. 5.

10. Kenney, *General Kenney Reports*, pp. 157–158.

11. Blakeley, *The 32D Infantry Division in World War II*, p. 81.

12. Letter Eichelberger to Milner, March 8, 1954, OCMH Files.

13. James F. Collins Papers, box 2, Military History Institute, oral history transcript, US Army Heritage and Education Center, p. 14; Harding's Diary, box 279, RG 319, National Archives and Records Administration, p. 12.

14. William H. Gill Papers, US Army Heritage and Education Center, p. 10.
15. Eichelberger Papers, box 2, p. I-198
16. Ibid., p. I-118.
17. Ibid.
18. Letter, Eichelberger to Milner, March 8, 1954, OCMH files.
19. Eichelberger Papers, box 2, p. E-17.
20. Ibid., p. I-58.
21. Ibid., p. I-30.
22. Letter Sutherland to Ward, April 6, 1951, box 282, RG 319, National Archives and Records Administration.
23. Chwialkowski, *In Caesar's Shadow*, p. 208.
24. Memorandum, March 23, 1951, subject: Chief Historian's Critique of Victory in Papua, OCMH Files.
25. Mayo, *Bloody Buna*, p. xiii.
26. The school solution is described in Schifferle, *America's School for War*, pp. 111–114.
27. Bischof and Dupont, *The Pacific War Revisited*, p. 10.
28. See also Richard L. Watson and Kramer J. Rohfleisch, "New Guinea and the Solomons," in Caven and Cate, *The Pacific*, p. 7; see also Gillison, *Royal Australian Air Force, 1939–1942*, p. 470; Joe Gray Taylor, "Air Superiority in Southwest Pacific," in Cooling, *Case Studies in the Achievement of Air Superiority*, p. 337.
29. Samuelson, *Love, War and the 96th Engineers (Colored)*, p. 47.
30. Sharpe, *Brothers Beyond Blood*, p. 23.
31. Toplin, *Reel History*, p. 204.
32. Berry, "No Time for Glory," p. 4
33. Ibid., p. 5.
34. Krenn, *The Color of Empire*, p.68.
35. Ibid., p. 71.
36. Reynolds, *In Command of History*, p. 285. There is a long history of Churchill's writing on history. See, for example, Rowse, "Sir Winston Churchill as a Historian"; Valiunas, *Churchill's Military Histories*. Reynolds, *In Command of History* is the most authoritative.
37. Quoted in Reynolds, *In Command of History* p. 351.
38. Ibid., pp. 354–355.
39. "New Guinea Army Command Revelations," *Barrier Daily Truth*, November 30, 1949, National Library of Australia, p. 1.
40. McCarthy, *South-West Pacific Area—First Year Kokoda to Wau*.
41. Peter Edwards, "Continuity and Change in the Australian Official History Tradition," in Grey, ed., *The Last Word?* p. 73.
42. Benedict, *The Chrysanthemum and the Sword*, p. 304.
43. See, for example, Yoshimi, *Comfort Women*; Argiby, "Sexual Slavery and the 'Comfort Women' of World War II"; Hayashi, "Disputes in Japan over the Japanese Military 'Comfort Women' System and Its Perception in History"; Nelson, "The New Guinea Comfort Women, Japan and the Australian Connection."
44. See, for example, Kishimoto, "Apologies for Atrocities."
45. See Pyle, *Japan in the American Century*.
46. Munster, "A History of Contact and Change in the Goroka Valley, 1934–1949," p. xii.

Bibliography

Adams, John A. *If Mahan Ran the Great Pacific War: An Analysis of World War II Naval Strategy*. Bloomington: University of Indiana Press, 2008.

Aldrich, Richard. *The Faraway War: Personal Diaries of the Second World War in Asia and the Pacific*. London: Doubleday, 2005.

Allied Geographical Section, Southwest Pacific. *The Native Carrier: Employment and Treatment of Native Carriers in New Guinea*. February 9, 1943.

Anderson, Joseph L., and Donald Richie. *The Japanese Film: Art and Industry*. Princeton: Princeton University Press, 1983.

Argiby, Carmen M. "Sexual Slavery and the 'Comfort Women' of World War II." *Berkeley Journal of International Law* 21/2 (2003): 375–389.

Arnn, Larry P. *Churchill's Trial: Winston Churchill and the Salvation of Free Government*. New York: Thomas Nelson, 2015.

Austin, Victor. *To Kokoda and Beyond: The Story of the 39th Battalion, 1941–1943*. Melbourne: Melbourne University Press, 1988.

AWM52. Australian Military Forces, Army Headquarters, Headquarters Unit, Land Forces Headquarters, War Diary. Australian War Memorial.

AWM52. 2nd Australian Imperial Force and Commonwealth Military Forces, Unit War Diaries, 1939–1945. Australian War Memorial.

AWM52. 25th Brigade War Diary. Australian War Memorial.

AWM54 492/4/62. Seizo Okada, "Lost Troops." 1946–1948, Australian War Memorial.

Ballantine, Duncan S. *U.S. Naval Logistics in the Second World War*. Newport, RI: Naval War College Press, 1998.

Barclay, Glen St. John. "Australia Looks to America: The Wartime Relationship, 1939–1942." *Pacific Historical Review* 46/2 (May 1977): 251–271.

Bassford, Christopher. *Clausewitz in English: The Reception of Clausewitz in Britain and America*. New York: Oxford University Press, 1994.

Bellafaire, Judith L., ed. *The U.S. Army in World War II: Selected Papers from the Army's Commemorative Conferences.* Washington, DC: Center of Military History, 1998.

Benedick, Ruth. *The Chrysanthemum and the Sword.* Boston: Houghton Mifflin, 2005.

Benere, Daniel E. "A Critical Examination of the U.S. Navy's Use of Unrestricted Submarine Warfare in the Pacific Theater During World War II." US Naval War College, May 18, 1992.

Berry, Sidney B. "No Time for Glory in the Infantry." *Assembly* 56/4–6 (March–April 1998).

Best, Antony. "Constructing an Image: British Intelligence and Whitehall's Perception of Japan, 1931–1939." *Intelligence and National Security* 11/3 (1996): 403–423.

Bischof, Gunter, and Robert L. Dupont, eds. *The Pacific War Revisited.* Baton Rouge: Louisiana State University Press, 1997.

Bix, Herbert P. *Hirohito and the Making of Modern Japan.* New York: Harper, 2000.

Blakeley, H. W. *The 32D Infantry Division in World War II.* Madison, WI, no publisher, 1955.

Bland, Larry I., and Sharon Ritenour Stevens, eds. *The Papers of George Catlett Marshall.* Vol. 3. Baltimore: Johns Hopkins University Press, 1993.

Borg, Dorothy, and Shumpei Okamoto, eds. *Pearl Harbor as History: Japanese-American Relations, 1931–41.* New York: Columbia University Press, 1973.

Borneman, Walter R. *MacArthur at War: World War II in the Pacific.* New York: Little, Brown, 2016.

Bourke, Richard Michael. "Root Crops in Papua New Guinea." *Proceedings of the 5th International Symposium on Tropical Root and Tuber Crops.* Manila: Philippine Council for Agriculture and Resources Research, 1979: 121–133.

Bradley, Phillip. *The Battle for Wau: New Guinea's Frontline, 1942–1943.* New York: Cambridge University Press, 2008.

Bradley, Phillip. *Hell's Battlefield: The Australians in New Guinea in World War II.* Sydney: Allen and Unwin, 2012.

Brawley, Sean, and Chris Dixon. *Hollywood's South Seas and the Pacific War: Searching for Dorothy Lamour.* New York: Palgrave, 2012.

Brawley, Sean, and Chris Dixon. *The South Seas: A Reception History from Daniel Defoe to Dorothy Lamour.* Lanham, MD: Lexington Books, 2015.

Brokaw, Tom. *The Greatest Generation.* New York: Penguin Random House, 1998.

Browne, Courtney. *Tojo: The Last Banzai.* New York: Da Capo Press, 1998.

Bulkley, Robert J. *At Close Quarters: PT Boats in the United States Navy.* Self-published. 2017.

Burch, Noël. *To the Distant Observer: Form and Meaning in the Japanese Cinema.* Ann Arbor: University of Michigan Library, 2004.

Cairns, Lynne. *Secret Fleets: Fremantle's World War II Submarine Base.* Welshpool: Western Australian Museum, 2011.

Calhoun, Mark T. *General Lesley J. McNair: Unsung Architect of the US Army.* Lawrence: University of Kansas Press, 2015.

Campbell, James. *The Ghost Mountain Boys: Their Epic March and the Terrifying Battle for New Guinea—The Forgotten War of the South Pacific*. New York: Broadway Books, 2008.

Carter, Worrall R. *Beans, Bullets and Black Oil: The Story of Fleet Logistics Afloat in the Pacific During World War II*. Newport, RI: Naval War College Press, 1998.

Caven, Wesley Frank, and James Lea Cate, eds. *The Pacific: Guadalcanal to Saipan, August 1942 to July 1944*. Vol. IV of *The Army Air Forces in World War II*. Washington, DC: Office of the Air Forces, 1983.

Chamberlin, Stephen J., Papers. US Army Heritage and Education Center.

Chwialkowski, Paul. *In Caesar's Shadow: The Life of General Robert Eichelberger*. Westport, CT: Greenwood Press, 1993.

CINCPAC Files, US Naval War College.

Cockrell, Philip Carlton. "Brown Shoes and Mortar Boards: U.S. Army Officer Professional Education at the Command and General Staff School, Fort Leavenworth, Kansas, 1919–1940." PhD diss., University of South Carolina, 1991.

Collie, Craig, and Hajime Marutani. *The Path of Infinite Sorrow: The Japanese and the Kokoda Track*. Sydney: Allen and Unwin, 2012.

Collins, James F., Papers. US Army Heritage and Education Center.

Cook, Haruko Taya, and Theodore F. Cook. *Japan at War: An Oral History*. New York: The New Press, 1992.

Cooling, Benjamin Franklin, ed. *Case Studies in the Achievement of Air Superiority*. Washington, DC: Center for Air Force History, 1994.

Coox, Alvin D. *Tojo*. New York: Ballantine Books, 1975.

Coox, Alvin D. "Flawed Perception and Its Effects upon Operational Thinking: The Case of the Japanese Army, 1937–41." *Intelligence and National Security* 5/2 (1990): 239–254

Curran, James. *Curtin's Empire*. Cambridge: Cambridge University Press, 2011.

Davies, Kevin. "Field Unit 12 Takes New Technology to War in the Southwest Pacific." *Studies in Intelligence* 58/3 (September 2014): 11–17.

Dean, Peter J., ed. *Australia 1942: In the Shadow of War*. Cambridge: Cambridge University Press, 2013.

Desrosiers, Laura L. "Operational Logistics in a Maritime Theater of Operations: The Buna Operation (11 July 1942–2 January 1943)." US Naval War College, February 13, 1995.

Dexter, David. *The New Guinea Offensives: Australia in the War of 1939–1945*. Series 1, Army, vol. VI. Canberra: Australian War Memorial, 1961.

Dilley, Michael F. *Behind the Lines: A Critical Survey of Special Operations in World War II*. Havertown, PA: Casemate, 2013.

Director of the Service, Supply, and Procurement Staff, Department of War. "Logistics in World War II, Final Report of the Army Service Forces." Washington, DC: Center of Military History, 1993.

Doob, Leonard W. *Public Opinion and Propaganda*. New York: Henry Holt, 1948.

Doolittle, Duncan H. Oral History, US Naval War College, December 1, 2004.

Doubler, Michael D. *Civilian in Peace, Soldier in War: The Army National Guard, 1636–2000*. Lawrence: University Press of Kanas, 2003.

Drea, Edward J. *In the Service of the Emperor: Essays on the Imperial Japanese Army* Lincoln: University of Nebraska, 2003.

Drea, Edward J. *MacArthur's ULTRA: Codebreaking and the War Against Japan: 1942–1945.* Lawrence: University Press of Kansas, 1992.

Duffey, James P. *War at the End of the World: Douglas MacArthur and the Forgotten Fight for New Guinea, 1942–1945.* New York: Nal Caliber, 2016.

Edgar, Bill. *Warrior of Kokoda: A Biography of Brigadier Arnold Potts.* St. Leonards, AU: Allen and Unwin, 1999.

Eichelberger, Robert L., Papers. Archives Collection, US Army Heritage and Education Center.

Enright, Kelly. *The Maximum of Wilderness: The Jungle in the American Imagination.* Charlottesville: University of Virginia Press, 2012.

Ferris, John. "'Worthy of Some Better Enemy?': The British Estimate of the Imperial Japanese Army 1919–41, and the Fall of Singapore." *Canadian Journal of History* 28/2 (August 1993): 223–256.

FitzSimons, Peter. *Kokoda.* Sydney: Hachette, 2010.

Foley, William A. *The Papuan Languages of New Guinea.* Cambridge: Cambridge University Press, 1986.

Frank, Richard B. *Guadalcanal: The Definitive Account of the Landmark Battle.* New York: Random House, 1990.

Frühstück, Sabine. *Playing War: Children and the Paradoxes of Modern Militarism in Japan.* Berkeley: University of California Press, 2017.

Gamble, Bruce. *Fortress Rabaul: The Battle for the Southwest Pacific, January 1942–1943.* Minneapolis: Zenith Press, 2013.

Gilbert, Martin, ed. *The Churchill Documents, 1941.* Vol. 16. Hillsdale, MI: Hillsdale College Press, 2011.

Gilbert, Martin, ed. *The Churchill Documents, 1942.* Vol. 17. Hillsdale, MI: Hillsdale College Press, 2014.

Gilbert, Martin, and Larry P. Arnn, eds. *The Churchill Documents, January–August 1943.* Vol. 18. Hillsdale, MI: Hillsdale College Press, 2015.

Gill, William H., Papers. US Army Heritage and Education Center.

Gillison, Douglas. *Air War, Royal Australian Air Force, 1939–1942.* Vol. 1 of *Australia in the War of 1939–1945.* Canberra: Australia War Memorial, 1962.

Ginoz, Naomi. "Dissonance to Affinity: An Ideological Analysis of Japanese Cinema in the 1930s." PhD diss., University of California, 2007.

Glass, Charles. *The Deserters: A Hidden History of World War II.* New York: Penguin, 2013.

Goldrick, James. "The Face of Naval Battle: The Coral Sea." June 2, 2016. http://navalinstitute.com.au/the-face-of-naval-battle-the-coral-sea.

Gole, Henry G. *The Road to Rainbow: Army Planning for Global War, 1934–1940.* Annapolis, MD: Naval Institute Press, 2008.

Grant, Lachlan. *Australian Soldiers in the Asia-Pacific in World War II.* Sydney: University of New South Wales Press, 2014.

Greene Jr., Channing M. "Canopies of Blue: The American Airborne Experience in the Pacific in the Second World War as a Case Study in Operational Art and Multi-Role Flexibility." School of Advanced Military Studies, United States Army Command and General Staff College, 2008.

Grey, Jeffrey, ed. *The Last Word? Essays on Official History in the United States and the Commonwealth.* Westport, CT: Praeger, 2003.

Grogan, Robert. "The Operation of Forward Surgical Teams in the Kokoda-Buna Campaigns." *Surgical History* 68 (1998): 68–73.

Gropman, Alan, ed. *The Big L: American Logistics in World War II.* Washington, DC: National Defense University Press, 1997.

Guard, Harold. *The Pacific War Uncensored: A War Correspondent's Unvarnished Account of the Fight Against Japan.* Havertown, PA: Casemate, 2011.

Ham, Paul. *Kokoda.* Tullamarine, Victoria: Bolinda Audio, 2012.

Hammel, Eric. *Carrier Crash: The Invasion of Guadalcanal and the Battle of the Eastern Solomons, August 1942.* Pacifica, CA: Pacifica Press, 1997.

Handbook on Japanese Forces. Washington, DC: US War Department, 1944.

Harries, Meirion, and Susie Harries. *Soldiers of the Sun: The Rise and Fall of the Imperial Army.* New York: Random House, 1991.

Hawkins, Glen R., and James Jay Carafano. *Prelude to Army XXI: U.S. Army Division Design Initiatives and Experiments, 1917–1995.* Washington, DC: United States Army Center of Military History, 1997.

Hayashi, Hirofumi. "Disputes in Japan over the Japanese Military 'Comfort Women' System and Its Perception in History." *Annals of the American Academy of Political and Social Science* 617/1 (2008): 123–132.

Iriye, Akira. *The Origins of the Second World War in Asia and the Pacific.* London: Routledge, 1987.

Ishida, Takeshi. *Japanese Political Culture: Change and Continuity.* New Brunswick, NJ: Transaction Publishers, 1989.

Japanese Army Operations in the South Pacific Area: New Britain and Papua Campaigns, 1942–43. Trans. Steven Bullard. Canberra: Australian War Memorial, 2007.

Johnson, Carl. *Mud over Blood Revisited: Stories of the 39th Battalion, 1941–1943, Kokoda to Gona.* Victoria: History House, 2012.

Joy, Robert J. T. "Malaria in American Troops in the South Southwest Pacific." *Medical History* 43 (1999): 192–207.

Jungwirth, Clarence. "Diary of a National Guardsman in World War II." World War II Veterans Survey, US Army Heritage and Education Center.

Jurens, William J. "The Evolution of Battleship Gunnery in the US Navy, 1920–1945." *Warship International* 28/3 (1991): parts 1–2.

Kahn Jr., Ely Jacques. *G.I. Jungle: An American Soldier in Australia and New Guinea.* New York: Simon and Schuster, 1943.

Keene, Donald. "Japanese Writers and the Greater East Asia War." *Journal of Asian Studies* 23/2 (February 1964): 209–226.

Kenney, George C. *General Kenney Reports: A Personal History of the Pacific War.* New York: Duell, Sloan and Pearce, 1949.

Kershaw, Ian. *Fateful Choices: Ten Decisions That Changed the World, 1940–1941.* New York: Penguin Press, 2007.

Kessenich, Arthur J. "This Is Your Life." World War II Veterans Survey, US Army Heritage and Education Center.

Kienzle, Robyn. *The Architect of Kokoda: Bert Kienzle—The Man Who Made the Kokoda Track.* Sydney: Hachette, 2011.

Kight, Otis. "Coral Sea and Other Reflections." Oral History. Pacific War Historical Society. http://www.pacificwar.org.au/Yorktown/HeatCombat.html.

Kishimoto, Kyoko. "Apologies for Atrocities: Commemorating the 50th Anniversary of World War II's End in the United States and Japan." *American Studies International* 42/2–3 (June–October 2004): 17–50.

Kituai, Ibrum K. *My Gun, My Brother: The World of the Papua New Guinea Colonial Police, 1920–1960.* Honolulu: University of Hawaii Press, 1998.

Krenn, Michael L. *The Color of Empire: Race and Foreign Relations.* Washington, DC: Potomac Books, 2006.

Kretchik, Walter. *US Army Doctrine: From the American Revolution to the War on Terror.* Lawrence: University of Kansas Press, 2011.

Landis, Arthur H. *The Abraham Lincoln Brigade.* New York: The Citadel Press, 1968.

Leahy, Michael J. *Explorations in the Highland New Guinea, 1930–1935.* Ed. Douglas E. Jones. Tuscaloosa: University of Alabama Press, 1991.

Leary, William M., ed. *MacArthur and the American Century.* Lincoln: University of Nebraska Press, 2001.

Lee, Lloyd E., ed. *World War II in Asia and the Pacific and the War's Aftermath.* Westport, CT: Greenwood, 1998.

Lindbergh, Charles A. *The Wartime Journals of Charles A. Lindbergh.* New York: Harcourt Brace Jovanovich, 1970.

Lowe, James Philip. "Nadzab (1943): The First Successful Airborne Operation." MA thesis, Louisiana State University and Agricultural and Mechanical College, 2004.

Mack, John. *Code Breaking in the Pacific.* New York: Springer, 2014.

Manchester, William. *American Caesar: Douglas MacArthur, 1880–1964.* Boston: Little, Brown, 1978.

Mayo, Lida. *Bloody Buna.* Garden City: Doubleday, 1974.

McCarthy, Dudley. *South-West Pacific Area—First Year Kokoda to Wau.* Vol. 5 of *Australia in the War of 1939–1945.* Canberra: Australian War Memorial, 1959.

McGee, William. "The Mining Industry in the Territory of Papua in the Period Between World War 1 and World War 2." MA thesis, University of New England, 1992.

McLaren, John, "Nationalism and Imperialism—Australia's Ambivalent Relationship to Papua New Guinea and the Pacific islands." In *Ninth Biennial Symposium on the Literatures and Cultures of the Asia-Pacific Region.* Singapore: Unpublished, 1999.

Milner, Samuel. *Victory in Papua.* Washington, DC: Center of Military History, 1989.

Morton, Louis. *Strategy and Command: The First Two Years.* Washington, DC: US Government Printing Office, 1967.

MS 6538 George Johnston Diary, January 15, 1942, Australian National Library.

MS 9002 Propaganda Relating to the Japanese Invasion of New Guinea in World War II, Report of the Activities of the Far Eastern Liaison Office for Period June 1942 to September 1945, October 1, 1945, Folder 1 Box 1, Australian National Library.

Munster, Peter M. "A History of Contact and Change in the Goroka Valley, 1934–1949. PhD thesis, School of Social Sciences, Deakin University, 1986.

Myers, Michael W. *The Pacific War and Contingent Victory: Why the Japanese Defeat Was Not Inevitable*. Lawrence: University Press of Kansas, 2015.

Napier, Lionel Everard. *The Principles and Practice of Tropical Medicine*. Calcutta: Thacker's Press, 1933.

National Security Archive Project, George C. Marshall Museum.

Nelson, Hank. "The New Guinea Comfort Women, Japan and the Australian Connection: Out of the Shadows." *The Asia Pacific Journal* 5/5 (May 5, 2007): 1–22.

"No Glory, but Truth Is They Had Guts." *The Sunday Morning Herald*, August 26, 2006. http://www.smh.com.au/news/opinion/no-glory-but-truth-is-they -had-guts/2006/08/25/1156012735768.html.

Null, Gary. "Weapon of Denial, Air Power and the Battle for New Guinea." Report, Air Force History Museums Program, 1995.

O'Connell, John F. *Submarine Operational Effectiveness in the 20th Century: Part Two, 1939–1945*. iUniverse Publishing, 2011.

Oja, Yoshitake. *Konoe Fumimaro: A Political Biography*. Trans. Shumpei Okamoto and Patricia Murray. Tokyo: University of Tokyo Press, 1983.

Oral History Interviews with Thomas T. Handy, 1974. Collection: Dwight D. Eisenhower Library Oral History Collection, 1962–1998.

Orbaugh, Sharalyn. *Propaganda Performed: Kamishibai in Japan's Fifteen-Year War*. London: Brill, 2015.

Papers of the Department of Foreign Affairs and Trade, Government of Australia.

Partner, Simon. "Peasants into Citizens: The Meji Village in the Russo-Japanese War." *Monumenta Nipponia* 62/2 (Summer 2007): 179–209.

Pennington, Lee K. *Casualties of History: Wounded Japanese Servicemen and the Second World War*. Ithaca, NY: Cornell University Press, 2015.

Pike, Francis. *Hirohito's War: The Pacific War, 1941–1945*. London: Bloomsbury, 2016.

Powell, Alan. *The Third Force: ANGAU's New Guinea War, 1942–46*. Melbourne: Oxford University Press, 2003.

Provis, Peter. "'Track' or 'Trail'? The Kokoda Debate." *Flinders Journal of History and Politics* 26 (2010): 127–149.

Purchase, Lloyd, Papers. 1939, 1944. Australian National Library.

Pyle, Kenneth B. *Japan in the American Century*. Boston: Harvard University Press, 2018.

Rasmussen, Nicolas. "Medical Science and the Military: The Allies' Use of Amphetamine During World War II." *Journal of Interdisplinary History* 42/2 (Autumn 2011): 205–233.

Rautman, Alison E., and Todd W. Fenton. "A Case of Historic Cannibalism in the American West: Implications for Southwestern Archaeology." *American Antiquity* 70/2 (April 2005): 321–341.

Reardon, Steven L. *Council of War: A History of the JCS, 1942–1991*. Washington, DC: National Defense University Press, 2012.

Records of Headquarters, European Theater of Operations, United States Army (World War II).

Records of the Army Staff, National Archives and Records Administration.

Reed, Barry. "Endurance, Courage and Care: The Kokoda Campaign of Captain Alan Watson and the 2/4th Field Ambulance." *Journal of Military Veterans Health* 19/2 (2011): 32–40. https://jmvh.org/wp-content/uploads/2011/04 /JMVH-Vol19-No2.pdf.

Rees, Laurence. *Horror in the East: Japan and the Atrocities of World War II.* Jackson, TN: Da Capo Press, 2009.

Rems, Alan. *South Pacific Cauldron: World War II's Forgotten Battlegrounds.* Norfolk: Naval Institute Press, 2014.

"Report of the Commanding General Buna Forces of the Buna Campaign, Dec. 1 1942–Jan. 25, 1942." US Army Heritage and Education Center.

Reynolds, David. *In Command of History: Churchill Fighting and Writing the Second World War.* New York: Basic Books, 2005.

Reynolds, David, and Vladimir Pechatnov. *The Kremlin Letters: Stalin's Wartime Correspondence with Churchill and Roosevelt.* New Haven: Yale University Press, 2018.

Riseley, Jerry B. "Adjutant's Journal: Second Battalion, 503d Parachute Infantry." Typescript, 1943, Herbert Hoover Archives.

Riseman, Noah. *Defending Whose Country? Indigenous Soldiers in the Pacific War.* Lincoln: University of Nebraska Press, 2012.

Roberts, Tom D. C. *Before Rupert: Keith Murdoch and the Birth of a Dynasty.* Queensland: University of Queensland Press, 2015.

Robertson, John. "Australia and the 'Beat Hitler First' Strategy, 1941–42: A Problem in Wartime Consultation." *Journal of Imperial and Commonwealth History* 11/13: 300–321.

Rose, Kenneth D. *Myth and the Greatest Generation.* London: Routledge, 2007.

Ross, Steven T., ed. *U.S. War Plans, 1938–1945.* Boulder: Lynne Rienner, 2002.

Rothgeb, Wayne P. *New Guinea Skies: A Fighter Pilot's View of World War II.* Ames: Iowa State University Press, 1992.

Rowse, A. L. "Sir Winston Churchill as a Historian." *Huntington Library Quarterly* 25/3 (May 1962): 165–179.

Samuelson, Hyman. *Love, War and the 96th Engineers (Colored): The World War II New Guinea Diaries of Captain Hyman Samuelson.* Ed. Gwendolyn Midlo Hall. Champagne: University of Illinois Press, 1995.

Sarles, Ruth. *A Story of America First: The Men and Women Who Opposed U.S. Intervention in World War I.* Ed. Bill Kauffman. Westport, CT: Praeger, 2003.

Schifferle, Peter J. *America's School for War: Fort Leavenworth, Officer Education, and Victory in World War II.* Lawrence: University Press of Kansas, 2010.

Schom, Alan. *The Eagle and the Rising Sun: The Japanese-American War, 1941–1943.* New York: Norton, 2004.

Services Around the World—The Army Air Forces in World War II: Pearl Harbor Through Guadalcanal. Vol. 7. Washington, DC: Office of the Air Force, 1983.

Sharpe, George. *Brothers Beyond Blood: A Battalion Surgeon in the South Pacific.* Austin: Diamond Books, 1989.

Shigeo, Misawa, and Minomiya Saburo. "The Role of the Diet and Political Parties." In *Pearl Harbor as History: Japanese-American Relations, 1931–1941*, eds. Dorothy Borg and Shumpei Okamoto, pp. 321–324. New York: Columbia University Press, 1973.

Sledge, Eugene Bondurant. *With the Old Breed: At Peleliu and Okinawa.* New York: Presidio Press, 2007.

Spark, Ceridwen. "Whites Out? Historicising the Relationship Between Australia and Papua New Guinea." *Journal of Pacific History* 4/2 (September 2005): 213–219.

Spector, Ronald H. *Eagle Against the Sun.* New York: Vintage, 1985.

Spencer, Bill. *In the Footsteps of Ghosts: With the 2/9th Battalion in the African Desert and the Jungles of the Pacific.* Sydney: Allen and Unwin, 1999.

Stanner, William E. H. *The South Seas in Transition: A Study of Post-War Rehabilitation and Reconstruction in Three British Pacific Dependencies.* Sydney: Australasian Publishing, 1953.

Stark, Niel B. "Engaged in the Debate: Major Albert C. Wedemeyer and the Victory Plan in Historical Memory." Fort Leavenworth, KS: School of Advanced Military Studies, Command and General Staff College, 2017.

Steele, M. William. *Certain Victory: Images of World War II in the Japanese Media.* Armonk, NY: M. E. Sharpe, 2008.

Stoelb, Richard A. *Time in Hell: The Battle for Buna on the Island of New Guinea, The Story of the Company F, 127th Infantry, 32nd Infantry Division, Wisconsin National Guard.* Sheboygan, WI: Sheboygen County Historical Research Center, 2012.

Stoler, Mark A. *Allies in War: Britain and America Against the Axis Powers, 1940–1945.* London: Hodder Arnold, 2005.

Stroup, Russell Cartwright. *Letters from the Pacific: A Combat Chaplain in World War II.* Columbia: University of Missouri Press, 2000.

Subcommittee on the United Nations Charter, US Senate, Committee on Foreign Relations. *Review of the United Nations Charter: A Collection of Documents.* Washington, DC: US Government Printing Office, 1954.

Sumida, Jon, and Daniel Moran. "Review of *If Mahan Ran the Great Pacific War: An Analysis of World War II Naval Strategy.*" *Journal of Military History* 73/4 (October 2009): 1295–1297.

Symonds, Craig. "For Want of a Nail: The Impact of Shipping on Grand Strategy in World War II." *Journal of Military History* 81/3 (July 2017): 657–666.

Tanaka, Yuki. *Hidden Horrors: Japanese War Crimes in World War II.* London: Routledge, 1997.

Thompson, George H. *The Toughest Fighting in the World: The Australian Campaign in New Guinea in World War II.* Yardley, PA: Westholme Publishing, 2011.

Thompson, George Raynor, and Dixie R. Harris. *The Signal Corps: The Outcome: Mid-1943 Through 1945.* Washington, DC: Center of Military History, 1991.

Threlfall, Adrian. *Jungle Warriors: From Tobruk to Kodoka and Beyond—How the Australian Army Became the World's Most Deadly Jungle Fighting Force.* Sydney: Allen and Unwin, 2014.

Toler, Irwin G. *Disillusionment at Age 21.* Self-published. No date.

Toll, Ian W. *Pacific Crucible, War at Sea in the Pacific, 1941–1942.* New York: Norton, 2012.

Toplin, Robert Brent. *Reel History: A Defense of Hollywood.* Lawrence: University Press of Kansas, 2002.

Umphrey, Olivia. "From Screen to Page: Japanese Film as a Historical Document, 1931–1959." MA thesis, Boise State, May 2009.

United States–British Conversations Report. Exhibits of the Joint Committee, Pearl Harbor Association.

United States Department of State. *Foreign Relations of the United States: The Conferences at Washington, 1941–1942, and Casablanca, 1943.* Washington, DC: US Government Printing Office.

United States Army Headquarters, Japan. Assistant Chief of Staff, G3, Foreign Histories Division, Japanese Monograph No. 45, History of Imperial General Headquarters Army Section, US Army Heritage and Education Center.

United States Strategic Bombing Survey (Pacific), reprinted. Maxwell Air Force Base, AL: University Air Press, 1987.

Valiunas, Algis. *Churchill's Military Histories: A Rhetorical Study.* Lanham, MD: Rowman and Littlefield, 2002.

Vickery, Edward Louis. "Telling Australia's Story to the World: The Department of Information 1939–1950." PhD thesis, Australian National University, 2003.

Walker, H. N. "Psychological Warfare in the South-West Pacific." *Army Journal* 298 (March 1974): 49–64.

War Department. FM 100-5, *Field Service Regulations, Operations*, May 22, 1941. Facsimile reprint. Fort Leavenworth, KS: US Army Command and General Staff College Press, 1992.

War Office. *Infantry Training: Training and War 1937.* H.M.S.O., 1939.

Wark, Wesley K. "In Search of a Suitable Japan: British Naval Intelligence in the Pacific Before the Second World War." *Intelligence and National Security* 1/2 (1986): 189–211.

Weinberg, Gerhard L. *Visions of Victory: The Hopes of Eight World War II Leaders.* Cambridge: Cambridge University Press, 2007.

Welburn, M. C. J. *The Development of Australian Army Doctrine, 1945–1964.* Canberra: Strategic and Defence Studies Centre, Research School of Pacific and Asian Studies, Australian National University, 1994.

White, Geoffrey M., and Lamont Lindstrom, eds. *The Pacific Theater: Island Representations of World War II.* Honolulu: University of Hawaii Press, 1989.

White, Osmar, *Green Armour.* London: Allen and Unwin, 1945.

Willmott, H. P. *The Barrier and the Javelin: Japanese and Allied Pacific Strategies February to June 1942.* Annapolis, MD: Naval Institute Press, 1983.

Winton, John. *Ultra in the Pacific: How Breaking Japanese Codes and Cyphers Affected Naval Operations Against Japan, 1941–45*. Norfolk: US Naval Institute Press, 1994.

Wolfe, William. *The 5th Fighter Command in World War II*. Vol. 3. Atglen, PA: Schiffer, 2014.

Yagami, Zazuo. *Konoe Fumimaro and the Failure of Peace in Japan: A Critical Appraisal of the Three-Time Prime Minister*. Jefferson, NC: McFarland, 2006.

Yoshimi, Yoshiaki. *Comfort Women: Sexual Slavery in the Japanese Military During World War II*. New York: Columbia University Press, 2002.

Index

About the Book

In 1942, US and Australian forces waged a brutal war against the Japanese in the jungles of Papua New Guinea. Plunged into a primitive, hostile world in which their modes of battle seemed out of place and time, they fought, suffered, hated, starved, and killed in muck and mud.

James Carafano's vivid history brings this all to life. Ranging from detailed descriptions of specific battles to accounts of the fates of prisoners and the crucial role played by New Guinea's Fuzzy Wuzzy Angels, Carafano chronicles the grueling, and ultimately successful, Allied campaign, telling a tale of war at the very edge of human endurance.

James Jay Carafano is vice president of the Kathryn and Shelby Cullom Davis Institute for National Security and Foreign Policy, as well as E. W. Richardson Fellow, at the Heritage Foundation. His previous publications include *G.I. Ingenuity: Improvisation, Technology and Winning World War II; Waltzing Into the Cold War: The Struggle for Occupied Austria;* and *After D-Day: Operation Cobra and the Normandy Breakout.*